# APHRODITE HOUSE

&

OTHER PLAYS
BY JACK RANDOM

RANDOM PLAYS, VOLUME II

CROW DOG PRESS
TURLOCK CA USA

# APHRODITE HOUSE

## & OTHER PLAYS BY JACK RANDOM

### RANDOM PLAYS, VOLUME II

Published by
Crow Dog Press
1241 Windsor Court
Turlock CA 95380

## Copyright 2016 Ray Miller

All rights reserved. No part of this book may be reproduced in any form or by any means, electronic or mechanical, including photocopying, recording, or by any information storage and retrieval system, without permission in writing from the publisher.

Cover art adapted from Sandro Botticelli's Primavera, circa 1482.

ISBN-13: 978-0997788334
ISBN-10: 099778833X

# APHRODITE HOUSE

*&*

*OTHER PLAYS*

*BY*

*JACK RANDOM*

# PLAYWRIGHT'S NOTE

The first twenty years of my writing experience centered on playwrighting. This is the second volume of my plays. The first volume (*D'Arc Underground & Other Plays*) included *Fosdick & Muldoon, Nighthawks Café, Geronimo's Revenge, Queen of the Lonely Hearts* and the title play, *D'Arc Underground: A Jazz Play in Sixteen Choruses.*

I did not realize until compiling these collections that all the plays in the first volume evolved around a theme of faith. That same theme looms large in the second volume as well. It figures. Anyone who chooses art in any of its forms, as the center of his or her life, has taken a leap of faith. The life of an artist is a constant struggle, even for those who find monetary and critical success in their field.

The works included in this volume are certainly varied: I wrote *Nashville Round* after I uprooted my life in central California, married and moved to the city of music. It chronicles the dreams and ambitions of those I met there. I wrote *Heroes* on the theme of hero worship. *Aphrodite House* is an exploration of the power of women and the fate of romantic love. *Ringed Women of the Forbidden Forest* explores goddess mythology. *Reason's Reckoning* is a chronicle of the life and times of Tom Paine. *Scenarios* is an indictment of the American government's response to the terrorist attack of September 11, 2001.

The plays in this collection date from the early to mid eighties and reflect varied interests and stages of personal development. The young romantic is definitely here (*Aphrodite House, Nashville Round*) as is the profound

## JACK RANDOM

influence of Joseph Campbell (*Heroes, Ringed Women*). Here too is the influence of the immortal one: William Shakespeare (*Ringed Women, Aphrodite House*).

In general, my plays have sometimes been criticized as lacking action. They tend to be word plays and despite my intermittent efforts I could not inspire theaters to engage them. I nevertheless continued to write for the stage until I moved from California to Nashville, Tennessee, in the early nineties.

I transitioned from plays to fiction toward the end of my five-year stay in Nashville. When my short story "Burning Churches" was published in AIM Magazine, I realized that there was a greater market for my fiction. I later published my first novel *Ghost Dance Insurrection* and decided to leave playwrighting behind. While I still love the theater it seems clear the theater does not return my affection.

The plays in this collection are what they are. I make no apologies and hope that they will strike the interest of some enterprising artistic director. Should any theater wish to stage any of these works, you will find they are available at a fair price: Free.

Jack Random
November 27, 2016

# TABLE OF CONTENTS

NASHVILLE ROUND — 9
A Play in Two Acts

HEROES — 57
A Drama in Two Acts

RINGED WOMEN — 103
Of the Forbidden Forest

APHRODITE HOUSE — 151
A Play in Two Acts

SCENARIOS — 205
A Play in Eight Scenes

REASON'S RECKONING — 247
The Age of Tom Paine

# NASHVILLE ROUND

## A PLAY IN TWO ACTS

## SETTING

A bar in Nashville. The entryway is visible downstage left. There is an exit upstage right that leads to a backroom off stage. We see several tables and chairs backed by a partial bar. Act one takes place on Christmas evening. Act two takes place one evening the following summer.

## CHARACTERS

NASHVILLE JACK: A singer-songwriter and poet of the Nashville beat.
JOHN: A singer-songwriter and last of the troubadours.
MACK: Sound technician and musician.
RODRIGO: A singer and entertainer, the romantic voice of our times.
ANNABELLA: A singer-songwriter and one who dances by moonlight.
LAURA LEE: A singer. Who am I without my man?
FLINT: New wave slam poet.
BARTENDER
OTHER VOICES: Heard but not seen.

## ACT ONE

(Lights go dark. Voices are heard along with the sound of guitar picking and strumming in the background.)

VOICE 1: My name is Jo-Jo Jackson. I'm from Detroit, the land of motor vehicles and unemployment lines. Came to Nashville three years ago this coming Christmas. This here is a song I wrote for my pops who just lost his job. [sings] It was only seven year ago, a life or two it seems... [fade]
VOICE 2: Hi, I'm Amy. Amy Bellamy. Been here in Nashville about...what time is it? No, I've been here three months. It's been a hell of a ride. They told me I had to have a train song so here's mine. [sings] From the open fields of barley wine to the Carolina shore... [fades]
VOICE 3: Hi, y'all! I'm from Nashville. [laughter, crowd noise] Alright, I feel like I'm from Nashville. Been here so long I'm beginning to dream in the round. Here's one I wrote on the way over here. It's about Dallas or Chicago or New Orleans, anywhere but Nashville. [sings] As I gaze upon the skyline that claims mine as its own... [fades]

[Lights up on a bar scene. NASHVILLE JACK stands among the patrons, speaking in the halting melodic style of jazz poets in a former time.]

JACK: Heartbeats / beaten / down the path / to wisdom / in a bottle. In a knowing / glance / where the heart beats / no more. In the shadow / of fallen angels / in the breath of a thousand voices / Souls of a thousand songs / Beat of a thousand rhythms / where every pen has a thousand writers / and every song is a story / and I am one / on the streets of Nashville. Poet of the hungry soul / Spokesman of the

## JACK RANDOM

underside / The cowboy king / The gypsy queen / The fathers of country music / The mothers of the heart song / Where the prince of fools reigns supreme and tears are miracles of light / On the streets of Nashville / where everything looks better / with a bottle of beer / through the window at Brown's [cheer and applause] Blessed are the silver tongues / for they shall be heard / Blessed are the pretty ones / for they shall be observed / The troubadours of truth / the preachers of wisdom / come and go on the streets of Nashville // But for every blessing hides a curse / the plain and simple common ones / whose truth is no less telling / whose wisdom is as compelling / in the shadow of the chosen ones / on the streets of Nashville.

[JACK bows dramatically to cheers and applause.]

MACK: Come over here, buddy, let me buy you a drink.
JACK: [complies, sits] Thanks. I need one.
MACK: Where have you been hiding?
JACK: On the row. Main Street. I've been mixing with the real people. What about you? Working?
MACK: I've been out of town trying to line up a few things.
JACK: Same old story. It never changes. That's what I like about this town.
MACK: Same here. I couldn't wait to get back to town, grab a beer at Brown's, see the boys, shoot the shit. Same old, same old.
JACK: Yeah. I hate it.
MACK: Hate it, love it. It's all the same.

[General lights fade; spot up on JOHN at the door.]

JOHN: I used to like this town. Now it belongs to the punks and the college boys and the new age pretty boys with their pretty college girls. They all think they're going to make it in the music biz. The old timers don't come out any more. They know better. It's not the same. You make the same rounds, hit the same joints, see the boys, shoot the shit but something's missing. At first you can't put your finger on it. Then it hits you. All the old boys have given up. Now it's just a game. It's going through the motions because you've got nowhere else to go. You talk about busting out, doing something new. You get drunk and go home. The next day you can't figure out what you were talking about. You write a song but it doesn't have the fire it used to have. It's just what you do. That's why you keep on doing it. Same old, same old.

[Spot fades; general lights up.]

MACK: Hey Johnny! Good to see you, looking good, looking good. How's the biz?

JOHN: I can't complain. Had a good time, made some bucks and made it back alive.

MACK: You know the problem with you? The problem is you don't know how lucky you are. Look at me. Look at Jack. All the boys. What have we got to do but hang out and shoot the shit? Same old, same old.

JOHN: Yeah? And the problem with you is you don't know how lucky *you* are!

MACK: [smiles] I guess you're right. So what do you say, buy me drink, take a load off.

JOHN: That's exactly what I had in mind.

JACK: Let the word go forth! Mack the stack who lay's the tracks at Jack's is getting high with the boys out back.

BARTENDER: Hey boys, keep it down will ya?

JACK: You're most humble and obedient servant begs your indulgence.

[JOHN, JACK and MACK move offstage to the back. Lights fade and a spot comes up on RODRIGO, the self-proclaimed romantic voice of our times. He raises his hands to acknowledge his adoring fans.]

RODRIGO: No, no, don't get up! [looks around] Where are the boys?
BARTENDER: Out back.
RODRIGO: [looks to the audience] It's not easy being an entertainer of entertainers, the gracious host, the maker of merry, the romantic voice of our times. For one, you have to make an entrance. It doesn't always work out but someone's got to do it. That's my job. Keep a smile on their faces. Keep the conversation moving. Keep the spirits flowing. The laughs, the songs, the repartee, that's what people want and they're willing to pay for it. Who wants poetry? Who wants to see some poor slob crying in his beer? Okay, sometimes you feel like shit. Is that any reason to bring everyone down? You want to be a star you've got to play the part. Always up, never down, that's my motto! Always on, never boring, that's the way I roll! That's my job. I'm a star but nobody knows it. Not yet. The boys know it. If the time comes when they need a lift, I'm there. [to the bartender] Hey, let the boys know I'm here!

[Spot fades, lights up. RODRIGO raises his hands as JOHN, JACK and MACK re-enter.]

RODRIGO: Hey!
JACK: The romantic voice of our times!

[All form a circle around him.]

RODRIGO: How are my little people? Still rising with the sun and working your butts off until you're too tired to make love with your women! You're beautiful! I love you!
MACK: Where's the little lady?
RODRIGO: [looks to his arm] I don't know! I thought

she was glued to my elbow!
JOHN: Looks like you've lost her...again.
RODRIGO: Rodrigo Verde never loses his woman!
MACK: I know a few who might dispute that.
RODRIGO: One in particular. She begged me to take her back. She got down on her knees and pleaded with her little heart in her hands. [goes down on his knees] "Rodrigo, please! I'm down on my knees! I beg you please forgive me! I know you can't help it if all the women in the world want you! Who wouldn't?" [stands] I said, "While you're down there." No, no, I joke. I said, "Get up, woman! You embarrass yourself! No one leaves Rodrigo, the romantic voice of our times, and comes back! You had your chance! I'm sorry."
JOHN: Same thing happened to me.
MACK: That's not what I heard.
JOHN: What did you hear?
RODRIGO: Hey boys, it's Christmas! Revelry and joy! Let's not dwell on the setbacks of life. We're here, we're alive, good friends and good people! Enjoy, mi compadres!
JACK: Here, here! [a toast] To all good friends through all the years! Bartender, drinks around! Bring us a little joy in a bottle!

[General lights fade. Spot up on ANNABELLA at the door.]

ANNABELLA: The moon is in Gemini and the cards are right! I feel like dancing on the wind with a thousand angels! Christmas is a time of joy, a time when love comes out of hiding, the spirit rejoices and bliss fills the air with the sound of wonder and awe. Fire and water, wind and earth, song of the goddess, carry me to ecstasy! Tonight is the night of the enlightened ones. Let me dance on moonbeams! Let me soar among the stars! Let the wisdom of the ages speak to my soul! Let me sing in harmony with the beauty of all things! Let me believe! Let me believe. Let me know only the love that is the center of life! Let me live the dream of the poets! Let me be loved! Let me be loved.

[Spot fades; general lights up as ANNABELLA enters.]

RODRIGO: Annabella! Sweet Annabella! Song of my soul! Queen of everything! How sweet of you to come!
ANNABELLA: Sweet of you to be here. Where's the little lady?
RODRIGO: Gone away! I'm a free man. Now at last I'm free to be me. Now at last I can take you back in my arms and hold you! Let me feel your warmth and tenderness!

[They embrace.]

MACK: Hey, step aside! Give someone who really needs it a chance.
ANNABELLA: Mack! [embrace] I had a dream about you.
MACK: Yeah? I had that dream too.
ANNABELLA: I don't think so but hey, how are you?
MACK: Great. Never better.
ANNABELLA: Still seeing that pretty little thing?
MACK: Well...
ANNABELLA: Oh no! She looked good on you.
MACK: Well...
ANNABELLA: You'd just better call her and tell her how you feel. Listen, I know what I'm talking about. She was just what you needed, a little loving and feminine wisdom!
MACK: Well...
ANNABELLA: John! [embrace]
JOHN: Annabella!
ANNABELLA: When did you get back in town?
JOHN: Just last night. How the hell are you?

# RANDOM PLAYS

ANNABELLA: Great, just great. How's the road?
JOHN: Had a great time. You working?
ANNABELLA: Research. I've got a few songs brewing. They're dancing in my head right now. Can you hear them?
JOHN: Maybe I do. What's this I hear about a new man in your life?
ANNABELLA: You heard right. Love happens when you least expect it. Who knows? Maybe this time it'll work out.
JOHN: When do we get to meet him?
ANNABELLA: Why? You want to look him over? Make sure he's good enough? Give him the stamp of approval?
MACK: It's a male bonding thing. Takes a hell of a man to satisfy the Queen of Everything.
ANNABELLA: He's man enough.
JACK: If he isn't, you know where to find me.
ANNABELLA: Jack!
JACK: How are you? [embrace] You still writing those ethereal, surrealistic, existential, mystical dream songs that no one can quite figure out?
ANNABELLA: You've got to write what you hear in your head, darling.
JACK: Truer words were never spoken. You keep on doing it – no matter what they say. Someday they're bound to catch up to you. If they don't, you'll be a star in heaven.
ANNABELLA: I already am. I just need someone to bring me back down to earth.
JACK: Look no further. I'm your man.
ANNABELLA: Too late for you, Jack. You had your chance and you threw it out with the trash.
JACK: Who is he? A songwriter?
ANNABELLA: He's a regular guy. He has a job, likes baseball and watches TV.
JACK: You're kidding. As if that will work.
ANNABELLA: Why wouldn't it?

# JACK RANDOM

JACK: He's not one of us. Think about it. Why should he put up with you and your lifestyle? Out all night, always on the go, always short of cash, you think he can handle that?
RODRIGO: Don't listen to him, princess. He's got his head up his ass. We wish you all the happiness in the world. God knows you deserve it, putting up with us all these years.
MACK: [toast] Here, here! You've got that right.

[They all drink.]

ANNABELLA: Thanks, boys, a woman needs all the support she can get.
RODRIGO: [another toast] To Annabella! May she find eternal bliss or at least three meals, free drinks and a man who adores her!
ANNABELLA: I'm not sure I like that.
RODRIGO: Okay. To your first major recording contract!
ANNABELLA: I'll drink to that.

[They drink. Light shift to spot on LAURA LEE at the entryway.]

LAURA: Oh God, here I am again! Will they even know me? Will they say, hey, how the hell are you? Or will they let me slide by like I'm not even here? Why do I even bother? Sometimes I wonder but then I say to myself: It's what I've chosen. It's what I want. I know the odds. Sometimes they want me, other times they don't. Sometimes I make a connection, cut a deal and get a gig. Other times I just get used. Sometimes I just go home. Home? That's a laugh. Where is home anyway? A thousand miles, a thousand years, a thousand tears and fears and jeers and cheers away. Maybe I should have stayed home. The rodeo queen marries the football star and raises a houseful of snotty little kids. Not for me. I've still got a shot. Hellfire, I'm a

# RANDOM PLAYS

damned good looking woman with a damned good voice! Kathy Mattea's got nothing on me! If she made it, I can make it too. Even if I don't I want to be close to those who do. This is where I belong. Close to the music. I'll take my chances.

[Light shift to general lighting. LAURA LEE enters.]

LAURA: John! How the ya been, cowboy?
JOHN: Well, well, Laura Lee. I've missed ya, darling.
LAURA: Have you now?
JOHN: Yeah, me and the boys were just talking about you.
LAURA: Is that right?
RODRIGO: Don't worry. Just the good stuff.
LAURA: That's what I was afraid of. Annabella, how are you?
ANNABELLA: The stars are shining bright and I'm feeling fine. Got my feet on the earth and a song on my mind.
LAURA: Good, good. Haven't seen you in a while, darling.
ANNABELLA: I've been out of the circuit. Research and development.
LAURA: It's good to see you. You're looking fine, mighty fine.
ANNABELLA: It's my time, darling. The moon's in Gemini and Saturn's on the rise.
LAURA: I can tell. What's his name?
ANNABELLA: Why does everything have to be about a man? It could be a song, a deal or anything.
LAURA: Who is he?
ANNABELLA: A guy from my hometown. Fairy tale stuff.
LAURA: Sweet.
JOHN: Hey Laura, you want to join me and the boys out

back?
    LAURA: You know me. Always ready and willing.
    JOHN: Annabella?
    ANNABELLA: I'll catch up to you. I want to take in the scene.
    JOHN: Suit yourself.

    [JOHN and LAURA exit. Spot up on JACK at the bar.]

    JACK: The last troubadour and the rodeo queen, gypsy princess and the prince of fools, fathers of country music and mothers of song beneath our feet, all is in its place, all is well. The city of music has its roots, roots that bind and ground and hold us in place. We are the seekers of the Golden Fleece! The ancient potion of magic from which the muses sing and music springs and songs without voice are heard gracing the Nashville skyline. The dream is the nightmare. Light and darkness, the curse and the blessing, a story that binds us all on the streets of Nashville.

    [Lights up on JOHN at the center of attention; spot out.]

    JOHN: Here we all are! How long has it been since we all got together, the whole gang of us?
    RODRIGO: It's been a while. Six months?
    JOHN: Not like we used to. Why is that?
    RODRIGO: Everyone's busy. We've grown up.
    ANNABELLA: Speak for yourself.
    MACK: He can't. He's the romantic voice of our times.
    JACK: None of us have grown up. We're children disguised as adults. Sitting around a campfire telling ghost stories. That's why we came here and why we found each other. That's why we're still here.
    RODRIGO: I've never sung at a campfire and I can't stand kids! Little brats jumping around and screaming: look at me! Look at me! It's just business. We used to be

carefree, bathing in the company of our fellow artists. What better way to spend the time when we had so much of it to spend? Now we've got the rent to pay, doctor bills, water and electricity. Hell, it never ends! We can't live like we used to live.

MACK: I don't know about you, golden boy, but I had to pay the rent back then too. I just don't have that kind of energy any more. I can't be hanging out with the boys all night and still get up and go to work.

RODRIGO: And then there's the women. In the old days if I wanted to go downtown and hang, the little lady went with me or kept her mouth shut. Now she rags. [crosses his fingers to form a cross] Back, woman, back!

JOHN: Is that how you remember it? I remember it different. The women complained every bit as much as they do now. The difference is we never listened.

RODRIGO: What do you think, Laura Lee?

LAURA: Hell, I was never one to do the ragging. Far as I can tell, there ain't much change. The men do the ragging on me!

ANNABELLA: It takes a special kind of man to understand the likes of us, darling.

MACK: Like your man?

ANNABELLA: That's right. He's someone who appreciates the lifestyle of an artist.

MACK: You have to be one to understand one.

ANNABELLA: He is. He's a writer.

JACK: So much for the regular guy.

ANNABELLA: You can be both.

JACK: The hell you can.

RODRIGO: The point is: Some of us still hang out and some of us don't. You can always find me here! Laura Lee's usually here. John holds court when he's in town. Mack flakes but he always comes back. We're the regulars. That leaves Annabella and Jack.

MACK: Maybe they've got better things to do than hang

out with the boys. Maybe we're not good enough for them.

JOHN: Give it a rest, Mack.

JACK: He's right. We do have better things to do. We write. These are working hours. The truth is you're pretty much past your writing days. You live off your laurels and there's nothing wrong with that. You've recorded some of the best songs in the history of rock. At least you have laurels. Rodrigo's an entertainer. Dust off the old chestnuts, give it a polish and you're ready to go. Mack's a tech who probably wishes he was still a player.

MACK: I am a player.

JACK: Okay. You're a tech and a player. Laura Lee is a singer. This is business to you guys. This is networking. It's keeping up a public image, mixing and making contacts, finding out who's doing what where. You need it but it's death to a writer. I mean, we have to get out to find out what the people are feeling. We have to do our research but the real work is home alone.

JOHN: So according to you this is all a waste of time.

ANNABELLA: He's not saying that. This is where we connect to the real world. It's the real Nashville. It's anything but a waste. He's right about one thing though. We've got to strike a balance. If we were out here every night like we used to be, we'd both be dead or gone. It takes too much out of me. But I love you guys. I envy you. I wish I could hang out every night, go home and write a song, get up in the morning and play. I just can't do it anymore.

MACK: Neither can we. We're fooling ourselves if we think we can. We're drinking ourselves to an early grave. Hell, I got to get out of this town before it swallows me.

LAURA: You love it, Mack. You couldn't leave if you wanted to.

MACK: I love everything that kills me: wild women, drugs, booze, cigarettes and fast driving. I love you too, baby.

JOHN: Maybe it's time we reconsidered our approach to

life.

RODRIGO: You must be high! We do what we do because we love it and we do it well. It's the Nashville round and we're at the center of it all. Hell, we are the Nashville scene! What would it be without us? We have a good time.

JOHN: You think this town couldn't get along without us? Think again. Right now there are a few hundred guys and gals lined up to take our spots. They're ready and willing to sit at this table, shoot the same lines, and fill the night with random noise. We're not important. We live off this town; not the other way around.

RODRIGO: No one takes the place of Rodrigo! My fans would not allow it. Okay, maybe. But even if they would, what would we do?

JOHN: We'd go home and live a life. Who knows? Maybe we'd come up with a few songs, a new act, a new harmony. We might just get our shit together.

RODRIGO: We have our shit together! This is it! It doesn't get any better than this.

JOHN: What do you think, Jack?

JACK: Doesn't matter. I don't know what I'm talking about most of the time and even then, I don't know much.

JOHN: You know more than we do.

JACK: I'm not making judgments. I'm just explaining why I don't hang out more. You do what you want.

MACK: That's a relief because I'm not ready to go home.

ANNABELLA: Neither am I. Let's forget all this rationalization and have a good time.

RODRIGO: You speak my language!

JACK: Bartender! Another round for my forlorn friends!

BARTENDER: You got it!

[Lights fade; spot up on JACK.]

# JACK RANDOM

JACK: LA, New York, Dublin, Chicago, New Orleans, Austin... I chose Nashville. Then Nashville chose me. Oh, what a lucky man I am! I am a child of the Midwest. I know what roots are. The town will chew you up and spit you out if it doesn't like the smell of you. If it does, it lays itself wide open like a bar princess with a thing just for you. She's a powerful lover. She takes hold of you, you take hold of her and you don't let go. You make love every night and every day you call her home. It wears you out. You learn to pace yourself before you burn out. She's got a beat and a rhythm that carries you through. All you've got to do is follow. You don't push or try to lead. She loves harmony. It's what makes her work.

[Spot fades; general lights up.]

RODRIGO: So what's this I hear about you working at Frontrunner?

ANNABELLA: I'm recording a few songs.

RODRIGO: Originals?

ANNABELLA: Some are mine, others are covers. They've got an image they're trying to sell.

JACK: Don't let them sell you out.

ANNABELLA: I wouldn't know how. They wanted to call me "Gypsy."

JACK: Now where'd they come up with that?

ANNABELLA: I couldn't go along with it. It's a part of me but it's not me.

JOHN: Stick to your guns, sweetheart. They'll package you if you let them. Fix you up with ribbons, bows, straw hats and overalls, get you a band you don't like and that's it. You're stuck. You can't live up to it and you can't get out.

MACK: Frontrunner's good. They're the best. If they want to take you on, listen to them. The last thing you want to do is get stuck on the round going nowhere fast.

JACK: Like everything else, like life itself, it's a

balancing act. Stay true to yourself and sell your talent. How are they treating you?
ANNABELLA: Fine for the most part. They'd treat me better if I were a man.
MACK: That's an old song, princess. Don't lean on it. It ain't going to change while we're still breathing.
ANNABELLA: It's got to change. There are too many good women out there. At least I'm working with a woman producer. That's something.
MACK: How is she?
ANNABELLA: Virgo with Scorpio rising. She's tough and she won't stop pushing.
MACK: Good for her!
RODRIGO: How's Cowboy taking it?
ANNABELLA: Fine.
MACK: Sure. Like a cage lion, he's on the prowl.
ANNABELLA: He approved the deal. He's all for it. Anyway, he doesn't own me. What am I supposed to do? Wait another seven years for him to get around to recording and pitching me?
MACK: I'm on your side. Cowboy's great but he had his shot. Give someone else a chance.
LAURA: I think it's great. I'd kill to be working at Frontrunner!
JACK: I bet you would.

[Lights fade; spot up on JOHN.]

JOHN: I'm the only one here who's from Nashville. It's a place you come to from somewhere else. When the time comes, she calls you. She doesn't flirt. If she calls she's got something for you. There's no way around it. People from Nashville have a hard time understanding that some kid from Podunk, Arkansas, belongs here as much as anyone else. It's a gateway. It's a port in the storm that offers refuge to anyone who has something to give. It's not just Music Row and the Grand Ol' Opry. That's a small part of it. Nashville is a heart city. You can't fool her. She sings true or she doesn't sing at all. Yeah, I'm from Nashville. It's different for me. My grandpappy had the dream. My mama and papa kept it alive and passed it on to me. I'm glad they did.

[Spot fades; lights up. JACK is standing, entertaining.]

JACK: The 12$^{th}$ century troubadours gave love to the people to ease the pain of human suffering. Where are the troubadours now? Who needs music when the sidewalks rumble below our soles and the structures of old crumble at our feet? Where are the troubadours now? Gone the way of romance. Gone the way of chivalry. Gone the way of love. Gone … on the streets of Nashville. [bows to applause]

RODRIGO: Bring back the troubadours!

JOHN: We are the troubadours!

JACK: I hate to be the one to break it to you, John, but you are the last of them and I drink to you! [he does]

JOHN: I'm not sure what that means but thank you.

JACK: Another round, barkeep! Another serving of tears and moonbeams for the boys and girls of the round! For the last of the troubadours and our lasting memory!

RODRIGO: Who are the troubadours if not us? What are we if not the troubadours? We bring lyric tales of romance and sweet amore!

JACK: We are minstrels and you are our fool! The troubadours are dead.

RODRIGO: It is the drink that speaks, not you. Not the poet laureate of the Nashville beat. Not the muse of merry souls and wanton ways we all know and love. Not the spokesman for lovers and musicians and poets. Not you, Jack. You need a woman, my friend.

JACK: What I need is a new song. I need a beat I can run with. I need an epic poem I can set to music. I need a reason to believe that we're not just fooling ourselves. I need more than living the lie that we're all going to make it someday. I need more than broken dreams and stumbling in the dark after an all-night drink fest. I need more than going through the motions, playing the part of a child who refuses to grow up. I need to know we're not just jacking off in the round.

ANNABELLA: What else can we do but keep writing, keep working, keep hoping that someday it'll pay off? We're living the dream. It's the life we chose. It's not easy. It's not supposed to be. I've been told to give up, get a day job, you'll never make it, you can't sing country or folk or pop. You can't play, you can't write... I've never believed them and I'll be damned if I start now.

JACK: Annabella...you're light-years ahead of your time. You've got talent. We've all got talent. But talent doesn't pay the rent. Talent doesn't charge the fires. Talent doesn't keep us going year after year when all the people we used to know are gone. They had talent too. So what keeps us going, Annabella? What makes us different?

ANNABELLA: The dream. It's all we have. Live your dreams or your dreams will kill you.

JOHN: It's the only dream in town and we're the standard bearers. We hold the torch. We took the job. Nobody asked us. We're in it till the lights go down.

JACK: Is that really all there is? The dream? What about the fruits of our labor? What about the drive of the creative spirit? What about the need to connect with our fellow beings? Is this it? Is it all there is? A handful of friends hanging out in a bar? Writers looking for a song? Strangers in a cloud of smoke looking for a pickup, sobbing in their beers?

MACK: You make me puke. Primadonna songwriters, musicians, singers who don't like the hand you've been dealt? Check out, buddy. Throw in your cards. Cry in your own damn beer! You don't know how lucky you are.

JACK: How lucky am I, Mack?

## JACK RANDOM

MACK: You get to be upfront. You get the mike. You get a chance to sing your own songs. How many of us can say that? The crowd doesn't listen? Write a new song. You want a hit? Write for the people. But no, you're an artist! You've got to write for your soul! Well, go right ahead but don't whine about it. At least you have an audience.

JACK: That's right. You're a musician. I keep forgetting. You sold out to become a techie. You took the easy way out.

MACK: Maybe you're right but I like what I'm doing. It keeps me in touch and it pays the rent.

JACK: Keeps you in touch with what?

MACK: The music scene, what else? I love it. It keeps me going.

LAURA: Same here, Mack. I love everything about it: hanging out at the studio, singing backup, listening to songwriters in the round, talking shop with music people. We can't all write songs but at least we can stay in touch. It's enough for me.

RODRIGO: [raising a glass] Here's to the music scene! To songwriters who don't know how lucky they are and the rest of us who do! Here's to the music!

[They drink. General lights fade. Spot up on MACK.]

MACK: Nashville's a long way from Pensacola. That's where my family is. What's left of it anyway. My mama keeps telling me: "Give it up. There's nothing there for you. You belong with your family." I think about it sometimes. I think about it a lot. But something always holds me back. I'm Mack. I stack the tracks at Cowboy Jack's. The Row don't go without me. I'm damned proud of that. I like what I do. Sure, I do my share of bitching about it. We all do. But she's got me. She's got her hooks so far in me I can't take a shit without thinking about her. She's in my blood. She owns me body and soul. Nashville is my home now.

# RANDOM PLAYS

Music is my family. That's how it is. Can't shake it and wouldn't if I could. That's the way I like it no matter how much I like to grumble about it.

[Spot fades. General lights up. LAURA eases up to MACK at the bar, leaving JOHN, JACK and RODRIGO seated at a table. ANNABELLA sits apart, observing.]

LAURA: Hey, Mack.
MACK: Yeah?
LAURA: You look like you could use a little cheering up.
MACK: That I could.
LAURA: I'm your girl. Buy me a drink.
MACK: You've got it. [he does]
JOHN: I don't mean to belittle what you're going through, Jack, but it's nothing new. It's just a phase in the cycle to get yourself psyched for a new song.
JACK: It's more than that. You've got your gig. You're set, man. I need a break or it's going to break me.
RODRIGO: We all need a break. It's no excuse to rain on the parade.
JACK: How do you do it, Rodrigo?
RODRIGO: Do what, my man?
JACK: Keep your spirits up. You've been at it as long as I have.
RODRIGO: I've had my share of success. Another show, another woman, another crowd of adoring fans! Another toast, another round, as long as I've got a seat at the table I'm a happy man! Frankly, I don't know what you're complaining about.
JACK: The time will come when you lose that seat. You know that, don't you?
RODRIGO: May tomorrow never come.
JACK: I guess it's just me. There's something inside of me, like a second self, whispering so quietly I can't make out

# JACK RANDOM

the words, vague grumblings of discontent, it's not enough. It's just not enough.

RODRIGO: I'm telling you, Jack, you need a woman – someone to stroke the old ego, give you a rise and tell you how special you are. Damn it, man, you're the crowned prince of the Nashville poets!

JOHN: Does that work for you?

RODRIGO: Hell, yes! Nothing cures the blues like a little adulation.

JOHN: Maybe I've been seeing too many airheads.

RODRIGO: What's wrong with airheads? You tell them what to say and they say it. You make passionate love under the moonlight and go your way, the stars still dancing in her eyes! She thanks you, you thank her and everyone's happy!

JACK: I'm looking for a little more than that.

RODRIGO: Who isn't? In the meantime we get what we can. [JACK laughs]

JOHN: A little something to help us through the night.

RODRIGO: That's my man.

[Light shift to spot on ANNABELLA.]

ANNABELLA: I was on my way from Idaho, heading for New Orleans. I stopped in Nashville for a drink and a good time. Seven years later, I'm still here. I had a handful of songs and a life full of heartache, looking for a dream I've had most of my life. I still haven't found it but I've found a lot of kindred spirits. I've had some opportunities. Like carrots in the mist, they keep dangling in front of me, keeping me going. Maybe this time. I keep saying: One more year. If nothing happens by then I'll move on. But something always happens, like carrots in the mist, and I keep staying another year. It's beginning to feel like home.

[Spot fades. General lights up as RODRIGO approaches ANNABELLA.]

# RANDOM PLAYS

RODRIGO: Annabella!
ANNABELLA: Rodrigo!

[They embrace melodramatically.]

RODRIGO: You are looking radiant tonight!
ANNABELLA: You're looking pretty good, too. It must be the home life.
RODRIGO: When I'm with her, I think of you.
ANNABELLA: When I'm with her, I think of you, too. Isn't that strange?
RODRIGO: I'm serious. The sun never shines without remembering when you were mine and I was yours and we held each other under the stars.
ANNABELLA: Everything changes.
RODRIGO: Except us. This circle of friends remains the same. What the city of music brings together, neither time nor circumstance will ever part. Could you ever forget me?
ANNABELLA: You know I couldn't.
RODRIGO: When you're a star, will you still remember the little people, the ones who knew you when you were a struggling songwriter hanging with the bums on the row?
ANNABELLA: Are you saying I'm not a star?
RODRIGO: You are to me, beautiful. Someday everyone will know it.

[MACK joins them, followed by LAURA LEE.]

MACK: So...seriously...how's the home life?
ANNABELLA: It has its ups and downs.
MACK: I thought so. The fact is he's not one of us. He doesn't understand the life.
ANNABELLA: I'm not sure I understand it.
MACK: He came all this way. He must love you.
ANNABELLA: He does but it's a long way from home.

# JACK RANDOM

He misses his friends and family. I know what it's like. When I got here I didn't know anyone but I had my music. It opened the door.

MACK: He writes?

ANNABELLA: Short stories, plays, poetry – everything but songs.

MACK: You've got to get him out of the house, mix it up with the boys, make the rounds. What the hell is he doing? Hiding out? Digging himself into a hole?

ANNABELLA: I can't force him.

MACK: You're a woman. Use your persuasion.

LAURA: Stand by your man, honey. I know how hard it is to find a good man in this town. Everyone's got his own agenda. No time for love. If a man came to Nashville for me, you could bet the farm I'd stick it out.

ANNABELLA: I'm not saying it's over. I know how to hold on to a man.

MACK: Ain't that sweet. Makes me want to cry in my beer.

[Light shift to spot on LAURA LEE.]

LAURA: Every night I ask myself: Why am I still here? I lost my illusions along with my innocence. I'm not marketable. I know I'll never be a star. I'll never be anything more than a backup singer and a good-time girl. There's too many just like me…only now they're younger and prettier. They get the chances I used to get. Me? I'll hang out with the boys and pick up a gig here and there. But even if I'll never be a star, at least I can say I've known a few. That's enough. I like being where the music is happening. It's happening here and I'm in the front row. Who knows? Maybe I'll find love.

[Spot fades. General lights up.]

# RANDOM PLAYS

JOHN: Is it really so bad, Jack?
JACK: What's that?
JOHN: Hanging out with the boys, making the rounds, finding out what's happening, staying in touch. It's what we do. It keeps me charged up. It fills my gut with something other than the mundane. This is it, man. What more do you want?
JACK: New blood. We're getting old, John. We're set in our ways. I don't want to keep writing the same old song over and over. Something's got to change. It's a whole new world out there. The wall is down, rap is happening and kids are stirring things up again. We've elected a president who cheats on his wife. Czechoslovakia elected a playwright president and here we sit. We're behind the times.
JOHN: You want to go to Czechoslovakia? Everything that's happening in the world is happening right here. All we have to do is feel it. Maybe we've gotten lazy. Maybe we don't listen enough. Maybe we don't like what we hear. But it's all happening right here in Nashville. Shake it up, bud. Go out in the street and put your ear to the ground.
JACK: Yeah?
JOHN: Yeah.
JACK: Give me a sec.

[JACK rises, sets his mind as others turn to listen.]

JACK: She was a leathered goddess of the lower eastside. A motorcycle mama with her knees apart, inviting wet dreams and arousing animal instinct, her leathers tightly squeezing and caressing my desire. She took note and shot a knowing glance my way. "You're mine," she said in a whisper none could hear but me. "You're mine for the taking." I squirmed and felt the pulsing heat of primal urge rising from the black hole of no tomorrow. I resisted wagging my tongue and straightened my cool in the reflection of a bottle. "Come on," she whispered. "Give it a shot. What have you got to lose?" "Nothing," I answered by rote. "Nothing but my soul." Like a snake drawn to shadow, I slithered to her table and stood like a dumbstruck child without words. "It'll cost you," she whispered. "I know," I replied. "How much?" "How long?" she said. "Everything is time." I emptied my pockets. "Not here, my friend," she smiled. "I don't do this for anyone." I lowered myself as a commoner to a queen. "What's the deal?" I asked. She touched my hand with the tips of her fingers to remind me of her power. "You can look but don't touch." I smiled in submission. She knew I wanted more. But this would do. It would have to. She tightened her hold and sealed our secret bond, strutting without another word, toward the door, her hips dancing like waves of moonlight on black velvet. Once more into the streets, the barren, lonely, soulful streets of Nashville. Vanished without a trace. A drunken wet dream fantasy…on the streets of Nashville.

[He bows, all applaud.]

RODRIGO: The Jack is back! The heart of the Nashville beat! The poet of the lost troubadours! Lift your glasses, one and all! Give praise and thanks! To the last true master of word jazz!

[All drink. General revelry.]

JOHN: Does this mean you're buying?
RODRIGO: [to bartender] Put it on my tab!
BARTENDER: You've got it.

[General lights fade. Spot up on RODRIGO.]

RODRIGO: It's not easy being me. It always seems to hit me around this time of night. Nobody knows. I keep it to myself. I hide it like a bad song. Hey, I work as hard as anyone. I bust my ass trying to come up with a new angle, working out a new set, a new song, booking a club date, rounding up musicians, working on a video, getting time at the studio, on and on. Where does it get me? They all think I'm just a good-time guy, all play, all party, no sweat or tears. I'd kill for a break. So I ask myself: Why Nashville? I'm not really a Nashville kind of act. But I fell in love with this town. I love the row, songwriter's night, the round, the old cowboys, the pretty women and the bars. Nashville doesn't know it but she needs a guy like me, someone to show her off like the grand old lady she is. It doesn't matter what happens. Somebody dies or moves on, someone else moves right in. She doesn't miss a beat. Sure I belong here – even if I'm not a country boy. This is my town and I love it!

[Spot out. End Act One.]

## ACT TWO

SETTING: As before. The stage is dark. Voices are heard along with tuning instruments. Tumultuous applause rises and fades.

JOHN: It's great to be on the road again. Picking and playing some of our old favorites for the folks who never forget. Anybody want to hear something new? No, I didn't think so. Here's a little tune that went to number one back in the day when the things we dug were groovy. It's about a little girl we all know and love. One, two, three...

[Fade sound as music begins...]

VOICE: Here he is fresh from a tour of the crowned heads of Europe...and a few heads in Paducah...the last voice of chivalry and romance, the personification of charm and social grace, the romantic voice of our time, the one, the only...Rodrigo!

RODRIGO: I love you! I love you all! You wonderful, lovely people! It brings me great warmth and gives strength to my heart to be once again with the people I love! It makes me sad that I cannot take each and every one of you home with me tonight! If it were in my power I would make passionate love to all your women and buy each of your men a drink! My beautiful friends and devoted fans, I have a song in my heart for you and you and you, you sexy little thing. Maestro, the music please...

[Piano roll as sound fades.]

LAURA: Hi, y'all! It's great to be in the round again

with all these talented young people. I've been working the studio scene lately so if anyone needs a backup singer, I'm available. This is a song a good friend of mine back home in Texas wrote for me. It's about a rodeo queen who picked up one day and went to Nashville. She's still here. The rest, as they say, is her story.

[Guitar strums and fades. The sound of an electric guitar rises.]

JACK: Is anybody out there? Are you ready for this? A little old plugged in, electric lady land, cool-aid acid test sound. Ready or not, I'm ready to kick up some dust, raise the roof and get down to some serious rock and roll with a country soul. The reggae of the white middle class. The scat jazz of anarchy set to a down home country beat. Nothing's impossible if you believe like I believe and I believe in anything that's good or true or happening. After all I've been through, I'm still dragging that ball and chain...

[Electric music fades; accordion music rises.]

ANNABELLA: They tell me I've got to get out and mix with people so here I am. Another face in the round. Another song from the heart. For those who care, Mercury just went into Pisces and Saturn is opposing Mars so it's a good night for making connections if the spirit is willing. Mine is. Yours must be or you wouldn't be here. This is a song I co-wrote with a friend of mine. She's an old soul and a kindred spirit. It's about the ghost of a gypsy queen in the swamps of the old bayou.

[Accordion rises and fades. General lights up on the bar scene. MACK is at the bar as JOHN and JACK enter.]

MACK: Hey, boys! It's about time you showed! I was

about to make a new plan, catch the act at the Déjà vu!

[They shake hands and embrace.]

JACK: Good thing we're here. It's too damned hot for that action.

MACK: Tell me about it. Last time I went out there I about had me a heart attack!

JOHN: You wouldn't be the first. How are you, you old goat?

MACK: Never better.

JACK: You lying dog! Still missing that woman, aren't you?

MACK: What woman? I'm into a new relationship. Digital tracks.

JACK: Right.

MACK: At least you're looking better. The last time I saw you, you were pissing and moaning about the goddamned moon! Hell, I don't even know what you were talking about.

JACK: Neither do I, Mack.

JOHN: He just needed a little female companionship. The horns were showing. He's back "on the streets of Nashville." Gave me a little sample on the way over. Where's Rodrigo?

MACK: Said he had some business.

JOHN: He's always got some business. I don't know where he finds the time.

JACK: The man's got ambition. He's got more than any of us and he's running against the clock.

JOHN: Who isn't? But I'll tell you this: the man's got heart! He may never reach the stars but he's got his fans. He makes things easier for all of us. I love that guy.

MACK: He's a good man. I'd hate to be married to him but I can't imagine things around here without him.

JOHN: Why would you say that?

# RANDOM PLAYS

MACK: What? He's a womanizer! We all know that.
JOHN: It's an act. He's no worse than any of us.
MACK: I guess he's just better at it.
JACK: Speak for yourself.
JOHN: I don't know anyone in the business that isn't a womanizer.
MACK: Garth excepted.
JOHN: Annabella been around?
MACK: I saw her down at Cowboy's cooking up some new deal.
JACK: She can't shake him, can she?
MACK: He won't let her go. Cowboy loves her. Treats her like a queen.
JOHN: All the old guys love her. I don't know what holds her back. She's got style, writes her own songs, plays her own music. She's a Nashville original. You'd think they'd eat her up.
JACK: It takes more than talent. She's a fish out of water here in Nashville. The old boys love her but they don't know what to do with her. One day, who knows? She'll hit like a thunderstorm.
MACK: That'll be the last we see of her. It's hard enough to get her out of the house now.
JACK: She'll come out when the stars are right.
MACK: I'm going to give that girl a call. [steps to the side; to bartender] Hey, Mack, give the boys a drink on me!
BARTENDER: You've got it, Mack.
JACK: He's in love with her, you know.
JOHN: Who isn't?
JACK: Why don't we do something about it?
JOHN: It wouldn't be right. We like her too much.
JACK: Is that it? I always figured I couldn't stand the competition. One writer in the house is enough for anyone. Demands a lot of attention.
JOHN: It demands a lot of patience.

## JACK RANDOM

[Enter RODRIGO with flair.]

RODRIGO: Hey! Mi amigos!
JOHN: Rodrigo!
JACK: The romantic voice of our times!

[Embraces and commotion.]

RODRIGO: It's so good to be back with the people who love me! I can't tell you how deeply it touches me. It fills my heart with joy, my soul with humility; it makes me want to sing!
JACK: Save it for the act.
JOHN: I heard you put on a good show at Josie's.
RODRIGO: What can I say? All the little people love Rodrigo!
JOHN: Good to see you, you old womanizer.
RODRIGO: An ugly rumor. Can I help it if the woman throws herself at my feet and begs me to show her the meaning of love? I'm weak. I admit it! I take pity on them.
MACK: [approaching] Hey, Rodrigo!
RODRIGO: Looking good, looking good, how long's it been?
MACK: About half an hour.
RODRIGO: Time is an illusion, my friend.
MACK: Well, you're looking good too.
RODRIGO: Thank you, thank you. It warms my blood to have such good friends!
JOHN: What's the word?
MACK: You know Annabella. She sounded a little strange.
RODRIGO: Sweet Annabella, the love of my life! I sense that she is coming to me! I feel it as only a lover feels these things. Deeply and desperately! She cannot fight it! She cannot stay away!
JACK: She's got a new man. You know how that goes.

# RANDOM PLAYS

RODRIGO: Do you think he's jealous?

JACK: If he is, it won't last much longer. He'll be on the plane by Sunday morning.

JOHN: And Annabella will have a new song by Sunday night.

MACK: He's a nice guy.

JACK: That'll save him.

MACK: I'm just saying, I hope it works out.

JACK: It always does.

[Enter LAURA LEE with FLINT, a younger man. They turn and give him a look.]

LAURA: Hi, y'all!

MACK: How ya been?

LAURA: Never finer.

[FLINT shuffles to a corner table. JACK edges up to LAURA LEE.]

JACK: Hey darling, you want to join me out back?

LAURA: Not tonight, sweetheart. [moves on to MACK at the bar]

MACK: Who's your friend?

LAURA: A guy I met at writer's night. He's writes poetry. I caught his act at the White Bird.

MACK: Is he any good?

LAURA: He's wild. He's into the slam scene.

MACK: Interesting. Has he published?

LAURA: Didn't ask. Hey Flint, come on over here!

FLINT: [crosses, shakes hands] Hey man.

LAURA: This is Mack. He lays the tracks at Jack's.

FLINT: Cool. What does that mean?

MACK: It means I'm a techie.

FLINT: Cool. I'm Flint.

MACK: You got anything published?

# JACK RANDOM

FLINT: A couple pieces. There's no money in it.
MACK: You should write songs.

[JACK rises and prepares to recite a street poem...]

JACK: In the dark corner of a back alley club, whose owner is a bearded man with baggy khakis and a Dead tie-dye tee, still paying dues for leaving his poetry in the dusty cobwebbed attic back home in Paris, Texas, kindred souls form a circle and sing to no-one but themselves and God. Their spirits soar like a temperature-driven breeze against the pulsing, hammering beat pounding the street outside. They wear their hearts on their sleeves, battered, bruised and scarred like a hobo of somebody else's color. Tears form and well in the eyes of the singer, her voice shudders and strays, her studied hands unsteady, her song about home so long and far away. So gripping and so common, her curse to remember and know she can never return. Her memories do not exist outside her troubled mind. The circle moves and plays like a merry-go-round in heaven's playground. Songs of passion, songs of love, dreams of glory, visions of harmony, their lives are played out in mood swings like a roller coaster high. The troubadours, their faces lined in joy and sorrow, have come together for the last rites of all fallen angels whose wings still fly without them. Love, death and rebirth...in the round...on the streets of Nashville.

[He bows and the crowd applauds. FLINT stares.]

RODRIGO: Once again, dear friends, the poet laureate of country muse! Last of the word jazz musicians! The soul and spirit of the Nashville street!

[All drink except FLINT who rises.]

FLINT: The village idiot pounds his rubber drum!

# RANDOM PLAYS

Behold the shaker come to steal your hollow thunder! Tear down your phallic tinker toy and raise your lowered voices. Who roams the black of void? Who hears the beat of three? Who wears the mask of Kerouac? Who swims the deeper sea? Dissolve and fade the hallowed ground of yesteryear. Mound upon mound of garbage in and garbage out, a pyramid of virgin sacrifice to gods that don't exist and never did. Bring down the towering babble of secret truth and sorrow! Your long lost cows devoured by the worms of no tomorrow! The prodigal son rises from the dust and plunders the mother earth goddess in the dying embers of a setting sun. The poet stands alone against shrouds of mysticism, splitting mind and soul, divining light and sound, he rails against the lifeless drivel of tired wagging tongues and crushes the lily-white voice that tells us what we mean. The fruit is ripe and ready to be plucked! Shake hands with your selves and stack your bones on an epic burial ground! Jazz is the rhythm of the beat and dream is what's happening...on the streets of Nashville. There are no lies! There is only time and art and poetry and me.

[JACK takes the challenge; the slam down is on.]

JACK: Form without content; content without words; words without meaning; meaning without form. Mama's little dandy lion wags his tail and expects the mountain to bow its head in awe. Ain't gonna happen, little boy blue! Go blow your horn in someone else's garden. Go diddle your fiddle with other little boys who have no fear. The third strong wind blows the pretty little pedals off his tie-dye leather head and leave his naked soul cowering in the shadows of giants, playing dead. Form without content; content without words; words without meaning; meaning without form. The tattoo archetype markets his confusion, rebels without a clue and offers his delusions to the worshippers of despair who make virtue of misfortune. This is no place for little boys who fail to respect their elders and spit against the winds of time. There is no place for you and yours...on the streets of Nashville.

[He bows and acknowledges the applause. As FLINT readies for the next round, JACK retreats like a prizefighter to his corner where JOHN awaits.]

JOHN: [to Jack] Well, Jack, you said you wanted new blood and here he is! Are you ready for this?
JACK: I was born ready. I'll rip him to pieces, the disrespectful little punk!
JOHN: Don't underestimate him. He's a rebel. He's like you were twenty years ago.
JACK: You didn't know me twenty years ago.
JOHN: Maybe I didn't, maybe I did.

[FLINT takes the stage.]

FLINT: Ghost of a beatnik generation, son of a weary Leary, stalks his helpless prey, stokes his rusted gun and aims his poison tongue my way. Quake and tremble, shake, rattle and roll! The aging rhymer attacks my fearless soul. Not today oh weathered one! Not today oh venerable one! Not in this house of the rising sun! I know the clock that makes you tick! I know the blood that runs beneath your revered streets of Nashville! The soul of the South is sticks and bones! Its name is old Jim Crow! I passed your marker miles ago. You were gazing at the sunset, struck dumb and chasing acid dreams! I was high-speed cruising the waves of time and my time has come!
JACK: The mike is open at the punk rock sixties late café! New-agers make wagers on the coolness of things to come. Poets of the now speak in tongues, rhythms without rhyme, screaming of acid queens on ice. Even punks have dreams. Even the waitress has writer's eyes, her thoughts

# RANDOM PLAYS

beyond coconut cream, a chorus rages through her thirsty mind, the waitress is not what she seems. The stumble drunk mumbles in stuttered verse to none within his range, his vision blurred beyond focus, his words slurred beyond understanding, his dream surviving the rising tide of fools who claim no heritage. Hanging by a thin gray line, he glides on the stream of his consciousness. This is no common drunk. This is no common punk who limps and stumbles on the stump where his foot used to be, severed by his own hand to escape the grasp of imagined enemies. Nightmares are the dreams of those who lose their souls...on the streets of Nashville.

[Bows, applause, FLINT broods, JACK approaches.]

JACK: Relax, kid, I like you. Where you from?
FLINT: Chicago.
JACK: I thought so. The windblown city where every event is a happening and every resident is a performance artist. Their primary art is trying to outrage New Yorkers.
FLINT: It's where it's at. Major league.
JACK: Where are you really from?
FLINT: [laughs] Indiana.
JACK: Norman Rockwell, basketball, mom and apple pie. No wonder you claim Chicago.
FLINT: I was lucky. I got out early. Before the disease took root.
JACK: Why'd you come to Nashville?
FLINT: I heard they were lighting a fire here. So far they like my style.
JACK: Are you a poet or a rap artist?
FLINT: I don't like labels, man.
JACK: I'm a jazzman, myself. Word jazz is my thing.
FLINT: Kerouac, Ginsberg, Ferlinghetti.
JACK: More like Bukowski and Lord Buckley. Ever heard of him?

# JACK RANDOM

FLINT: Lord Buckley? Can't say that I have.

JACK: He's from Chicago. How long you been here?

FLINT: I've been in and out for the last few years.

JACK: Where have you been hiding?

FLINT: I get around.

JACK: You don't know anything about this town.

RODRIGO: He knows what he likes. He keeps coming back.

JOHN: He likes Nashville but does Nashville like him?

MACK: She'd have kicked his butt all the way back to Indiana if she didn't.

LAURA: She can always change her mind.

FLINT: I don't claim to know anything about this town. To me it's just another city. The only difference between Nashville and Chicago is size.

JACK: I've been to Chicago. It's all about sports, money and music – pretty much in that order. The street's a constant hustle. The only place you can hang and not feel out of place is a ball game.

FLINT: You went to the wrong places, man.

JACK: Maybe. Every city has its scenes but I'm talking about the core, the heart and the beat of the place. Nashville is music to the core. What's Chicago? I know this: Slam poetry is about as big in Chicago as professional ping-pong.

FLINT: Art is art, man. It doesn't matter how big it is. It's the scene. It's what's happening. Everything that's going on here is going on tenfold in Chicago.

JOHN: They got a Ryman's auditorium in Chicago?

MACK: They got women like Laura Lee?

FLINT: They've got everything, man.

LAURA: What the hell. Go back to Chicago then.

JACK: My man doesn't want to go back. They have too many slam poets just like him. He figures he can make his mark here in Hicksville. Big fish in a little pond.

FLINT: Hey, man, I like Nashville.

JACK: How can you like a place you don't know?

# RANDOM PLAYS

FLINT: I know what I like.

JACK: Let me tell you a few things about this town. Take notes. Maybe you'll learn something.

FLINT: You've got my attention.

JACK: First and foremost, this is only town in the world where the word writer means songwriter. It's the only town where every night is songwriter's night somewhere. It's the only town where the round is a group of people sitting in a circle playing and singing their own songs. Everywhere you go, any time of the day or night, any day of the week, the music is what's happening. It's what we talk about, what we get mad about and what we love. It's what gets us through hard times. When we dream, we dream to music. It's not just a line. It's reality. It's the heart of Nashville: City of Music.

FLINT: City of country music.

JACK: You haven't been around. We have every kind of music and the musicians to play it: gospel, jazz, rock, folk, blue grass, blues, reggae, soul, R & B and every variation of country. If it's got a beat, we play it here.

FLINT: Is that right?

JACK: Would I bullshit you?

FLINT: You might. I've heard you music people talk. Who's got a gig? Who needs a backup? Who's signing with who? Who's got a cut? Who's got publishing? Who's hot and who's not? Who's recording and what are they looking for? Sounds like business to me.

JACK: Everything's business when you're trying to make a living at it. That's what the dream is. We're trying to make a living at what we love. You want to make it in this town you'd better understand that.

FLINT: I just want to do my thing, man. I let the money take care of itself.

JOHN: [laughs] Sounds familiar.

JACK: [laughs] Well, kid, let's do our thing.

# JACK RANDOM

[JACK prepares.]

JACK: She was old enough to be his mother and smart enough to know better. A platinum blonde of the Marilyn mold, skirt split to the hilt of a well-contoured hip. Her deep brown eyes sleepy time seductive, her lips were poised for pleasure.

He was a contender for the King of Cool, cigarette dangling from his lower lip James Dean style, blue jean jacket, skull and crossbones, live free or die, his greased hair and brow frozen in textbook devil-may-care style.

She crossed her legs in the manner that draws all eyes, especially his. Pale gray clouds of smoke divided at her command, like Moses at the Dead Sea, and drew him in for a closer look.

A sign in ruby red neon flashed in the back of his brain, endangered cool, as her sweet lips formed a circle and the tip of her tongue gently grazed the edge of her upper teeth.

It moved him like an alto sax in minor key, blowing cool breeze through a steamy night on Bourbon Street. He stood when his legs let him and made his move with his hippest jazzman strut.

A distinguished gentleman in silver gray, moosed and two-tone shoes, padded shoulders, double breast, emerged from smoke and shadow to sit himself beside her with a smile that said too much.

As he motioned to the waiter she made him with her eyes: Kid of Cool grew up. "Sweet tease," he said through his disguise. "Sweet dreams of jaded kind."

She smiled and promised him a future...on the streets of Nashville.

[Bows, applause.]

FLINT: [prepares to counter] He is the Jack of Kerouac. He hears the beat of three. His is the word that must be

# RANDOM PLAYS

heard. The dharma bum of the Nashville jazz poetry scene, I raise my glass and offer praise and crown the jazzman king! Master of the beat, poet of the street, dream defender, sage of soul, shades of Miller and Bukowski, wingless messengers of wisdom, dark angels in disguise, rise to honor the wise: On the streets of Nashville!

[Applause as ANNABELLA enters. She is distraught but struggles to maintain. All eyes turn.]

ANNABELLA: Finally someone appreciates me!
RODRIGO: Annabella, mon ami! At last you return! At last I can feel the warmth of your embrace!
ANNABELLA: Cut the crap and buy me a drink!
RODRIGO: Such language from a little lady! It grieves me and brings pain to my poor heart!
ANNABELLA: It's been a long day. I'm ready to have a good time with my friends. Is that too much to ask?
RODRIGO: Bartender, give this woman a drink!
BARTENDER: What are you drinking?
ANNABELLA: Long Island!
BARTENDER: You got it!

[JACK takes FLINT aside.]

RODRIGO: That's pretty strong medicine, Annabella. What's wrong?
ANNABELLA: Everything. I don't want to talk about it.

[Light shift to JACK and FLINT.]

JACK: [to Flint] Hey kid, you're okay.
FLINT: Same to you.
JACK: You learned something tonight if you're smart enough to take the lesson.

# JACK RANDOM

FLINT: What's that?
JACK: Play to your audience.
FLINT: You have to have an audience to play to.
JACK: Hang in there. Your day will come. The point is: Some things are more important than art.
FLINT: Like a friend in need.
JACK: Welcome to Nashville!

[They shake hands. JACK approaches ANNABELLA. A circle has formed around her. FLINT retreats to his corner where LAURA joins him.]

JACK: Hey beautiful, how's it going?
ANNABELLA: Fine. I'm fine.
JACK: Sure you are. How are things at the studio?
ANNABELLA: It's hell. They want to steal my publishing. They're ruining my music. They treat me like a piece of furniture. I've had it with their self-adulation, always telling me how great they are and how lucky I am to be working with them. Damn it, they're lucky to be working with me! It's about time they gave me some credit.
MACK: That's how it is with them. Success goes to their heads. They can't stop tooting their own horn.
JOHN: You have a fight with the head witch?
ANNABELLA: I had to get out of there. I was mad enough to slap her around. I can't help the way I feel. When I hear the tracks, it doesn't move me. It bores me.
JACK: What exactly is the problem?
ANNABELLA: It's out of my hands. They ask me what I think. I tell them. Then they do whatever they want to do. It's not me anymore. It's not what I hear in my head. They've stolen my music.
RODRIGO: I'm sorry, princess.
MACK: Don't' take it too hard. You're not the first.
ANNABELLA: It'll be all over town by tomorrow. No one will work with me.

# RANDOM PLAYS

MACK: Hey, you can always go back to Cowboy's. The old guy loves you.

ANNABELLA: I'm thinking about it.

MACK: You've got to go where they value who you are as an artist.

ANNABELLA: I know. I should never have left.

JACK: Hold on, darling. If you can just hang on for a while, maybe it'll work out. Nashville's a small town. You don't want to burn any bridges.

ANNABELLA: I know you're right. I just can't take it anymore. I thought working with a woman would be different but it's the same old story.

JACK: It's business. Everyone's in it for their own. If you play your cards right you can come out of this with something in hand. Then it's your turn. You call the shots. Right now, bite the bullet, babe. They have all the cards.

ANNABELLA: It's not supposed to be like this. We're the artists. Without us they wouldn't exist.

JOHN: They only treat you right if you're a star. Otherwise you're sheep. You're supposed to be grateful they let you in the front door.

ANNABELLA: You've got that right.

RODRIGO: What's the matter with them? Don't they know you're already a star?

JOHN: Patience, Annabella. Your day will come.

ANNABELLA: I'll sleep on it, take some time, maybe I'll find the light.

MACK: [waits] I know you, Annabella. This is not just business. How are things with Joe?

ANNABELLA: Not good. He's packing his bags and moving back to California.

MACK: I'm sorry, princess.

ANNABELLA: I'm having one of those days, Mack.

RODRIGO: It could be worse, my dear.

ANNABELLA: Yeah, the moon could be in Scorpio.

RODRIGO: At least you still have your friends.

# JACK RANDOM

ANNABELLA: True. Where would I be without you guys?

MACK: Idaho, Oregon, New Orleans, anywhere but Nashville.

ANNABELLA: Funny you should say that. I've been thinking about getting out. Maybe I've been here too long. There are too many people and not enough space. It's turned into a business town and I'm tired of business. I need to be somewhere where I can breathe and relax and write.

RODRIGO: Holly shit, now you've got it!

ANNABELLA: What's that?

RODRIGO: The Nashville blues.

JACK: It's a disease. Something we go through twice a year like clockwork. The winters are too long and the summers are too damn hot. There's a song in it somewhere.

RODRIGO: Where would we be without the gypsy queen of everything? You're the finest songwriter in town. You can't leave us!

JACK: She dances on moonbeams and makes poetry out of dreams.

JOHN: Whatever you do, Annabella, stick with the music. You've been ahead of your time so long it's bound to catch up to you. It'd be a shame if you weren't around to enjoy it.

LAURA: If I had your talent, I'd be on top of the world. I'd wake up every morning and count my lucky stars. You've hung in there this long, you've got to stick it out. At least you're getting their attention.

ANNABELLA: That kind of attention I don't need.

MACK: Listen, girl, I've heard one of your cuts. Let me tell you something: it comes through. You stick it out. Take whatever they give you. Cry if you have to. Scream, knock down the wall, kick the dog, whatever it takes, but stick it out. This is your shot.

ANNABELLA: Thanks. I love you guys.

MACK: One more thing while I'm on a roll. Don't be so

# RANDOM PLAYS

quick to give up on Joe. He's a good man. He'll be there for you. As soon as you decide to let him in, he'll be waiting for you. I wouldn't tell you that if I thought I had a chance but I don't and I know how he feels about you.

ANNABELLA: Maybe you're right. I know I'm hard to live with. You guys make me feel like a queen. Maybe I should have problems more often.

RODRIGO: Don't push it. We've all got problems. Next week it's my turn.

JOHN: The hell it is. Who's the star of this show?

JACK: You are, John. You always will be. We just like to spread it around a little.

JOHN: Okay then, enough about Annabella, let's talk about me!

[Laughter as general lights fade. Spot up on JACK.]

JACK: Music and harmony. The inseparable force that brings us back when we stray too far and stumble in the dark. The force that binds us together and makes us stronger than we could ever be alone. It's bigger than any one of us. It's not about stars. It's about the music. It always will be. For all those who give up and move on to their normal lives, Nashville is the home of the Grand Ol' Opry. It's a ghost that will haunt them and a memory that will hide in the shadows of their minds forever. For those of us who stay – the Cowboy Queen, the Gypsy Princess, the salt of the earth and the last of the Troubadours, Nashville is a city of dreams.

[Light shift. Spot up on ANNABELLA.]

ANNABELLA: Love and hate. One minute I hate this town. The next it's the greatest thing that ever happened to me. I've always wondered what would have happened if I'd gone to New Orleans. People have said they'd love me there. They like people who are different. Some people say I'd be a hit in Europe. Who knows? I'm in Nashville and I'll stay here until it plays itself out. It's got a hold on me. It won't let go until it's finished.

[Spot shift.]

MACK: It's eight degrees in Pensacola today. I'm freezing my balls off in Nashville. Tomorrow I'm back in the studio, sweating blood stacking the tracks for some producer who's got nothing but crap to give me. Some would-be starlet will come up and unload a truck full of shit. On and on, same old same old and I love it. I'll come back to Brown's, have a few beers, talk shop and let it go. I'll be back tomorrow. Nashville's all right by me.

[Light shift.]

LAURA: What the hell am I doing with a punk rock poet? Poets don't need backup singers! Oh well, you never know what's going to happen in this town. That's what I like about it. Tomorrow night I'm back in the round. Maybe I'll meet a producer or some hotshot singer who likes my voice. Maybe I'll get lucky. Maybe not. Either way you'll know where to find me.

[Light shift.]

RODRIGO: A year from now everything will be pretty much the same. A lot of opportunities, a lot of promises, a lot of struggles and a few heartbreaks. It's all under the bridge. Five years from now maybe one of us finds success, one drops out and moves away, one settles down with a day job and leads a normal life. Ten years from now at least one of us dies. The parade of songs, singers and musicians goes on as if nothing ever changes because nothing ever does. But I'll be here and I'll have some stories to tell.

# RANDOM PLAYS

[Light shift.]

JOHN: I've had my fifteen minutes. Fact is I've had more than my share. I'm still living in the afterglow. That's something they can never take away. I know what it feels like. Old stars never fade away. They just get out of the house more often. Maybe I'm too old but I never get tired of it. The struggle, the stories, success, heartbreaks: It's an old story – as old as the rock mountains of Tennessee, as old as the pioneers on the Cumberland, as old as the music. I was born in Nashville. Someday I'll die here. That's the way I want it ... with an old song on the radio.

[Light shift.]

JACK: In the breath of a thousand voices, in the souls of a thousand songs, in the heartbeat of a thousand rhythms, to the pounding of a thousand drums; where every scene has a thousand writers, where every face tells another story and every tear is a miracle of light, where I am one with all... on the streets of Nashville.
Blessed are the silver tongues for they shall be heard. Blessed are the pretty ones for they shall be observed. But for every blessing hides a curse, the stars whose light never reaches earth, in the shadows of the chosen ones, where hope and dreams and I reside... on the streets of Nashville.

[Spot fades to black.]

End Act Two.

*HEROES*

## SETTING

A tavern in a secluded area near the west coast. The tavern is divided into three sections: There is a well-stocked bar with barstools up left. There is a tiled dining area with a table and chairs down center and a carpeted "memorial" room with a desk, easy chair, books, pictures and memorabilia up right. We see framed pictures of Einstein, Paine, John Lennon, DiMaggio, Marilyn, Bogart and Bobby Kennedy. The entry door is stage left. Night approaches as the play opens.

## CHARACTERS

**HERO:** Caretaker. A good-natured man who appears older than he is. He walks with a limp.

**JOE:** A traveler. Cautious but cool, he amuses himself with a healthy sense of sarcasm. He wears a Yankee cap.

**JENNY:** A free spirit who is uncommonly direct and honest.

**CHICO:** A classic bandito with an exaggerated accent.

**OLD WOMAN:** Caretaker.

**VOICES:** May be recorded or actors offstage.

## ACT ONE

[The orange of an approaching sunset seeps in the windows as the lights come up on the interior of the tavern.]

JENNY: [off] Hurry up! We're here!
JOE: We'd better be! My legs are about to drop off!
JENNY: [opens door, enters] If you'd have checked the water at the last stop...
JOE: [enters] Give me a break!
JENNY: Hello! Anyone here?

[JOE carries a sleeping bag. Both carry small packs. JENNY finds and lights a lantern.]

JOE: We never should have come on this trip. We should have taken a cruise to Hawaii. We should have gone to New Orleans for Mardi Gras. Nice hotel, drinks, fine dining...
JENNY: We thought it would be fun.
JOE: You thought...
JENNY: You agreed!
JOE: I was wrong. [looks around] Hello! [nothing] Just our luck, a twenty mile hike uphill in the middle of goddamned nowhere and what do we find?
JENNY: [unloading her pack] Relax. There's got to be someone here. They left the door open!
JOE: My guess? An axe murderer killed everyone here, chopped them up in little pieces and deposited them in garbage bags out back. So here we are... [looks around, roams up right to the memorial room where JENNY awaits] ...in some kind of mausoleum. Jesus, look at this place! Is this great or what?

# JACK RANDOM

JENNY: It's like a museum: Einstein, John Lennon, Bogart... who's this?

JOE: Tom Paine. He wrote the Rights of Man and Common Sense. One of the true founders of this nation. "These are the times that try men's souls..."

JENNY: What an odd collection. A scientist, an actor, a writer, there's no theme.

JOE: Heroes.

JENNY: What?

JOE: It's a collection of heroes.

JENNY: Whose heroes?

JOE: They could be mine! Joe DiMaggio, the Yankee Clipper! [picks up photo] Fifty-six game hit streak, 1941!

JENNY: Only one woman though. [starts to pick up photo] Marilyn!

[The barrel of a shotgun becomes visible through a window off left.]

HERO: Freeze! Don't move a muscle! Don't even think about it!

[HERO enters. He has the appearance of a mountain man.]

HERO: You with your sweaty paws on the Clipper, you ever been to a museum?

JOE: Sure.

HERO: You ever touched a Picasso?

JOE: No.

HERO: Why not? You felt like it, didn't you?

JOE: It never occurred to me.

HERO: Sure it did! It's natural. You see something you like, you want to touch it! You want to take it home with you! You wear a pin-striper, you think it gives you certain rights! It's only human. You are human, aren't you?

# RANDOM PLAYS

JOE: I am.

HERO: Sure you are. But a little voice in the back of your head tells you it's wrong. You can look but don't touch! You don't put your fingers on anything that might be more valuable than you are! It's called a social conscience! You have one of those?

JOE: Sure I do.

HERO: Put it down real slow! Exactly where you found it. [JOE complies] Now sit over there! [JOE sits at the table down center] Now you! [JENNY freezes] Don't even think about laying your hands on Marilyn! Now join your pin-striper friend! [she complies; he checks them out, lowers his shotgun and heads behind the bar] Well, you folks seem okay to me. Can't be too careful. A lot of wackos around here. I can't afford to trust no one! What'll it be, tequila or tea? [they fall silent as he pours three shots of tequila and pulls out three beers] Speechless, hey? Well now, you'll get over it. [serves them]

JENNY: What the hell!

HERO: After all, what choice do you have?

JOE: What do you mean by that?

HERO: Ah gee wiz, terribly sorry. I apologize! Now take a load off, relax, you've had a long hike. You're about as tired as a smoker in a marathon!

JOE: What do you mean we have no choice?

JENNY: How do you know about the hike?

HERO: I saw the two of you climbing up the hill. What's your name, son?

JOE: I'm Joe.

HERO: A fine name. Your folks give it to you?

JOE: Yeah. After Joe McCarthy I think.

HERO: You think?

JOE: They never said so but I got that impression.

HERO: I'm really sorry, I didn't want to make you two uncomfortable. You just can't be too careful.

JENNY: What do you mean we have no choice?

HERO: Did I say that?

JENNY: You did.

HERO: I must be losing it. You always have a choice.

JENNY: I want to know what's going on here. You threaten us with a shotgun? Not a great way to greet customers!

HERO: Customers? We haven't had customers in years.

JOE: This is a tavern, isn't it?

HERO: Once upon a time it was: Hero's Pioneer Tavern! That sign must be twenty years old. There used to be a lumber operation down the road but nobody drives up here anymore unless they're lost or trying to get that way. The point is: I don't see many folks these days and when I do I size 'em up before I dive in.

JOE: You've been watching us this whole time?

HERO: Yes sir.

JENNY: That hardly justifies the shotgun! Jesus, I thought you were going to blow us away!

HERO: I said I was sorry about that. I get a little touchy when someone gets too close to the display there. I know I should have made my move before things got carried away. But when you put your hands on the clipper it triggered a deep need for action. You don't mess with the clipper!

JOE: I'm sorry.

HERO: So you said. We're a sorry lot in a sorry situation so what do you say we make the best of it. That's what civilized people do, ain't it?

JENNY: Sure.

HERO: If I was you I'd just be glad you didn't put them grease pads on Marilyn. I don't know if I could have held myself back. That's something I can't abide. Something takes over and I can't control it.

JENNY: You really ought to put up a sign.

HERO: By God, that's a good idea!

[HERO walks behind the bar, pulls out paper and pen,

# RANDOM PLAYS

writes HANDS OFF in bold letters, pulls out hammer and nail, crosses to display area and nails it to the wall.]

JOE: [laughs] It's a little late now, don't you think?
HERO: No time like the present. That's what I always said. [returns to table, refills his shot glass and chases it with beer] Drink up and I'll pour you another one! [pours] Here's to Joe D, the greatest ballplayer this side of the Babe!
JOE: To the Clipper!

[They drink and HERO pours another round. All are sitting now.]

HERO: Having car trouble?
JOE: Yeah. "Chinka-chinka-chinka"... I don't know what it is.
JENNY: It might have something to do with the fact that we haven't checked the oil, the transmission fluid or the water in six months.
HERO: Yep. That might be it. Not much of a mechanic, are you Joe?
JOE: Afraid not.
HERO: Well, there are more important things in life.
JENNY: Not at the moment.
HERO: Not to worry. We'll get you back on your feet better than ever. First thing in the morning I'll hike down and take a look-see. If it ain't too bad I should be able to get you down to Solesby. There's a garage there.
JOE: We don't want to trouble you.
HERO: No?
JOE: If you've got a phone we'll just...
HERO: If I had a phone don't you think I'd have used it by now?
JENNY: Right. No phone.
HERO: Well, that ain't exactly right. I've got a phone, it just don't work. The fact is I ain't paid Ma Bell in what,

# JACK RANDOM

twenty years?
> JENNY: So we're stuck here.
> HERO: Pretty much. Unless you want to keep hiking.
> JOE: [shrugs, a toast] To Ma Bell!
> JENNY: To Marilyn!
> HERO: To Albert Einstein, the old codger!

[They drink. HERO pours another round.]

> HERO: Not to worry! We'll take care of you!
> JENNY: That's what we're afraid of.
> HERO: [aside] The missus seems a bit upset.
> JENNY: You think?
> HERO: Talk to her, will you?
> JOE: She's more upset with me than you.
> HERO: Oh, so that's how it is!
> JENNY: How's that?
> HERO: Got something against men folk, does she?
> JENNY: I'm right here!
> JOE: Sorry, babe.
> HERO: She seems upset.
> JENNY: I'm not!
> JOE: He's just saying...
> JENNY: Okay! You want me to be upset? I'm upset! [stands] And since the two of you are getting along so well, I'll hike back down to the car...
> JOE: Jenny, please. We're sorry. It's almost dark.
> JENNY: There's a flashlight in the car.
> JOE: Do we need a flashlight?
> JENNY: [thinks] I guess not. [sits] Let's get drunk!
> HERO: That's the spirit!
> JENNY: [toast] To John Lennon, the smart one!
> JOE: To Paul McCartney, the melodic one!
> HERO: To Joltin' Joe DiMaggio!

[They drink. HERO looks suddenly at the Hero display.]

# RANDOM PLAYS

HERO: What time is it?
JOE: [glancing at his watch] Eight twenty.
HERO: [crosses to window, looks out] Yeah, just about time. Lovely.
JENNY: What time is that?
HERO: Tea time. [crosses to bar, prepares three cups of tea] My own special mixture. It requires just the right touch at precisely the right moment.
JENNY: [crosses to window] Beautiful! What is it about twilight? The earth melting into a dying sun...like a woman taking her lover, giving herself to his desire in an explosion of fire! It's life and death, death and life – nature's daily orgasm before it gives way to the calm of night.

[HERO has delivered tea to the table. The tray also has a bell, candles and incense.]

JOE: My wife is a poet.
HERO: I can see that. I'm given to philosophy myself. And you?
JOE: Baseball.

[HERO laughs, lights three candles and incense, rings the bell.]

HERO: Tea is served!
JENNY: [returning] Sorry if I...
HERO: Apology not accepted. You were taken by the spirits. Our sunsets are known to affect people that way. It's a gift. The spirits would have been offended if you hadn't accepted their gift. [pours tea]
JOE: So what's the story? I mean, this place must have an amazing history.
HERO: History? Yes. Tea. [a toast] To Jack Kerouac!
JOE: Woodrow Wilson Guthrie!
JENNY: Bob Dylan and Joan Baez!

## JACK RANDOM

[JOE and JENNY sip. HERO drinks and pours.]

JENNY: [feeling it] That's strange. I see light and colors surrounding...everything.
HERO: It grows on you. [toast] Again! [they comply] To Bobby Kennedy!
JENNY: Jackie and John!
JOE: Honest Abe and Martin Luther King!
HERO: That's the spirit! [they drink, he pours]
JENNY: Once more! To Humphrey Bogart & Ingrid Bergman!
JOE: Liz and Burton!
JENNY: Bogie & Bacall!
HERO: To you, my friends!

[They drink. HERO pours.]

JENNY: Once more, to George and Martha!
JOE: Which ones?
JENNY: Either!
HERO: Take care, my dear, your heroes shape your soul.
JENNY: Washington. Is there anything wrong with George and Martha Washington?
HERO: Not at all...if they're your heroes.
JENNY: I don't think I have any heroes. It's child play. I don't even believe in them anymore.
JOE: It's just a game, Jen. Don't take it serious.
HERO: It is a serious matter. There are few things in life more important than keeping our heroes alive. If we allow them to die, the heroes within us will also die. If we honor and nourish that part of ourselves, we may awaken the sleeping hero within.
JENNY: Joseph Campbell. Flight of the Wild Gander. It's all very romantic but what does it mean to be a hero these days? One woman's hero is another's villain. I'd like to know what you think, mister... what is your name anyway?

# RANDOM PLAYS

HERO: I don't think much of names. Haven't used one in years.

JOE: Make one up. We've got to call you something.

HERO: A Man Called Something: That's a novel idea.

JENNY: It couldn't be that bad.

HERO: What name would you like?

JOE: What name would *you* like?

HERO: I wouldn't.

JENNY: John. I was thinking Henry but John is better.

HERO: John it is.

JOE: After Kennedy.

JENNY: Or John Huston.

HERO: A name is a name. [to Joe] You were interested in history.

JOE: That's right. I'm curious.

HERO: [to Jenny] And you want to know what a hero is.

JENNY: Sure. In real life. Not in the movies.

HERO: You believe in imaginary heroes?

JENNY: Sure. Imagined beings with superhuman qualities and powers.

HERO: Sure. Well. It won't be easy. The memory is a little foggy these days but I think I can manage. Let's see. Yes, it was 1843. That was the year this place was built. It was a man named...well...I can't remember his name. They called him Hero. He came out from Chicago. He had a dream about going west, staking a place for himself. He found a woman with the same dream and out they came. I believe it was the Oregon Trail. It was hot that summer, painfully hot, but they made it. They eventually took up in a place on the San Francisco Bay. Things were a little tight but they were happy. Just trying to build a little nest egg. Then the fire happened. She hadn't been feeling well when he left for work. She never made it out.

JENNY: How very sad.

HERO: Yep. Sadness is like a disease. It changed him. He became a recluse. Packed up and moved north to get away from people. This is where he settled. He built this cabin. He lived by hunting, fishing and trapping. As the years rolled by, other folks moved up this way. Good folks. Strong, independent folks. He watched them from a distance. Then one day stories began to travel up the coast about a band of thieves robbing and terrorizing folks. Stories of murder, rape and mayhem. He was high up on the hill when he saw them coming through the pass. A band of seven or eight men and they had a woman with them. She was tied and bound. Pretty little thing. She reminded him of…someone he once knew. [silence] He trailed them until they set up camp. He figured he could take them when they were sleeping but fate took its turn. Seems the stories were right. Soon as they'd built a fire and had a bite it became clear what they intended for their evening entertainment. The ugliest of them picked her up and slammed her against a tree. When she fought back he slapped her and threw her to the ground. That was it. That was all he could watch. He fired a shot right through the ugly man's temple and all hell broke loose. Bullets flying, screaming, yelling, running about. When it was all over, he took three shots: one to his neck, one to his gut and one to his leg. But he and a young lady were the only ones who lived to tell the tale.

JOE: That's quite a story.
HERO: Yep.
JOE: Is it true?
HERO: Every word.
JENNY: What happened to them?
HERO: Just like the story books. She nursed him back to health. They fell in love and lived happily ever after. He became a new man. Reborn. He came out of his shell. He never said no to a neighbor in need. He saved many a man and woman from desperate times and cruel twists of fate. They say not a soul on this coast wasn't beholden to him for something he had done. As legend has it, he's still here. He roams the coast range, protecting folks, guiding them out of

trouble, changing lives for the better.

JOE: Is that what you believe?

HERO: I'd have to take it with a grain of salt. No man's as good or as bad as legends make him. I believe we do what we can or what we have to do. No man wants to be the bad guy. We all want to be the hero. But without the bad guys there would be no heroes.

JENNY: There's something mysterious and spiritual here.

JOE: She was born romantic.

HERO: I can see that. What about you?

JOE: I'm a realist.

HERO: Meaning you believe in reality.

JOE: That's right.

HERO: I guess you must have a pretty good hold on what reality is.

JOE: Reality is a broken down car.

HERO: No room for doubt?

JOE: There's always doubt.

HERO: Good. That's all we need.

JOE: All we need?

HERO: For change, an awakening, a new way of looking at life! You ever fall out of a tree?

JOE: As a matter of fact I have.

HERO: Remember what the world looked like when you first came to? All fresh and new, bright colors, strange textures.

JOE: I remember the pain. I broke my arm.

HERO: That's all you remember?

JOE: That's all I remember remembering.

HERO: What a shame.

JENNY: I remember coming out of a fever once and feeling like the whole world changed.

JOE: Had it?

JENNY: I thought it had.

HERO: The world is a ball of clay. You mold with your

mind. All you need is a fresh perspective.

JOE: And a lot of money.

JENNY: Is that realistic or cynical?

JOE: Is that a rhetorical question?

JENNY: It really isn't a question at all.

JOE: What does that mean?

JENNY: Just that we could both use a new perspective.

HERO: [pours] Here, here! To Joe and Jenny and a fresh outlook!

JENNY: To you!

JOE: To heroes, one and all! [they drink] You haven't finished your story.

HERO: What story?

JOE: History! How did you come to be here?

HERO: Me? I don't know exactly.

JOE: Come on, you're not that old.

JENNY: Maybe he'd rather not say.

HERO: No, no, let's see. Many years ago I came to California with my wife. Unfortunately, we were separated. Circumstances beyond our control. I just sort of ended up here. Someone had to look after this place. Not much of a story, is it?

JENNY: Sounds like us. Except for the separation. Where do you come from?

HERO: Midwest. Indiana.

JENNY: Chicago area?

HERO: Give or take. Where are you folks from?

JENNY: How do you know we're not Californians?

HERO: Are you?

JENNY: No, we're from York, Pennsylvania.

JOE: We came to California by way of Chicago. We went to college there.

HERO: Really? How is Chicago these days?

JOE: Big. It was a few years back.

HERO: How big?

JOE: Very.

# RANDOM PLAYS

HERO: Five thousand?

JOE: Five thousand what? Bars?

HERO: Bars?

JOE: Yeah, on one block. I'm kidding. Chicago's huge. You can look out from the top of the Chrysler Building in all directions and never see the end. It spreads out as far as the eye can see – which generally isn't very far.

HERO: The Chrysler Building.

JOE: The tallest building in Chicago.

HERO: [puzzled] Why did you leave?

JENNY: I had a kid. He got a job. It's a common story.

HERO: Did you like it there?

JENNY: It was fun and exciting. There was always something going on: a play, a film festival, a jazz group at the tavern, a day game at Wrigley or a night game at Comiskey. We never stopped moving. It was great.

JOE: It was great while it lasted but it's no place to raise a kid.

HERO: You came to California for the child.

JOE: Yeah. That and the fact that I got a job here.

HERO: You needed a job.

JOE: I did. I'm a teacher.

HERO: They don't need teachers in Chicago?

JOE: Of course. But if you want to teach in the arts, you take what you're offered.

HERO: You're an artist!

JOE: Well... I teach art. Art appreciation and history. Jenny's a sculptor.

HERO: You appreciate art.

JOE: It helps to appreciate art if you teach art appreciation.

HERO: Do you enjoy teaching?

JOE: What's not to like?

JENNY: He's a good teacher. The students line up at his door. They love him.

HERO: No regrets?

# JACK RANDOM

JOE: None here. California's great! Mild winters and comfortable summers. It's great.
HERO: You like the weather?
JOE: Sure. You know what it's like back east.
HERO: [to Jenny] And you? No regrets?
JENNY: Some. Like I said there was always something happening there. I was engaged. I miss that life. But I'm a mother now. It's better for the kids.
HERO: Tell me about them.
JENNY: Billy is seven and Susie is five. They wanted to come on this trip but...
JOE: We needed some time together.
HERO: I'm sure they're beautiful children.
JENNY: They are. It's amazing how fast they grow up.
HERO: Would they have liked Chicago?
JENNY: I don't think so.
JOE: The smog, the crime, the crowding, the garbage, neighborhood gangs, street people... There's no room for kids to run around and play.
HERO: Chicago sounds like a terrible place.
JOE: For kids. Not for everyone.
HERO: I'm sure you did the right thing.
JENNY: I think so.
JOE: No regrets.

[Awkward silence.]

HERO: So now you're on vacation.
JOE: We're on our way to Seattle to see some old friends.
HERO: Sounds good.

[SOUND: We begin to hear the spirits of the night at low volume. There is a strange brew of chaos and comfort. JOE and JENNY are mystified. HERO is amused.]

# RANDOM PLAYS

JENNY: Do you hear that?

JOE: I do.

JENNY: It's almost like music.

JOE: It's twisted.

HERO: It's only the wind, the trees, the owls, creatures of the night. All perfectly natural. Nothing to be afraid of.

JENNY: [rises, moves to the window] I'm not afraid. There's something soothing about it. Comforting.

JOE: [passive, entranced] You put something in the tea.

HERO: It's just your imagination. The woods come alive at night. Relax and breathe it in.

JENNY: Something's coming. It rides the wind and the rain. I hear voices.

VOICES: [faint, rising, ethereal] Give in. Sacrifice. The moment calls to you. There is only the moment. Don't fight it. Give in. Seize it and be free!

[Thunder and lightning mask the entrance of CHICO. He is a classic Mexican bandito with six-guns in hand and a roaring laugh.]

CHICO: Stay where you are! Well, well, well, what have we here? Three stinking cowards cowering in the night, afraid of their own shadows. What are you afraid of, my dear? Chico won't hurt you! Chico is here to protect you! [JOE rises, CHICO points a gun his way] From who? From him for example. What's that? He is your husband! He is not worthy! He is weak. He is a worm. [HERO laughs] What are you laughing at, old man?

HERO: I laugh at fools.

CHICO: Who are you, old man? [JENNY starts to move away from the window] Don't move! Just like him I have eyes in the back of my head. [examines HERO] What are you? [to Jenny] You! Over there! [JENNY joins Joe at the table; CHICO pulls over a chair and sits, holstering his guns and pulling out a knife] Well, well, well, it's going to be a

## JACK RANDOM

long night. Relax. Take a load off. What? You are still scared? [the knife] This? I am sorry. I must keep it. For protection. [indicating Hero] From him. I'm very good with this, old man.

    HERO: I'm sure you are.
    JOE: Look, why don't you just...
    CHICO: Say it! Who knows? It might be important.
    JOE: Why don't you just go?
    CHICO: Go? Why don't I just go? [laughs] You think I want to be here? I was brought here against my will! By the old man, I think.
    JOE: Well then, why don't you let us go?
    CHICO: Go! [JOE and JENNY rise to leave.] Wait a minute. There is a problem. I don't want to be alone...with him. You understand. You can go but your wife must stay.
    JOE: Right. We stay.
    CHICO: If you insist!
    JENNY: Wait. What if Joe goes and I stay?
    CHICO: Well, there's an idea! You like that idea, old man?
    HERO: I like it fine.
    CHICO: No, no, no, it's no good. I like her better than you. She is better company.
    JOE: Right. We stay.
    CHICO: If you insist.
    JENNY: What do you want with us?
    CHICO: I told you. Ask him.
    HERO: [speaking with his mind] Go ahead, Chico. They won't believe you. Nobody believes you.
    CHICO: You think he's your friend. Go ahead and tell them! You brought me here! I am tonight's entertainment! I know this old man! [to Hero] You're right, they don't believe me and we are getting nowhere. Okay, let's play a little game. Let's find out who we are dealing with. [to Jenny] Who are you, mija?
    JENNY: I'm Jenny.

# RANDOM PLAYS

CHICO: What's in a name? Shit would still stink if you called it a rose. Who are you?

JENNY: I'm a mother and a wife. I teach when I have time. I sculpt, I draw and I take care of the kids.

CHICO: It's a beginning. [to Joe] And you?

JOE: I teach. I'm a father.

CHICO: What do you teach?

JOE: The arts.

CHICO: All of them?

JOE: Yes.

CHICO: You must be a very smart man. Until now I thought that art was only one thing. There are many horses but art is one. I am not so smart.

JOE: Photography, painting, sculpture, architecture, literature, on and on.

CHICO: [to Jenny] What do you teach?

JENNY: The arts.

CHICO: That's very interesting. Don't you think that's interesting, old man?

HERO: Yes.

CHICO: We agree? What do you know? [to Joe] What do you do when you are not teaching art?

JOE: Go to movies, theater, ball games, play some golf, go to museums, restaurants...

CHICO: [to Jenny] And you?

JENNY: Pretty much the same.

CHICO: You do these things together?

JENNY: Sometimes.

CHICO: This too is interesting. You do the same things, sometimes together, sometimes with other people.

JENNY: Someone's got to take care of the kids.

CHICO: The kids? Where are they?

JENNY: Home with a sitter.

CHICO: They should be here.

JOE: Thank God they're not.

HERO: [speaking with his mind] Ask them how they feel

about each other.

CHICO: Why?

JENNY: We needed some time alone.

HERO: [with his mind] Ask them.

CHICO: Why?

JOE: People do it all the time. We needed some time. What's so hard to understand?

CHICO: [laughs] Up to your old tricks, old man! [to Joe] I understand. When a man and a woman are having problems, they leave the kids at home. What are these problems?

JENNY: Everyone has problems. It's normal.

CHICO: You are having normal problems?

JOE: Yes.

CHICO: I am not a normal person. Maybe you noticed. I do not know what normal problems are.

JOE: It's between us. Why should we tell you?

HERO: [mentally] He wants to know how far you'll go. He wants to see if he can challenge you.

CHICO: [to Joe] You are challenging me? That is not very wise, senor.

JOE: [scoffs] You storm in here in this ridiculous Pancho Villa costume and an absurd Hollywood accent! You're not fooling anyone! You're just a two-bit thug!

CHICO: Let me tell you where we differ, little man. You believe your eyes. [sniffs] I believe my nose. You act like a brave man but my nose tells me it is a lie. You are a frightened man who is trying to save his pride but it does not work. I have a big knife. Maybe you noticed? I have guns. This gives me power. You? You have nothing. [moves to Jenny] You have your woman, your kids at home, your problems. [cuts off a lock of Jenny's hair] A souvenir. You will tell me your problems but first we will have a drink. [to Jenny] You will bring me that bottle of tequila. [sits as JENNY complies] We will all sit down and we will talk about our problems. Old man, you will join us.

# RANDOM PLAYS

HERO: Why not?
CHICO: [to Jenny] Glasses! You will bring glasses!

[JENNY brings tequila and glasses, sits.]

HERO: [mentally] We don't need no stinking glasses!
CHICO: You are a very funny old man but no one laughs. [to Jenny] You will pour. [she does] You have great power, viejo, but you too have a problem. You like these people. You would not do anything to endanger them.
HERO: Let's drink! To Chico!
CHICO: To you, old man!
HERO: To Joe and Jenny!

[HERO and CHICO drink; JOE and JENNY do not.]

CHICO: You do not like the toast? You will drink anyway! [they comply] Now we play the game. I will tell you what your problems are and you will tell me if I am right or wrong.
JOE: How do you know we'll tell the truth?
CHICO: I know by my nose.
JOE: Right. You read minds. If you already know the answers why bother to ask?
CHICO: What I know is what I know. It does not interest me. Reality bores me. It is perception that interests me. It is more powerful than the truth. It is so powerful it can disguise the truth. Only the spirits know. But you do not believe in spirits. You believe only what you see. That is your problem.
JOE: I'm a realist. It's not a problem.
CHICO: Your wife can tell you what the problem is.
JENNY: I don't know what you're talking about.
CHICO: Sadly, you do not tell the truth. She sees you are threatened and she protects you. You are a lucky man! When you are home she will say: You're problem is you

have no dream! There is no romance. Where is the man she fell in love with? The things you worry about destroy you but they are not real. They are not important.

JOE: I'll take the bait. What am I worried about?

CHICO: Money.

JOE: We have all the money we need.

CHICO: Of course. You have always had the money you need but it is never enough. You want more. You want security. You want comfort. You want more. You began your journey not knowing how much it would cost you. Now you have arrived and you realize it cost your soul. You are afraid. You cannot go back.

JOE: I don't want to go back.

CHICO: Maybe. Maybe not. But it worries you. You can only go on and you wonder if you have lost the one thing you cannot bear losing: your wife's love.

JOE: [pause; to Jenny] This is the part where you say something.

CHICO: She will lie for you.

JOE: I don't want her to lie. I know there's some truth to it and I'm sorry. He's right about one thing: I'd do anything not to lose you.

JENNY: You've never lost my love. You never could. I thought I'd lost yours. I wondered what I did or didn't do.

CHICO: It is moving, so very moving.

HERO: [mentally] Don't push it too far.

CHICO: I must. We must. We cannot stop until all the cards are on the table.

HERO: [mentally] I'll stop you if you do.

CHICO: You cannot stop me, old man, but you may try. [to Joe] I am very sorry but I must tell you now what you have felt in your heart a long time. Your wife has not been faithful.

JENNY: He's lying.

CHICO: She misunderstands my words. She thinks I speak of adultery. She has not given her body. She has given much more. She has given her love. Not the love that is yours but the love that has grown while she has grown. It is the love you could not receive. You were too busy. I tell you now what you already know. She is not to blame. She pays more than she owes. You will forgive her now and maybe she will forgive you.

JOE: Who the hell are you?

CHICO: Why trouble yourself with what you cannot understand?

JOE: [to Jenny] It's true, isn't it?

JENNY: I wanted to tell you but I couldn't. I didn't want to hurt you.

JOE: It doesn't matter.

JENNY: It does.

JOE: I'm sorry. It's my fault.

CHICO: So very touching! Now, my dear, I must tell you something.

HERO: [mentally] Do not!

CHICO: You worry too much, old man!

HERO: [mentally] I warn you!

CHICO: You have lost the guts God gave you!

JOE: I don't know what's going on here or who you're talking to but I know what you're going to say and I'd like to tell her myself.

CHICO: If you insist.

JENNY: You don't have to say it. Believe me, I know.

CHICO: You disappoint me, chica! Just when we were about to have such a good time you spoil the fun! You should be punished...but how?

HERO: Let's have a drink and think about it.

CHICO: A good idea! Careful, old man, I may get to like you!

HERO: Just a while ago I was thinking the same about you.

CHICO: But now? Good. I don't wish to think what would happen if we became friends. [to Jenny] Pour! [she complies; they drink; to Hero] It's your turn, old man! Who are you?

HERO: You know who I am.

CHICO: I know but our friends do not.

HERO: Are you sure?

CHICO: Did you tell them?

HERO: Can't say that I did. I told them a story. I think maybe they're beginning to put it together.

JENNY: You're Hero and he's the bandit.

CHICO: Shame on you, old man. You've been telling stories again! What did I do this time? Kill a baby? Torture a nun? Slaughter a village?

JOE: Murder, terror, robbery.

CHICO: [thinks] You are hiding something. Why? [rises, paces] What could be so terrible? You think I don't know? You think you can disguise your thoughts with nursery rhymes? [stops] Oh. That is a terrible thing. [to Hero] You should be ashamed, old man. Such lies!

HERO: [a toast] To horrible lies and ugly banditos!

CHICO: To scumbag gringos who tell filthy stories!

JENNY: To innocent bystanders…

JOE: And happy endings.

CHICO: That's good. I like it. Drink! [they drink]

JENNY: I'm going to be sick.

HERO: [points off right] Down the hall.

CHICO: Go! We don't want your stinking puke all over the place!

[JENNY exits stage right.]

JOE: I think you've had enough fun at our expense. There's no need to take it any further. We've played our parts. You win. We're intimidated. What else do you want? You want us to beg, plead for mercy, what?

CHICO: You are not having a good time?

JOE: If it's all the same to you, we'd like to go.

# RANDOM PLAYS

CHICO: Relax, take a load off, have a drink.

[JENNY enters.]

CHICO: Trouble with the window, mija?
JENNY: No trouble.
CHICO: Ah well. I let it pass. Your husband wants to go.
JENNY: Does he?
CHICO: He is not having a good time.
JENNY: Imagine that.
CHICO: What? You are not having a good time either?
JENNY: No. As a matter of fact I think the both of you are very cruel men.
CHICO: Both of us? It breaks my heart. I like you so much! You are sure you don't like me just a little?
JENNY: I despise you.
CHICO: Such strong language. You are sure you will not change your mind?
JENNY: Not likely.
CHICO: But possible?
JENNY: Not possible.
CHICO: You don't know how much it saddens me to hear this. I was so looking forward to the rest of our evening together. It is the old man's fault, you know. He has poisoned you against me. But if you are sure... [shrugs, to Hero] Shall we let them go?
HERO: Where would they go?
CHICO: Who knows? Anywhere but here. They are not happy.
HERO: We were getting along fine before you came.
CHICO: Oh, so it's my fault? [to Joe] You see? It's very complicated.
JOE: Nothing complicated about it. We walk out that door and never return.
CHICO: Where would you go?

# JACK RANDOM

JOE: Does it matter?
CHICO: You would stay in these woods?
JOE: So what?
CHICO: You are a braver man than me, senor.
JOE: We'll take our chances.
CHICO: Okay! Alright! I tried. I did my best! Did I not, old man?
HERO: You can only try.
CHICO: Go then…but be careful.

[JOE and JENNY grab their bags and go to the door. As they open it, a blast of lightning and thunder rumbles the entire building. The storm rages with the voices of spirits under. They freeze, close the door and turn back. CHICO shrugs, smiles.]

CHICO: I told you.

[Fade to black.]

End Act One.

## ACT TWO

(Lights up. Everything is as it was. JENNY seems increasingly lost, dazed, wandering.)

JOE: Who are you?
CHICO: You are speaking to me?
JOE: Quit jerking us around! I'd like to know who you are, what you are and what the hell is going on here!
CHICO: What do you think I am?
JOE: You look like a man but…
CHICO: You don't believe your eyes?
JOE: I don't believe anything anymore. No man has the rain, the wind, thunder and lightning at his command! I don't know what you are! I'm beginning to think this is all a dream! You're not real!
CHICO: What is real? What is a dream? It is all the same. If you were an Apache, gringo, you would know that.
JOE: I'm not Apache.
CHICO: No. You are a coward. You deny what you cannot understand and cannot control. You call yourself a realist but you are only a coward.
JOE: I'm not afraid of you.
CHICO: A coward is a man who pretends he is not afraid.
JOE: What does it matter? I am afraid. I'm afraid of you and [indicates Hero] him and the spirits outside this door. I'm afraid of evil.
CHICO: Evil? Now you will tell me what is good and what is evil? Pretty soon you might make me mad! You don't want to make me mad, pendejo! It is good you are afraid. I am strong and you are weak. You find yourself in a world you do not understand. You have no map, no

compass. You have nothing to guide you. Welcome to my world, pendejo! It is a world of spirits!

JOE: Then I'm right. You're not real.

CHICO: Again you disappoint me. I give you truth and you shit on it! I feed you wisdom and you spit it out! Soon I will begin to lose faith.

JOE: Deny it then.

CHICO: What's to deny? Todos son espiritu! I am a spirit! The old man is a spirit! A very powerful spirit! Espiritu fuerte. The wind, the rain and the trees: All spirits! Your wife is a very interesting spirit and you, little man, are a spirit too.

JOE: Bullshit! [sarcastic] We're all spirits! Bullshit! We're real and you're not!

CHICO: So you say. [pulls out a bandana and lays it across his forearm; pulls out his knife, slices his palm and holds it up as blood runs down his arm] If you cut us, do we not bleed? [wraps the bandana around the wound] You pretend to know but you do not know. You pretend to understand but you cannot see beyond your sight. You are a child in this world.

JOE: This is a nightmare!

CHICO: Should I cut your heart out to wake you up? What is a dream? What is a nightmare? Do you think you have created me? I laugh at your foolishness! [grabs JOE by the shirt, stares at him face to face] Look at me, pendejo! Who do you see?

JOE: You're not real!

CHICO: The truth is in front of you but you do not see!

JOE: It's an illusion! I don't believe it!

CHICO: There are no illusions! You don't need to believe! You know! There are some things you know in your heart and this is one!

JENNY: That's enough! [to Hero] Stop him!

HERO: It is not for me to stop him.

JENNY: If you want to torture someone, try me!

# RANDOM PLAYS

JOE: Stay out of it, Jenny!

CHICO: An interesting proposal! But I am patient. Your time will come. Now is the coward's turn.

JENNY: He's no coward! You don't have a clue!

CHICO: I say he is a coward! Cobarde miedoso! He knows the truth but he doesn't have the guts to face it! He sees what he sees but will not name it! He is a coward!

JOE: I'm not afraid!

CHICO: Then tell the truth! Look into my eyes and tell me what you see?

JOE: I see...myself.

CHICO: [nods, then laughs] Yes. I am you and you are me and we are one with the spirits of the night. Your wife feels its pull! [JENNY moves to the windows] She feels it in her bones! We cannot imagine how they call to her!

JENNY: [entranced] It's true. They are inside me. I feel them in my soul. It's warm and comforting. I belong with them. I'm one of them. The wind has deep blue eyes, dark with passion. They fill me with desire. They promise me a world beyond the senses, a world of beauty and power...

CHICO: Now you will see!

[HERO rises but keels over as if kicked in the gut.]

JENNY: I want to be with them!
HERO: Help her!
CHICO: Now you will understand!
JOE: What can I do?
CHICO: It is beyond your control!
HERO: Tell her you love her!

[JOE goes to her, embraces her.]

CHICO: It is too late!
JOE: I love you, Jenny!
CHICO: There is nothing you can do!

# JACK RANDOM

JENNY: I belong with them!
JOE: I've loved you since the first time I saw you!
CHICO: She is no longer here!
JOE: But I swear to you I've never loved you more than I do this moment!
CHICO: She belongs to us now!
JOE: Fight back, Jenny!
CHICO: Let go! You know where you belong!
JOE: I love you!

[JENNY collapses in his arms.]

HERO: [moving up right to the sanctuary of heroes] Bring her here.
JOE: [carrying JENNY to the sanctuary] Dear God, thank you. Thank you.
CHICO: [smiling] You think it's over? It is only beginning.
HERO: We almost lost her.
JOE: How? To what?
HERO: To the spirits you do not believe exist.
CHICO: He believes now!
JOE: Will she be okay?
HERO: Yes but she is in great danger.
CHICO: Tell the truth, old man. There is no danger. She is enchanted! Another moment and she would have been an angel!
HERO: You lie! A spirit is not an angel!
CHICO: A little lie. I get excited. A passionate woman is something to behold! Does she ever feel that way with you, pendejo?
JOE: She did. A long time ago.
HERO: There are many forces at work here. Some are familiar and some are not.
JOE: What can I do?
CHICO: You are asking him? You might as well ask the

moon. After all I've done for you, this is what you do? You are a fool. You think the old man is your salvation? He is your damnation! But I have tried. There is nothing more I can do. [sits and pours tequila]

HERO: Your wife is a special soul. The spirits of the night are attracted to her beauty, her passion and her desire. It arouses them. They thirst for her as other men do. Maybe you've noticed.

JOE: I have.

HERO: Have you been jealous?

JOE: Yes.

HERO: Good. That will help.

CHICO: Give it up, viejo! It's out of your hands.

JOE: What do they want?

HERO: They want her soul. To them she is a rare jewel. They see her passion and they sense her weakness. Emotions stir them but they can't succeed unless there is doubt. Doubt is the window through which Jenny may pass.

JOE: What can I do?

CHICO: Nothing! You are good at it!

HERO: You drunken fool!

CHICO: Can a ghost get drunk?

JOE: Tell me.

HERO: Whatever happens, Jenny can never doubt your love. You stopped them because she believed you. You made her remember when your love was strong. The window closed but they'll be back. This time they will be stronger. To fight them you must rediscover your faith – not only in Jenny but also in yourself. You must rise above yourself to be worthy of her love. You have said you love her; now you must convince her. She must believe you love her more than life itself.

CHICO: That is a problem.

HERO: What are you babbling about?

CHICO: He cannot convince anyone if it is not true.

JOE: It is true.

# JACK RANDOM

CHICO: It is only words. When it comes to action, you are a coward! You are not worthy of this fine woman! You would not risk your life for anyone!
HERO: If he's right, she's lost.
JOE: He's wrong.
JENNY: [coming to] Where am I? What happened?
JOE: You're safe, baby. You were lost for a while but you're back and you're safe.
CHICO: For now but not for long!
JOE: I'll protect you.
CHICO: You could not protect her from a dog!
JOE: You want me? Come on!
HERO: He's not important. You're not fighting him.
CHICO: That's true. I am not important. I could take your head off with my little finger but I am not important.
HERO: [unspoken] Stay out of it!
CHICO: You're right. It is not the time. I will sit and drink your tequila and count the ticks of the clock. The time will come.
JOE: What's he talking about?
HERO: Nothing. He's touched.
CHICO: I heard that!
HERO: Talk to her.

[HERO crosses to the bar, sits.]

JENNY: What happened?
JOE: You were in some kind of trance. It was as if the spirits of the night possessed you. When you came out of it, you passed out.
JENNY: I don't remember much. Voices. Feelings. You told me you loved me and I reached out.
JOE: Thank God you heard me. I don't think I could live without you.
JENNY: There have been times I've wondered. I thought you might want to live without me. I thought

somehow I held you back.

JOE: I know, Jenny. I wanted you to feel that way. I think I wanted to punish you.

JENNY: Why?

JOE: For making me feel old. You're still young. You're full of energy and idealism! You still believe in right and wrong. You follow your heart. You live in the moment. In so many ways I'd lost that.

JENNY: I didn't mean to make you feel old.

JOE: I know you didn't. It was how I felt about myself. I didn't want to change and I didn't want to feel guilty so I blamed you. I was the realist and you were the fool.

[HERO has prepared tea and now serves it to them.]

HERO: Here we are. Something special to soothe you both.

JENNY: Thank you.

[JENNY sips as CHICO laughs.]

JOE: Wait!
HERO: You must learn to trust an old man.
CHICO: I warn you again. It is a mistake.
JENNY: It's okay, Joe. I trust him.
JOE: I guess you're right.
CHICO: Don't say I didn't warn you!
HERO: [to Jenny] How do you feel?
JENNY: Strange. Wonderful. [starts to rise]
HERO: No. [indicates the sanctuary] It's safer here. Evil spirits are afraid of heroes.
JENNY: A sanctuary! How can you doubt someone who worships Marilyn?
JOE: You're right. [sips tea]
HERO: [crosses to bar, sits and closes his eyes] I'll leave you two alone now. They'll be back but not for a while.

CHICO: It may be sooner than you think!

HERO: There's a lot you have to talk about.

JENNY: He's right.

JOE: [pause] Where to begin?

JENNY: I know you wanted to leave me.

JOE: I thought I did.

JENNY: If it wasn't for the kids, you would have.

JOE: No. That was an excuse. I was scared. [waits] I have to tell you something.

JENNY: You had an affair. I know. Who, when, where – I know.

JOE: Do you forgive me?

JENNY: [waits] I could have killed you. I wanted to confront you about it but every time I tried something stopped me. I'd like to think it was love but I think it was fear. I didn't want to start all over. [waits] I hated you.

JOE: I understand. I hated myself. I hate myself now for hurting you. I can only tell you I've changed. I know that's what they all say but it's true. I'm sorry for what I did and I swear I'll never knowingly hurt you again.

JENNY: Is that enough? Why should I believe you?

JOE: I can only tell you I need you and I need you to believe in me. I know that words aren't enough. I'll do anything. I just don't know what to do.

JENNY: Try. That's all. Just try.

JOE: I promise you I will.

JENNY: [waits] My turn. My confession. I wanted to have an affair. I wanted to cause you the same pain you caused me. But it was more than that. I wanted to feel something more than a mother's love. I was looking for it. So when the opportunity came, I took it. You didn't know, did you? He was a friend of yours.

JOE: I didn't know. I don't want to know.

JENNY: It felt right. There was no guilt and no shame. But when it came right down to it, neither of us could go through with it. I don't know why. Maybe I'd already got my revenge. I betrayed you in my heart.

JOE: We've made a mess of it.

JENNY: We have but we're still here and we're still together. We can't change what happened but we can go on. It's strange. Even tonight, after all we've said, after all we've been through, I feel more alive than I have in God knows how long.

JOE: Jenny, don't you know what's going on here? These spirits, whatever they are, hallucinations or whatever, they're after you. I can't explain it but if I lose you tonight, I've lost you for good.

JENNY: They can't take me unless I want to go. I don't know how I know but its true.

JOE: They're not what they seem. They're evil. You have to fight them.

JENNY: Fight them? How?

[The sound of the storm begins to rise.]

CHICO: [standing] Wake up, children! They are coming for you! We must use our time wisely. You have had a good talk? Yes? No? You understand each other? Yes? No? Don't worry about it. There is nothing you can do.

HERO: That is not true.

CHICO: You know something I do not?

HERO: Don't pay any attention to him. He's a fool who likes to meddle in other people's lives.

CHICO: And you do not? [to Joe] You still believe in him? After he gives you drugs? After he tells you lies?

JOE: I don't know what to believe or who to trust.

CHICO: That is a beginning. He tells you his heroes will protect you. [crosses to display] Who are these heroes? They are spirits... not unlike the spirits of the night. [thunder cracks as he picks up Joe DiMaggio] This one. Who is he?

JOE: Joltin' Joe DiMaggio. One of the greatest ball players of all time.

CHICO: He plays ball?
JOE: Baseball. He used to play. He's dead now.
CHICO: He is your hero?
JOE: Yes.
CHICO: Because he plays ball?
JOE: It was the way he played and how he carried himself. He made everything look easy. He played with grace and humility. He never acted like he was better than the rest of us even though we all wanted to be him. Off the field he was a simple man. Dignified. He knew what he believed in and he lived up to it.
JENNY: Then he married Marilyn.
CHICO: Who is this Marilyn?
JENNY: [crosses to pick up picture] May I?
HERO: Of course.
JENNY: Isn't she beautiful?
CHICO: I like her very much – almost as much as I like you.
JENNY: She was a goddess – a Hollywood goddess. She was every man's dream but she was also so sensitive, vulnerable and so innocent. She just wanted to be loved. Not by the whole country, not by every man, but by one man. She was a lot like Joe really. It's a shame it couldn't last.
CHICO: She left him?
JENNY: They left each other. My heart goes out to them even now. They never stopped loving each other.
CHICO: [reflects] A jilted lover and an insecure actress? These are your heroes? [indicates Einstein] Tell me about this one, the one with the crazy hair.
HERO: The smartest man who ever lived. His theory of relativity will one day enable humans to travel in time. Without Einstein we could not have split the atom, creating the most powerful force in history. We used that knowledge to end the Second World War.
CHICO: He invented a bomb?
HERO: He gave us knowledge.

# RANDOM PLAYS

CHICO: Without that knowledge we would not have the bomb? How many lives would be saved if your hero never lived?

HERO: You miss the point. Einstein was a scientist. It is not his responsibility what others do with the knowledge he revealed.

CHICO: He gives matches to his children and expects them not to start a fire. No, my friend, it is you who miss the point. It is not what you intend; it is what you do that matters. [moves to the picture of Humphrey Bogart] This one. What is he?

JOE: Humphrey Bogart. A great actor.

CHICO: Another movie star?

JOE: That's right. He played the tough guy with a heart of gold. Hard on the outside, soft on the inside. He always stuck his neck out for the woman he loved, a friend in need, his partner or the greater good.

CHICO: It is the movies! It is easy to be strong in the movies. [moves to Tom Paine] And this one?

HERO: Tom Paine. He wrote Common Sense and The Rights of Man. Without Paine, this great country of ours might not have been a republic.

CHICO: A writer? Words are cheap. What did he do?

HERO: A writer writes and sometimes what he writes can change the world. He had a part in two revolutions. He marched with the soldiers in America and he was imprisoned in France. He risked his life.

CHICO: But he did not fight. He left that to others who had more cajones than he did. And the others?

JENNY: Bobby Kennedy and John Lennon. Lennon was a singer, a musician and songwriter. He recorded some of the greatest songs of his generation. He believed in peace and justice and love. He gave up on the world to become a parent. When he came back to the world he was gunned down by a crazy man. Just like Bobby. Bobby Kennedy was *my* hero. He was hope. He wanted to end the war. When they killed Bobby, they killed hope. He would have been president and the world would be a better place today.

CHICO: A singer and a politician. [shakes his head] I don't understand you people. I laugh at you. These are no heroes! They are movie stars and people who give words, not actions! Did you even know these people? Do you know what was in their hearts?

JOE: It's not what we know. It's what we feel. These people represent our ideals. They were who we want to be.

CHICO: You don't care what the truth is?

JENNY: The truth is what we believe and what we feel in our hearts.

CHICO: Your heart never misleads you?

JENNY: Never.

CHICO: You married him!

JENNY: I did. I would again.

CHICO: He does not believe as you believe!

HERO: Doesn't he?

CHICO: What do you say, pendejo?

JOE: I say... anyone who disrespects John Lennon, Bobby Kennedy, Albert Einstein, Tom Paine, Joe DiMaggio and Marilyn Monroe... is a miserable excuse for a human being.

CHICO: Words! Only words. So... you are all against me? Good. I like it that way. It will make victory even sweeter. Tell me more about these heroes. How can you worship people who are so unlike yourselves?

HERO: They all believed in something greater than themselves.

JOE: They believed in a better world.

JENNY: They believed that what counts most is what is in your heart.

JOE: They believed in love.

HERO: And they gave everything for their beliefs.

CHICO: [reflects] I am touched. But what do they have to do with you?

# RANDOM PLAYS

JOE: They make us want to be better.

CHICO: Fools! You cannot be better than who you are. It is not possible.

HERO: It is possible.

CHICO: We shall see. [to Joe] You believe in your heroes?

JOE: Yes.

CHICO: Like you believe in your wife?

JOE: Yes.

CHICO: What would you give for this belief?

JOE: Anything. Everything.

CHICO: You would not lie to Chico?

JOE: I might but not about this.

CHICO: Good. You will have your chance. [closes eyes] They are coming! Soon they will be here. Then we will see.

HERO: [unspoken] You surprise me, my friend. You're beginning to play fair.

CHICO: There is no sport in hunting squirrel. I will make him into a wolf! Well, maybe a fox.

HERO: [unspoken] I think you like him.

CHICO: [aside] I like his wife much better. [louder] You know what I see when I look at your heroes? Sorrow.

HERO: There is sorrow. There's always a price to pay. We can't live up to them just as they couldn't live up to themselves. But if you look beyond the sorrow, you see hope and love and greatness. That's what we see. The greatness.

[JENNY rises as the storm grows closer, louder.]

CHICO: They come to you! Can you feel them?
JENNY: [shudders] In my bones.

[JOE rushes to her as she moves to the windows. He takes hold of her.]

# JACK RANDOM

JOE: Fight them!
HERO: You can't force her. You must convince her.

[The following dialogue overlaps as the storm grows louder along with the spirits. They whisper: *Jenny, Jenny, come with us! We are your destiny! You belong with us! Believe in us! etc.* It is a cacophony of sound.]

JOE: [to Hero] I've said I love her.
CHICO: Can you hear them?
HERO: Patience.
CHICO: Their voices are sweet like music!
HERO: The time will come.
CHICO: They call to you!
JENNY: Joe? Where are you?
CHICO: You cannot resist them!
JOE: I'm here!
HERO: Then you must act!
CHICO: Can you feel them?
JOE: I'm here! Look at me.
JENNY: I can't.
CHICO: Closer and closer!
JOE: Try, Jenny!
JENNY: I feel them!
CHICO: They will not let go!
JENNY: They're inside me!
JOE: Fight them, damn it!
HERO: The moment will come.
CHICO: Let go!
JENNY: It's beautiful!
HERO: Then you must act.
JOE: They're evil, Jenny!
CHICO: He lies!
JOE: Look beyond the mask!

[JENNY looks directly at JOE.]

# RANDOM PLAYS

JENNY:  Come with us!
JOE:  Are you crazy?
JENNY:  I'm asking you.
JOE:  What about Billy?
CHICO:  Who is this Billy?
JOE:  And Susie?
JENNY:  They'll understand.
CHICO:  Who is this Susie?
JOE:  That their parents are gone?
JENNY:  We'll take them with us.
JOE:  This isn't you.
JENNY:  Do you love me?
JOE:  You can't mean it.
JENNY:  [smiles wickedly] But I do!

[The storm rages and lifts JENNY toward the sky.]

CHICO:  She is no longer of this world!
JOE:  Speak to me!
CHICO:  She cannot hear you!
JOE:  Come back to me!
CHICO:  She belongs to us now!
JOE:  I love you!

[A blast of wind hurls JENNY to the floor. CHICO pounces, knife in mouth, forcing her legs open, ripping her clothing.  JOE dives at him, knocking him to the floor. Chico rolls and pops up, knife in hand, poised for a showdown.  They freeze and gaze into each other's eyes. Chico tosses his knife to the floor at Joe's feet. Joe snatches it as Chico pulls his shirt open and stands with his arms extended and palms outward.  Joe raises the knife to strike. Freeze.  Spot on CHICO and JOE.  Spot on JENNY, up and awake.  Spot on HERO, smiling.  Black out.]

[It is morning.  Lights up on JOE and JENNY sleeping on

an open sleeping bag. Enter the OLD WOMAN as morning light spills in. She opens windows and birds sing. The old woman smiles at their sleeping presence, fetches mugs and pours coffee from a thermos. JOE awakens and then JENNY. They take in the scene and the old woman in silence. HERO is gone. CHICO is gone. The heroes on display are gone, the case that held them empty.]

OLD WOMAN: Coffee? [they rise and join her at the table] I'm sorry if I startled you. I'm the old woman who looks after this place. [they look at each other] I see you've met Hero. He's a legend around these parts. A ghost story. It's surprising how many people swear they've seen him, talked to him, even spent the night with him. Never mind the door is locked. I bring a thermos of coffee just in case. I brought tea once but they wouldn't touch it. A couple from out Iowa way.
 JENNY: Do you know him?
 OLD WOMAN: Hero? I've had a few talks with him. The truth is I kind of like the old goat. He's welcome here.
 JOE: When did he...?
 OLD WOMAN: Die? A long time ago. Did he tell you the story of the bandit?
 JENNY: He did.
 OLD WOMAN: And the young lady?
 JENNY: Yes.
 OLD WOMAN: The story is true. I looked it up. It made the papers in San Francisco.
 JENNY: What happened to them?
 OLD WOMAN: He didn't tell you? They lived a long and happy life. He lived here and she lived down the way. They often visited.
 JOE: They lived apart?
 OLD WOMAN: They did. I suppose they both wanted their independence.
 JENNY: Were they happy?

# RANDOM PLAYS

OLD WOMAN: By all accounts, they were as happy as a man and a woman can be.

JENNY: Regrets?

OLD WOMAN: None at all. Or so the story goes.

JENNY: Did they have children?

OLD WOMAN: Heavens, yes! They all moved away one by one. A great, great grandson came to live here once. He was a remarkable man. He'd met with some misfortune and wanted to get away from it all.

JOE: What happened to him?

OLD WOMAN: One day he up and left. He said this place was haunted.

JOE: He got that right!

OLD WOMAN: He went back to his life. He was running away, you see. Hero set him straight. He still visits. "Came to see the heroes," he says.

JOE: Where are they?

OLD WOMAN: Who?

JOE: The heroes. [crossing to display] The pictures and postcards: Einstein, Marilyn, DiMaggio, Paine...

OLD WOMAN: Paine? That's a new one. I'm afraid, dear man, they were never here. Figments of the imagination I suppose.

JENNY: [crosses to display area] No, no, they were here. We held them in our hands.

OLD WOMAN: I can only tell you what I know. We have no use for any display here. It's mystifying, I know. The human mind is capable of conjuring any number of things. Reality can be illusive. Sometimes I wonder if they aren't real. Who's to say? You're not the first to have seen them and if I know Hero you won't be the last.

JOE: I'm guessing a lot of people come back here.

OLD WOMAN: Yes, quite a few. Maybe we should open it back up.

JENNY: You should. You really should. We'd come back. It's a wonderful place.

OLD WOMAN: Somehow I think it might be best to leave it as it is. It's a special place to so many people. I wouldn't want to frighten the spirits away.

JENNY: Maybe you're right.

OLD WOMAN: Of course, if you'd like to visit… I'm just down the road about a half a mile. You can't miss it.

JENNY: We will. Thank you. Won't we, Joe?

JOE: We'll bring the kids next time.

OLD WOMAN: By the bye, how did you manage to find this place?

JOE: The car overheated.

OLD WOMAN: [nods] Well, you'll have no more trouble with the car.

JOE: Are you sure?

OLD WOMAN: As sure as I can be.

JENNY: [waits] What about Chico the bandito?

OLD WOMAN: Is that what he calls himself these days?

JOE: Quite a character.

OLD WOMAN: Don't think too badly of him. We all have our parts to play. His may not be appealing but it is necessary.

JENNY: We couldn't have done without him.

OLD WOMAN: Exactly.

JOE: [eyes his coffee] Listen, I think maybe we should hit the road, babe.

JENNY: [waits] Maybe so.

OLD WOMAN: Everyone's in such a hurry. You have somewhere to be?

JENNY: Somewhere to go and a lot to talk about.

OLD WOMAN: I'll bet you do.

JOE: We were heading to Seattle but I think we might be heading home to pick up the kids for a camping trip. What do you think, Jen?

JENNY: I'd like that.

[They gather their things.]

JENNY:  We'd like to thank you for everything.
OLD WOMAN:  It's been my pleasure.
JOE:  If you happen to see Hero, tell him I'm grateful for all he did.
OLD WOMAN:  You believe in him?
JOE:  He's a hero to me.
JENNY:  Thank him for me too.  I'll think of him and his friend whenever I look at the stars.
OLD WOMAN:  I'll tell him.
JENNY:  Until next time
OLD WOMAN:  Until then.

[Exit JOE and JENNY.  The OLD WOMAN begins cleaning up.  Enter HERO.]

HERO:  Hello, dear.  Have they left?
OLD WOMAN:  They have I'm afraid.  All your guests seem to leave early.
HERO: [sitting] I guess they do.
OLD WOMAN:  They were very grateful.
HERO:  Were they?
OLD WOMAN: [kisses him] More than you know.

[Lights fade.]

End Act Two.

# *RINGED WOMEN*

## *Of the Forbidden Forest*

## SETTING

The play takes place in the four kingdoms of an ancient world, the royal court of Talmus, the path of an enchanted forest, the magical realms of Sira, Terra and Ariel – the deep cave, the land of the lakes, the sacred mountain and the throne of inner light.

## CHARACTERS

TALMUS: King of the Light Dwellers
ARMON: Son of Talmus
MAGI: Guardian of the Forest
SIRA: Ringed Woman of the Underworld
TERRA: Ringed Woman of the Earth
ARIEL: Ringed Woman of the Heavens
JINN: Seeker
DIABLO: Guardian of the Tomb
SANTERA: Guardian of the Maze
LEONA: Enchantress
ELENA: Betrothed to Armon
BEAST: Elena's Master

(The roles of Talmus, Jinn, Diablo, Santera and the beast may be played by one actor, the roles of Leona and Elena by one actress. The incantation may be recorded.)

## ACT ONE

INCANTATION OF THE RINGED WOMEN:
The earth, the air, the fire, the water. Return, return, return, return...

The earth, the air, the fire, the water. Return, return, return...

[The incantation continues as lights come up to reveal ARIEL, TERRA and SIRA dance round and round.]

RINGED WOMEN: [as one]
May the circle grow complete.
May the circle be unbroken.
May the circle be filled with enchantment.
Earth, fire, wind and rain: Return, return, return.
Wind, fire, water and earth: Return, return, return.
Air, dirt, heaven and flame: Return, return, return.

ARIEL: Banishment shall be your blessing. Return, return, return.
TERRA: Thirteen moons shall be your journey. Return, return, return.
SIRA: The thirteenth moon your journey's end. Return, return, return.

[Lights to black. Incantation fades. Lights up to reveal the prince, ARMON, before the throne of TALMUS.]

TALMUS: Why do you come before me in this public forum? Why do you take the place of a common citizen who has need of such a hearing? You are my son, my prince, my prodigy. Do we not sit at the same table where we take our meals? Do we not walk the same halls and inhabit the same chambers where we receive our royal guests and entertain our privileged fellows?

ARMON: We do, my gracious lord.

TALMUS: Withdraw then and seek more private counsel where a father may throw off the weighty robes of sovereignty and open his heart to his beloved offspring.

ARMON: Pardon, my lord, I cannot. I have had visions that move my heart more than all the splendors of this royal court, visions that instruct me in heavenly wisdom and foretell what cannot be foretold, visions that speak in voices enchanted, voices I cannot deny for to deny them would be to deny myself.

TALMUS: Who has not had visions? The strange inhabitants of sleeping minds. Yet we are not ruled by them. Be wary, my son, of that which dares not show itself before the holy flame of the gods' fire! It deceives the mortal eye.

ARMON: My visions fear not the light of day for they are the bearers of light itself. They emerge from darkness as the sun rises to our eyes. They reveal myself to myself. This scene they lay before me: Myself the humble servant bent before your lofted view, you with the heavy hand of judgment seated above, the eyes of the kingdom around us like a circle of stars. This I have seen, my royal father, and thus I come before you.

TALMUS: We set aside our prudent counsel and speak as royal lord to loyal subject, master to servant, for our very foundation is affronted and the duties of this crown cannot be cast aside. You must speak most candidly of these visions that fear not the light of the heavenly father. You must tell all that we may judge and seat you in your rightful place.

ARMON: With your leave, my royal grace, you move me to my purpose. I have had these visions a fortnight. When they came to me I first thought to live without sleep. I paced my quarters every night, ingesting special potions to keep my mind alert and forestall sleep yet still the visions came. They are visions of dark and unending night, descending into the deepest tunnels of the underworld where monsters thrive and fear takes every form and guise.

TALMUS: These are nothing more than creations of the mind, visions that prey on fear and inhabit the frightful soul. Let go your fear and grip the solid earth. These horrors will not hold.

ARMON: So thought I, your grace, but when I went beyond the range of imagining, beyond the point where none may go and return unaltered, a brilliant shaft of light appeared before me, streaking upward to heaven's gate. That part within that bears no thought and seeks not understanding instructed me to kneel in humble servitude. I did so and ascended. Where formerly I sank now thrice that distance did I rise. Where all was darkness now was light. Where all was sorrow now was joy. A throne appears, transparent with an inner glow, as if the seed of all creative force was born within. Then three tunnels of darkest shadow sprang forth to point the way: One to the lakes of a towering forest, the second to a deep cave beneath the rock mountain, a third to the heavens. Awestruck I beheld the illumination of darkness and the emergence of three angelic beings, a trinity of the ancient goddesses, the ringed women of earth, air and water.

TALMUS: We know these beings from sacred text. They inhabit the forbidden forest where it is said they have majesty over all beings within their realm. What more we know we cannot say. Our honor pledges for reason hidden and cause unknown to speak no more. Yet we do not know this throne whereupon we think a royal inhabitant may challenge our sovereignty.

ARMON: I know not, my lord. I know only that it hosts the Ringed Women whose light forms its very essence.

TALMUS: What say these luminous spirits who have so enraptured you that you forget your place and solemn duty? Do they have voices? Do they speak to you?

ARMON: They do, my lord. They speak of a kingdom

that has thrown off its sacred spirit. They speak of darkness without light, fire without water, force without direction, power without compassion. They foresee famine and disease born of poison in the air, the water and the earth. They speak of a crown that loses its luster and a throne supported by the light of mirrors.

TALMUS: Take care, noble prince, for they instruct you to the edge of treason. I am the wearer of this crown. I am the bearer of this regal trunk whose ancient roots must hold me to its duty and bind me with honor. Tether thy tongue for soon I must cast off my paternal affection and take on the dignity of the crown.

ARMON: I bow before you, my king, and hold you in highest esteem yet now I come to my purpose. I am summoned and I must go. I hear the call of the goddess and I must follow to the forest wherein the Ringed Women reign. I do but ask a father's blessing.

TALMUS: [rising] It is forbidden!

ARMON: It is for Kings to forbid and Kings may lift the barriers imposed in former times. What purpose it served I do not know but that purpose is now lost and serves none but the forces of repression. This is the truth the visions reveal.

TALMUS: I am foresworn!

ARMON: You are King and cannot be foresworn.

TALMUS: [pacing] The crown is myself and it forswears me! Should I bow to the goddess? Should I yield to the Ringed Women, our ancient adversary, who regard us as enemies as we regard them? This is the very root of our rule! It cannot be! The light cannot yield to darkness or the ruler to the ruled. The great wall of opposing force is our strength! It protects us and holds us in our appointed place. The forest is forbidden for it is darkness and we are light!

ARMON: Forgive me, my lord. I too am foresworn and cannot be moved from my duty.

TALMUS: Not moved? Foresworn to voices others cannot hear, visions others cannot see? Obedient to our enemy? Go then but take not the blessings of this crown! King have you none! The throne you leave behind is empty for it has no heir! The forest be your kingdom now! Banished! Go and speak no more of blessing for upon the honor of this robe if you set foot upon our soil again, it shall hold your final rest. Yet shall we be merciful for you have been a good and loyal son. I offer up the light of the thirteenth moon that you may make repentance and reclaim your honored place. If you fail to appear before this court at the appointed hour, never again will you be greeted by our friendship. Mark our words, hold them to your heart and go.

ARMON: [rising] The Ringed Women foretold: Banishment shall be your blessing, thirteen moons shall be your journey, the thirteenth your journey's end. Fear not, good father, for I shall keep the appointed hour to set things right.

TALMUS: May it be so. For though we have our kingly duty, our heart is heavy with sorrow. We cannot throw off our former affection as the serpent sheds its skin. May the Gods go with you! May they protect you and guide you to our heart once more. Go! We cannot bear to dwell upon this parting.

[Lights fade. Spot up on MAGI.]

MAGI: Sorrow walked with the young prince along the path to the forbidden forest. He wandered in the emptiness of the endless night. He walked alone, isolated and detached. He followed the trail of a thousand paths, slept beneath a sky of a million stars, bathed in the waters of a hundred streams, yet he remained alone in the darkness that bears no light. At last, when he had found peace, when he understood the beauty of solitude, when he grew small enough within himself, I greeted him at the forest gate.

[Enter ARMON at the gate.]

# JACK RANDOM

ARMON: Are you a man?

MAGI: I hold the vision of a man and take his place upon the earth. If all that I am is not a man then no man stands before you. [sits on bench] Come be seated beside me that we may share this view.

ARMON: Who are you that I should sit beside?

MAGI: I am Guardian of the Forest. I am its watch and holder of the key. The gate I keep keeps you from your destiny. Here you must pass to walk among the inhabitants of the forest. Who are you that wants my favor but will not sit beside?

ARMON: [sits] Pardon, kind sir, my name is Armon. I come from the kingdom beyond the forest. How long I have wandered I cannot know. I am lost. All that walks before appears as it was behind. I have seen no man, woman, no being of any kind till you.

MAGI: You have traveled in the sorrow of a dark heart where none may walk with you. In solitude you have learned a second sight that led you to my greeting.

ARMON: Are you sent to guide me?

MAGI: I am sent to meet you, greet you and tell you what I may.

ARMON: Speak then for I am eager to begin my journey.

MAGI: Your journey has begun but I will speak of things that are to come. You are young and need guidance for your growth. You choose the Forbidden Forest as your master as the forest chooses you. She will teach if you are willing. She asks only that you open your heart and clear your mind. She will guide you if you are worthy. There are many tests along the path. The lessons of the journey are many. Their number is that of space and time.

ARMON: You speak in riddle yet would I know: What is the number of space and time?

MAGI: The number of space is four: the four kingdoms, four corners, the boundaries that confine. Three is the number of time: the past, present and future.

# RANDOM PLAYS

ARMON: The number of space and time is seven.

MAGI: The number is not mine yet it is more than five and less than nine. Odd, isn't it?

ARMON: Give me the first that I may better judge your wisdom's worth.

MAGI: He that judges wisdom proclaims his own folly.

ARMON: Is that the lesson or your reply?

MAGI: The first lesson is fear: to fear not but greet it as a friend. He that runs from fear flees his journey's end.

ARMON: By my upbringing, he that runs from fear is called a coward while he that runs to greet her is called a fool.

MAGI: Let him run not and fear not what he is called.

ARMON: You counsel against haste: to run neither to nor from but walk or stand or sit and be not moved.

MAGI: A man may travel far without movement. Yet he that would walk the long path to wisdom must walk with patience as his companion. He that hurries forward leaves not the past behind. He gathers no blessings and sees not the guiding signs.

ARMON: Patience is the second lesson. It sits well for often has my father advised. Let's hear another.

MAGI: You must know the smallness of your being to know the greatness of your call for he that is grown small shall be as one with all.

ARMON: Already I have witnessed myself grown small yet I remain lost and know not the greatness of my calling. This lesson cannot stand alone.

MAGI: Much may be learned in knowing not.

ARMON: Your words rest heavy in my thoughts, bearing the weight of ancient wisdom. Tell me more.

MAGI: To know wisdom is to know that wisdom is beyond knowing: To whom it is unknown, to him it is known. The one knowing knows not. Understood not by those who understand, it is understood by understanding not.

ARMON: You throw my thoughts in circles that such

wisdom is bestowed by one who claims it not.

MAGI: Even so.

ARMON: So deep in meaning it would spend a lifetime in contemplation yet by my count it is only five.

MAGI: He must have faith that is not bounded; he must rise though he is grounded.

ARMON: What is it that flies yet remains upon the earth?

MAGI: Is it not the spirit of a man?

ARMON: So it is for any man may dream. In visions waking and asleep I have visited the stars and walked upon the moon and soared with celestial travelers as company. This then is the sixth lesson. The seventh and by its keeping greatest lesson remains.

MAGI: He must know love in all its faces; he must know pain to gain its graces.

ARMON: Love? My mother's love denied me, I know only a father's love for his son.

MAGI: A mother's love cannot be denied. Have you no other?

ARMON: None but love of virtue bequeathed by my father yet even he I have defied in coming to your gate.

MAGI: You have done what a son must do. Look not behind but to the path ahead. You are free to walk among the dwellers of this forest.

ARMON: I am a stranger in a strange land, unguided and alone, yet by my intuition I place my trust in you.

MAGI: I have but one guidance: walk freely.

ARMON: You know the ways of the forest. You hold its knowledge and its wisdom.

MAGI: Ask no more than what is freely offered. Take no less that what is freely given. Your path unfolds. Seek no further guidance for it is yours alone. None may lead you. You alone must surrender yourself to follow. Direction can only lead you astray. You must walk the path that none may walk but you. Choose not for that which you seek chooses you.

ARMON: I seek the Ringed Women.

MAGI: [stunned] They are known to you?

ARMON: I have seen them in my visions. They have summoned me to this journey.

MAGI: A sacred journey indeed. How may one say what is known and what is not? I say you must follow your heart. To do so you must know your heart. The light follows the darkness. It is a long journey, my son. You must fight until you learn acceptance. You must struggle until patience is your friend. You must suffer to know happiness. If you seek love you must know loneliness. If you seek wisdom you must follow to your journey's end. There is no other way.

ARMON: Will we meet again?

MAGI: [closing and opening his eyes] We will.

ARMON: Is there no more you can tell me?

MAGI: Only that I go with you. The gate opens to those of pure heart and worthy cause. It opens for you now.

[A light appears upstage. ARMON moves to it and kneels as if in prayer.]

MAGI: [to audience] He crossed the great barrier and beheld with new eyes the majesty of the Sacred Forest. He beheld the greatness of the journey at once and that understanding froze him to that spot of earth where the two worlds meet in darkness and in light. Fastened there as string to bow he fixed his mind to understanding understanding not. For three days and four nights he knelt in thought and meditation, eyes directed to his inner being, and each night he struggled against his conscious mind to free himself from all his thoughts and false learning. At length he was visited by a vision in the shadows of the tallest pines.

[The RINGED WOMEN appear above. Incantation.]

# JACK RANDOM

RINGED WOMEN: [as one] May the circle be completed. May the circle be unbroken. May the circle be enchanted. Earth, fire, wind and rain. Return, return, return. Wind, fire, water, earth. Return, return, return. Air, soil, heaven and flame. Return, return, return.

MAGI: On the fourth day he rose [ARMON rises] to walk among the people of the forest. He became a trusted one. He exchanged ideas with its inhabitants and always he thanked them. He was given a part in the sharing and smoked from the pipe of the long root. He saw the Ringed Women who spoke to him.

[ARIEL, TERRA and SIRA appear, veiled in fog and shadow, and circled in rings of darkness and light.]

ARIEL: The way to wisdom is confusion. I am your guide, your vision and your protector.

SIRA: The door to faith is doubt. I shall be both. I am your teacher and tester, your dragon and slayer. In me you shall know fear and learn courage. I am your strength.

TERRA: If you would know kindness, seek the beast within you. I am the earth your mother. I am love and cruelty. I am wisdom. I am the white light on the darkest night.

ARIEL: If you seek light, face the darkness.

[Exit RINGED WOMEN. ARMON rises and circles the stage. Enter JINN in simple clothing.]

MAGI: He did not speak but felt the truth of their words. It was then that Jinn, a fellow seeker and servant of the forest, came to him.

JINN: You have smoked the long root. You have seen the Ringed Women.

ARMON: Yes.

JINN: I too have seen their majesty and heard their song.

# RANDOM PLAYS

ARMON: Did you speak to them?

JINN: I did not. Like you I fear and yet I am not afraid. I understand but I do not.

ARMON: Who are they? What secrets do they hold?

JINN: They are the oldest inhabitants of the forest. They reside in the far mountains where no mortal being may climb. They take refuge in the deep cave where none but true believers may descend. They live in the heavens beyond the stars where only dreams may wander. They appear to us in the shadows of the night. It is said they have reached the journey's end. It is said they are the soul of enlightenment. Are you a seeker?

ARMON: I am. I seek the path not chosen.

JINN: I am Jinn of the forest dwellers. I too am a seeker. I will choose your path for you. It is intended that I do so. The spirits of the deep cave call to us.

ARMON: [shaking hands, embracing] I am Armon of the land beyond the forest. I have dreamed of the deep cave.

JINN: Then we follow your dream. We will walk the mountain path to the fountain of the great passage. There the path parts and you must choose.

[ARMON draws a circle and designs in the soil down left, pulls a pouch from his belt and gives an offering in the four directions before kneeling to pray.]

MAGI: They set out the next morning. The path was long and arduous. Their packs grew heavy on their shoulders as they marched for three days. Each night Armon prepared a shrine before the tallest tree and offered his prayers.

ARMON: Oh spirits of the ancient forest, hear my plea. I come to you with open mind and open heart. Give me the vision to know the path. Give me the patience to follow it. Give me the wisdom to conquer my fears...

[SIRA appears veiled in shadow and light.]

SIRA: I am Sira, sister of the deep cave. I am the fountain of creation and death. I am your deepest fear and greatest hope. I am the womb and the grave. Why do you call me?

ARMON: My people need hope. Despair weighs upon our souls. Our soil is barren. Our air and water is poisoned. Our spirits no longer soar with the wind...

SIRA: Do you wish your spirit to fly...or to free your people?

ARMON: By freeing myself I seek to bring my people the flame that enlightens. I wish to show my people the path.

SIRA: Do not fear. My sisters and I will guide you.

ARMON: All the fears I once held vanished with the vision of your beauty. I seek the counsel of the cave spirit.

SIRA: It is good you fear me not as most mortal men do for I may speak only to those who have no fear. You will face fear again, Armon. The dragon that lives within you will not be conquered in a single battle. The struggle must grow to the heart. The heart must be strong. The vision must be clear.

ARMON: My heart is strong for I place it in your hands. My vision is clear for you are my vision.

SIRA: Will you walk the path within? Will you descend into the pit of darkness that you may pluck the light of wisdom for your people?

ARMON: I will. My path is chosen and my heart follows.

SIRA: It follows wisely for opportunity passes in the beat of a heart. When you hear from me again you will have faced your greatest fear. Should you rise to conquer you may begin your journey anew.

ARMON: My journey is long already. How much longer must it be?

SIRA: The journey begun has already found its end. It is written in a language that may not be known to mortal men. It is known to me and my likeness. You must neither take comfort nor fear the known end for what is known may yet be unknown and that which hides in darkness now may be revealed. That which is revealed may return to darkness.

Behold this sacred crystal [she holds the illuminated crystal before him]: It holds the power of vision and the strength of faith. It is the light in your darkness. It is the darkness of light. Behold and feel its power within.

ARMON: It holds my eyes to the journey before me.

SIRA: Do not allow fear to blind you for now you must descend. Know that I go with you and remain with you always.

ARMON: I descend without fear into the heart of the dragon and know it is the guardian of my soul.

[Enter ARIEL and TERRA. The Ringed Women chant as one, ethereal music accompanying.]

RINGED WOMEN: Descend, my child, son of my sons, chosen of the land beyond the forest. Plunge into darkness that you may behold the light. Surrender to the void that you may be renewed. Song of the Jains and the twenty-four saviors comfort and protect you! Descend to the eighteen degrees of nothingness!

[Incantation, music under.]

SIRA: Te Kore: The Void.
ARIEL: Te Kore tua tahi: The First Void.
TERRA: Te Kore tua rua: The Second Void.
SIRA: Te Kore nui: The Vast Void.
ARIEL: Te Kore roa: The Far-Extending Void.
TERRA: Te Kore para: The Serene Void.
SIRA: Te Kore whiwhia: The Unpossessing Void.
ARIEL: Te Kore rawea: The Delightful Void.
TERRA: Te Kore te taumaua: The Fast Bound Void.
SIRA: Te Po: The Night.

# JACK RANDOM

ARIEL: Te Po teki: The Hanging Night.
TERRA: Te Po terea: The Drifting Night.
SIRA: Te Po whawha: The Moaning Night.
ARIEL: Heenay mahke moeh: The Daughter of Troubled Sleep.
TERRA: Te Ata: The Dawn.
SIRA: Te Au tu roa: The Abiding Day.
ARIEL: Te Au marama: The Bright Day.
TERRA: Whai tua: Space.

[Decisive drum roll and gong.]

RINGED WOMEN: [as one] From the void, space. From space, the air. From the air, fire. From fire, water. From water, earth. Earth, wind, fire and rain: Descend into darkness, return to light!

[ARMON has descended into the dark void. DIABLO appears as a demon.]

ARMON: Who are you that appears like a serpent in the fires of darkness?
DIABLO: I am your enemy! I am the one who blocks your path. I am all that you despise. Your journey's end is to peer into these eyes with love in your heart. Then may you have wisdom. Then may you become yourself.
ARMON: Stand aside! My purpose is below!
DIABLO: You will not pass till I am satisfied.
ARMON: [considers] How then would you be satisfied?
DIABLO: I would know the dreams of your deepest sleep. I would know the shadows of your soul. I would know the demons of your hidden self.
ARMON: These are things that cannot be known to strangers who hide in darkness lest they become phantom cave dwellers who steal the soul to leave the spirit wandering in despair.

DIABLO: Then here we will remain till I am no longer a stranger. Here we will look into each other's eyes till we see the mirror of ourselves. You shall know my being as I know yours lest you pass into a world from which you may not return.

ARMON: I do not fear you.

DIABLO: Yet you fear my passing – as well you should. One who knows not the light of darkness, who knows not the dark angels who reside within, cannot pass without deadly peril.

ARMON: I know what I fear. I fear losing hold of the solid earth. I fear being afraid. I fear losing my way, my soul, my dreams, my love, my life and all that I cherish more than my life.

DIABLO: Do not fear what is not known. He is not lost that is himself. Your soul resides within you. The earth in all its treasures surrounds you. You must embrace your fears that you may bring them to your cause. Yours is a long, hard journey with many trials. You will need all your strength and all your allies. This is but the beginning but here you must face your dragon.

[Spot up on MAGI stage left as ARMON kneels and DIABLO circles him.]

MAGI: He knelt before his nemesis. He fell into a trance and descended deep into himself. Through eighteen stages of darkness he descended in space and time, past the sirens of desire and the shadows of passion, past the illusions of pleasure and pain, past the wandering souls of confusion, past the demons of vengeance and despair, until he arrived before the dragon of this deepest self.

From the talons of six legs dripped the blood of a million damned souls: betrayals and cruelties of heart. Flames spewed from its gaping mouth, releasing a stench of remorse. From his enraged and burning eyes, visions of his darkest fear, the birth incubus, emerged: Rape of the goddess, murder of the god, by the hands of an anguished son. Fires of his inmost being raged within and without. He felt his skin peel back in flames, his flesh flushed aside and his pain enveloping his senses. He surrendered his self and all that he knew before this moment.

[A raging fire transitions with a bang into a cloud of smoke. DIABLO is gone and SIRA emerges in his place.]

Kneeling before the dragon of his own creation, he opened to the heavens like petals to the sun. A bright light appeared and at its center her eyes opened. Seven crystals adorned her brow, angels danced on distant clouds and songs beyond human voices filled the air.

ARMON: Goddess of truth and light, I am reborn without fear! I have faced my dragon and survived. I am your servant and slave as you have freed me from the great darkness of my inner soul!

SIRA: You have freed yourself, Armon. You have earned my blessing. The path you must walk is chosen. You will not often see me for I am not often seen yet you will feel my presence beneath the soles of your feet. I am gravity. I hold you to the earth. My strength will give you balance. I will comfort you when you sleep and give you resolve when you awake. I give you this precious stone [she does so] as a symbol of my blessing. Honor it for it is my love.

Now you must return to the world of light. You will walk the path to the deep forest where my sister awaits. The journey is long but you will not tire. There are many who would lead you astray but you will not follow. You will find your way through the maze of confusion. The Dog Star will guide you in your hour of need. You have conquered your most basic fear, my son, and now you need patience. You must build the foundation upon which your faith will be grounded.

# RANDOM PLAYS

MAGI: Humbled by the magnitude of the blessing she bestowed, he lowered his lips to the hem of her garment and as he did so he felt her warmth engulf his mortal being. At once he felt his smallness and it gave him comfort. His eyes turned within and he felt his body rise from the force of her presence within.

[Lights out on SIRA as she exits.]

MAGI: When next his consciousness returned he walked the path to the deep forest, home of the Earth Goddess, embodied in the Lady of the Lakes where she resides. In the visions of the pipe she appears as Terra, the Ringed Woman of the Earth and Water. In her realm none but the brave may survive. Here the towering pines house ancient spirits and the owl is a sacred being. Here are many shadow spirits, gypsies, thieves and false shamans, banished from the village of the forest people. Few have dared to enter the realm of Terra for to do so they must pass through the maze of confusion. With each step the path narrows, the climb steepens and the trees appear taller before his eyes. Armon begins to question his own senses when he encounters Santera, guide and protector of the maze.

[Enter SANTERA, a forest dweller.]

SANTERA: You are on the path to the deep forest?
ARMON: I am on the path.
SANTERA: Do you seek the Lady of the Lakes?
ARMON: I seek the sister of Sira, known to me as Terra, mother of earth.
SANTERA: It's your good fortune I have found you. I will serve as your guide.
ARMON: I seek no guide. It is a path I must walk alone.
SANTERA: You are brave but foolish. No one should walk the path alone.

ARMON: Your words speak truth but I seek no guidance.

SANTERA: Then we are both lost but let my sorrow be my own.

ARMON: I am not a man to turn away from another in need. How may I serve you?

SANTERA: You have your own journey. I would not delay you from your destiny.

ARMON: My destiny must wait. Speak for I would hear your tale.

SANTERA: I have no tale but I would speak of my own journey if you would listen.

ARMON: Speak. I will listen.

SANTERA: Like you I seek enlightenment. I have heard the call of the Ringed Women. They spoke to me and charged me with this task: Seek out and guide a worthy traveler through the maze of confusion. A thousand days I have waited. I saw at once you were the one. Even your refusal bears witness. Yet I fear for I remember the words of the Goddess of the Moon and the Heavens: Let not the worthy soul pass unaided. For neither you nor he will return to the light.

ARMON: Now I must choose and choose wisely.

SANTERA: So must we both.

ARMON: But you have chosen. You have pronounced me worthy.

SANTERA: What is done may be undone and yet I believe you worthy.

ARMON: What reward are you promised?

SANTERA: Freedom. For though I serve as guardian of the maze I am confined until my task is complete. Your safe passage is my own.

ARMON: I met a wise man who counseled me to walk the path not chosen. Since you would choose for me, the terms of his counsel are met.

SANTERA: Then let us delay no longer for it is written

that I should guide and you should follow.

ARMON: His wisdom also counseled patience.

SANTERA: Patience is wise when the path is uncertain but when the path lies before him a man should not wander.

ARMON: The wise man said: My path is my own. Accept no guidance for none may guide you.

SANTERA: This wisdom leads in circles. Surely it is not wise to enter the maze alone. Many have tried and many have failed. Their souls cry out each night. They are lost where none may find them. They seek guidance now that once was offered and refused.

ARMON: You have offered before?

SANTERA: Not I. Others that came before me.

ARMON: No one in these one thousand days?

SANTERA: None worthy. I let them pass. In the maze they wander still.

ARMON: How did you judge them unworthy?

SANTERA: They judge themselves. I am blessed with second sight and can perceive the purpose of a man.

ARMON: What is my purpose by your sight?

SANTERA: You serve your people. You seek the wisdom of the goddess that you may return and save them.

ARMON: You know much for one who is confined.

SANTERA: I know only that which is revealed.

ARMON: Have patience for now I must make communion with my heart.

SANTERA: Forgive me. I am overcome by the joy of knowing. With each word my certitude grows. I have chosen well and now must wait for your destiny to join with mine.

ARMON: [kneels] Great Goddess of the Earth and all things living within the light of darkness, come that I may be comforted by your advice. Candle of eternal flame, reveal what cannot be disguised. Sira, mother to the sacred light below, give me the strength of balance that holds me to my path. Terra, lady of the lakes and sacred pine, cleanse my mind of all that came before that I might choose not.

[TERRA appears in a vision above. SANTERA does not hear their exchange.]

TERRA: Who is it that beckons me with praise?
ARMON: It is I, Armon, from the land of the light dwellers.
TERRA: I know you.
ARMON: I have seen you in my visions.
TERRA: As I have seen you in mine. My sister speaks well of you.
ARMON: I am beholden for the blessing she bestowed on me.
TERRA: Hold on to it. It serves you well.
ARMON: I have come to the maze of confusion where I am offered guidance.
TERRA: The worthy should not be denied.
ARMON: I cannot judge his worth.
TERRA: Yet judge you must. Go with him yet be not led. His purpose will be revealed.
ARMON: I thank you for your counsel.
TERRA: [receding] Look to the Dog Star in your hour of need.

[Exit TERRA. ARMON rises.]

ARMON: I will go with you.
SANTERA: You choose wisely.
ARMON: I choose not for you have chosen me.
SANTERA: So I have. Let us begin.
ARMON: I have but one request.
SANTERA: Speak and it is done.
ARMON: Allow me to go before you. Should I wander from the path alert me that I should right my way.
SANTERA: It is strange but let it be so. Go forth and I

will follow. But take care for any false step may be your last.
SANTERA: I need not fear with you to prevent it.
ARMON: I need not fear with you to prevent it.
SANTERA: I will do my best. Let us begin.

[ARMON fastens a scarf as a blindfold. Seeing this, SANTERA fastens a stone to a garment.]

SANTERA: [offering the stone-free end of the garment] Take this, my worthy friend, whilst I take hold the other end so that we may not be separated. Take care for the maze is darkness itself.
ARMON: [blindfolded] I do so. But do not seek to alter my course with well-intentioned tugs and pulls. My path must not be altered.
SANTERA: On my honor I will hold it plainly as a dead weight might do.

[ARMON exits cautiously, moving into darkness as SANTERA remains behind.]

SANTERA: What fool is this who plays more to my liking than even my imagination could devise? I follow for though he will surely be lost I must know the precise location where he plants himself beyond return. There I will confront him and play the part of savior. On the other hand, if his path is true, I will intercede and lead him astray.

He guards his pouch as if some secret treasure it contains. Who knows what a fool treasures? A lock of his loved ones hair? A token of private value? We shall see. What is his is mine. For none may pass that take Santera's hand.

[Exit SANTERA following Armon. Spot up on MAGI.]

MAGI: Secure in the counsel of the Lady of the Lakes, Armon paces himself slowly through the maze, weighted by a stone, taking care that each step is unguided by desire.

# JACK RANDOM

Santera lurks behind, his glee hardly contained. His amazement grows as Armon's blindness guides him true. The maze opens before him as Santera revises his treachery. With half the maze behind and half ahead, the false guide springs forth in pretended joy.

[Lights up on ARMON and SANTERA, who grabs him by the arms.]

SANTERA: Rejoice, my friend! You have reached your journey's end!
ARMON: [waits] Your counsel is false. There is no end here.
SANTERA: There is, noble one! Unmask! [circles Armon as he speaks] Before you lies the path to the lakes where the lady awaits you. Even now her radiance appears in the distance. Behold the fruits of your success!
ARMON: Your weight stays behind while your voice travels. What spirit is this that carries not his own body yet claims the figure of a man?

[SANTERA yanks the stoned garment from Armon's grasp and removes the stone.]

SANTERA: I deceive you, fool! I am not a man. The stone I fastened to your tail guided you. I did not know the magic it possessed until I saw it walk you through the darkness without misstep. Yet now you are undone. The stone is mine and I alone may walk the maze to its end.
ARMON: [removes the blindfold] What is your purpose?
SANTERA: I seek the treasure withheld.
ARMON: You have the stone. Is that not enough?
SANTERA: The stone? That which was mine is mine still! I seek that which you hold to your side and guard as if with jealous love.
ARMON: What you seek cannot be given.

# RANDOM PLAYS

SANTERA: Why else would I desire it?

ARMON: Leave me lest I grow angry at your impertinence! You are false and cunning! To receive a gift such as this wants honor and humility! You possess neither and will not receive this sacred gift by my hand!

SANTERA: I ask no more than what is required. I see that you are a man of honor. You have passed the first test. Now you must pass the second. You must sacrifice that which is dear. I am but a humble servant to the lady you seek. Would she require less than what is treasured most?

[We begin to hear the voices of lost souls.]

ARMON: Is there no end to your deceit?

SANTERA: I play my part. To deceive is my duty just as yours is to seek. Who shall say which is the greater service? Listen! Hear the voices of all who came before you! Listen! Hear the sound of despair! The lost souls in infinite darkness call to you!

ARMON: Let them call. My way lies ahead.

SANTERA: I am the holder of the stone!

ARMON: It holds no greater magic that any other.

SANTERA: I see. So the true magic lies in the treasure you hold in your pouch.

ARMON: There is no magic but that which resides within a man's heart.

SANTERA: Why then do you blind yourself?

ARMON: To free myself.

SANTERA: You are blinded by sight? How then will you stop your ears? A thousand plugs would not block out these voices of despair!

[The voices grow in number and volume.]

ARMON: The honor you have thrown away cannot be restored.

SANTERA: Listen to the voices! Will you join them?

ARMON: I fear not.

SANTERA: There is another way but only if you place your trust in me. I offer you full confession for I see you will not be satisfied with less. The Lady of the Lakes placed me here with a blessing and a curse. I alone shall know the way of the maze for as long as I remain within. But if another should find the way then I am lost and will spend my days wandering with the lost souls.

ARMON: You are a prisoner by choice.

SANTERA: I am until such a man undoes me.

ARMON: You are forewarned. Leave this place for I will find the way.

SANTERA: Should I depart without reward? I have served long and well. I have gathered treasures others can only dream: crowns of gold, jewels of the four kingdoms, stones of enchantment, potions to every purpose, books of hidden knowledge and more. All that you can carry is yours.

ARMON: What use have I for your treasures? You cannot tempt me with wealth or magic of any kind. They make their keepers slaves as they have rendered you.

SANTERA: Go then! Let it be so! Come what may.

[ARMON scans his surroundings.]

SANTERA: How speaks your honor now? What? Lost your bearings? The way that was is vanished! The way that is no more! Three times I have marked you: once in anger and deception, once in anguish and despair, and again in sweet temptation! All is lost in confusion! Swirl and swarm and fog! What was right is now wrong for he is lost that stays too long!

[Exit SANTERA. Spot up on MAGI.]

MAGI: Under the spell of Santera, Armon's mind

returned to all that was before. His spirit wandered aimlessly though his body held its place. Santera longed for Armon's treasure but he dared not disturb the spell. Soon he would collapse under the weight of infinite confusion. Santera waited as Armon drifted in a sea of strange imaginings. Then, in the great distance a light appeared to him and Armon remembered the words of the lady Terra: Look to the Dog Star! He raised his head as the heavens opened and the Dog Star gazed down on him. There came a light between them that took the form of a brilliant monarch butterfly. As it floated through the dark unending sea Armon knew he had mastered the mystery of the maze. Santera looked on in horror as Armon gave himself to the flight of heavenly beings. A thousand points of light enveloped him and he knew at once they were the lost souls of the endless maze.

He found himself on the path once more, in the deep forest of the towering pines, and walked in quiet solitude, his heart filled with joy. He received the blessings of all that graced his mortal senses, the wind whispering harmonies and the earth in all its glory reverberating a divine melody. He came at length to a clearing where the path divided and paused to take in the sight. This was his next lesson. He closed his eyes to seek the guidance of his inner being. But inward sight sprang outward and he was drawn to the figure of a man sitting where the one became two.

[Lights fade.]

End Act One.

## ACT TWO

(MAGI sits where the path divides. ARMON approaches him.)

ARMON: My spirit soars to find you at this clearing!

MAGI: As does mine, my son. You have traveled far and done well. Six moons have circled since last we met.

ARMON: Has it been so long?

MAGI: Long and yet not so long. Sit that we may share this view. [ARMON sits at his side] Time is an illusion by which mortal beings pay tribute to the great circle of here and there. That you have come this far in so few steps is wondrous strange and rare. Your strength is great and your magic is strong.

ARMON: I have none but that which is captured in my heart.

MAGI: It is magic enough. You have battled and befriended fear. You have found second sight. You have learned to focus your mind and center you being. You have judged wisely that you may discover wisdom. The gifts you have gathered are great. The souls you have freed watch over you. Yet all that is behind is less than that which lies ahead. The end you seek is highly priced and will not yield to those who would not hold it to their hearts. Yet this consolation will you have: the greater the battle, the more glorious the triumph.

ARMON: I fear not. I have learned the greatness of the journey and the smallness of my part. That which is within reaches outward and carries me to an end that is mine alone.

MAGI: I would know more. Tell me of your home and those who guided you in childhood that you should come so far. Who is the father of such a son? Who is the mother of the chosen one?

ARMON: My father is a good man and a hard king. Without his crown he is kind and gentle, patient and wise. He taught me to love all living things. To love nature for her infinite beauty and all creatures that walk the earth or bathe in her waters or breathe her air. He taught that to love others is to love oneself. He taught that a royal birth may be lost if not guarded by worth. He held that no man may be king who loses the respect of his people.

MAGI: You speak of a man who is wise and worthy. Is this man not the king?

ARMON: He is yet he is ruled by laws that none may see but him. The forest is forbidden. The passage to enlightenment is blocked. The air, the earth, the water and all the earth's beings are held in servitude. How can this be? It is beyond my understanding.

MAGI: Your understanding grows with each step you take. Kings and kingdoms may journey as well as a prince. What of your mother? Has your kingdom no queen?

ARMON: I cannot say. My mother is not known to me for when I was but a suckling infant, my father a wandering prince, in a far away land I know not where, I was pulled from my mother's breast.

MAGI: This tale is most strange. Could not your father return to this far away land to claim his queen?

ARMON: The land is enchanted or so it is said. A spell was cast. She is lost where none may look to find yet she remains his queen for he had no heart to seek another.

MAGI: He speaks well of her?

ARMON: As a man would speak of love itself. To hear him tell it, her voice is more glorious than the song of the Sirens, her beauty more striking than the twin peaks of Parnassus, her enchantment greater than the muses in all their revelry.

MAGI: It pleases me to know that love is your source.

ARMON: Why do you inquire of things that to you can

have but passing interest?

MAGI: I am as the owl, the eyes of the forest and its memory. When time unfolds and people wish to hear the tale, the task will fall on these shoulders.

ARMON: So be it. Yet who would hear such a tale?

MAGI: Even those who watch with interest now. But your journey beckons. The path before you divides. Would you seek guidance?

ARMON: I seek no more than what is freely given. Even then the path is chosen. Is it not so?

MAGI: It is and yet there are means that may serve you. [draws a circle on the ground with his staff] If a man with inward sight, who holds the secret of the maze and the blessings of light, stands within this circle and turns him once to the left, twice to the right and back again, the path that is not chosen chooses to unfold. [ARMON stands in the circle] Great circle of all that is and all that is not, let that which is two return to one – the father, the mother and the chosen son.

[Exit ARMON on the path not chosen.]

MAGI: No longer did he shoulder doubt. No longer did he question that which is beyond his understanding. For though the path that was divided now revealed itself as one, he did not hesitate but began his climb to the sacred trinity of water in the high cliffs. Here the Lady of the Lakes awaited him. Here on the high ridge where the dying embers of the setting sun dance with moonbeams on the lakes below, where the shadows of the tall pines appear as mountains in darkness, the young prince faced his greatest test. Even the inner vision may be deceived where the eyes welcome the heart and desire calls to the soul.

[LEONA appears in silhouette.]

MAGI: She appears as a statue in deepest, darkest onyx,

# RANDOM PLAYS

a silhouette in the radiant glow of sunset. At first sight a pulsing warmth springs from the core of his soul, as if the wellspring of his inmost self had suddenly been set free. It radiates, swallows him whole, stealing his breath and shrouding his vision. As he steps to greet her the muscles of his body stay him and mortal time stands still. A jolting pain grips him from within. Instinctively, he calls: Sira!

[SIRA appears above enshrouded in fog.]

SIRA: Yes. It is I who stops you! It is passion that leads you forward and love that for a borrowed moment holds you back. Now I must release you but hear me: When you peer into her eyes, mine shall you see. When she holds you to her breast, mine shall warm you. When she runs her fingers through your hair, my blessing will comfort you. For the length of her enchantment, my lips, my legs, my loins and every part of me shall be her stead. Alas, when passion is spent and desire yields to honest affection, you will see her as she is. Go now. I release you.

[Exit SIRA as LEONA steps into the light.]

ARMON: Vision of the holy night, who are you that casts this spell?
LEONA: I am one who waits in quiet solitude. I wait for you, my prince.
ARMON: Are you the Lady of the Lakes?
LEONA: I am the maiden, Leona. Do you seek the Lady?
ARMON: She is my destiny. I seek what is in my heart.
LEONA: The eyes give welcome to the heart.
ARMON: If it be so, my heart has found a home.
LEONA: I, too, have a heart and one that burns as Aphrodite's did. Would that you could feel it.
ARMON: My heart pounds as the ocean greets the shore.

It summons me and I would follow where it leads.

LEONA: Your desire is my own. Come and we will join our hearts, our limbs, our core and every part. We will drink from passion's cup the nectar that makes lovers drunk.

[ARMON goes to her. They embrace and drink from the cup of desire.]

ARMON: Till now I have but thirsted. This joy I have only dreamed.

LEONA: Dream no more, sweet prince. For on this night and in this nest of love's divine pleasure, I am yours and you are mine. Seek no more the Lady of the Lakes or any other for I will not share your love and affection. Give me the promise that unbinds a woman's desire.

ARMON: By the blood that burns within my loins I do swear.

[Lights fade on ARMON and LEONA as they recline together. Spot up on MAGI.]

MAGI: Gripped in the temptress Leona's spell, Armon released his desire in the arms of love. As her words foretold, Sira of the Deep Cave took the temptress' place. From this strange coupling a child of darkness and light would spring, a boy who would be king and a tale that would be told. But hold for this is not the present story. Armon sleeps in ignorance and bliss. His passion subsides as a flower folds to night. When his eyes open to the morning light the spell is broken and the temptress appears to him without disguise.

[Spot out. Lights up on ARMON in prayer and LEONA rising.]

LEONA: Is this the posture of a man who has tasted

ecstasy and bathed in the arms of his promised love? Is this the proper greeting for the object of his desire?

ARMON: It is the posture of a fool who sees now that a heart may be deceived by passion. It is the greeting for the deceiver from he who has been deceived.

LEONA: Have you been deceived?

ARMON: You know I have.

LEONA: What do you see that before you could not see?

ARMON: I see you as you are – an aged one whose desires are but memories.

LEONA: Why then have you not fled? What stays you from your journey when that which held you is no more?

ARMON: My word is my honor and my honor is my cause. I have given my oath.

LEONA: That which is given falsely cannot bind you by honor.

ARMON: I was blinded from within. I saw through desire's eyes. The deception was born from my own weakness.

LEONA: Are you a mortal man?

ARMON: By she that gave me life I am.

LEONA: Then cast your inward blows aside. No mortal man can escape Aphrodite's net.

ARMON: If this is so, it is a cruel fate for I remain your servant by my oath.

LEONA: Would you serve me even now?

ARMON: If it pleases you.

LEONA: Your sense of duty touches me where I had thought to feel no more. I once was a mortal praised for her beauty throughout the seven realms, courted by princes from every court. They offered jewels and treasures if only I would wed yet none would I have. Too much did I enjoy the courting and the romance. Alas I was offered what I could not refuse: eternal life. To be immortal and never know the sorrow of growing old and withering until death. [laughs] I too was deceived by my own desire for little did I know eternal life is not eternal youth.  Mine is a fate most cruel and yet fitting for I will age until the sun no longer shines.  Though I have spells and potions to give my former beauty to men's eyes, I am old and will never know the comfort and blessing that is death.

ARMON:  Your beauty is more honest now than it was before.

LEONA:  You flatter me to gain my favor.

ARMON:  It is not my nature to flatter.

LEONA:  You are a good man and I release you of your duty if only to relieve myself of your honest pity.

ARMON:  I thank you. [bows] There is a part of me that would stay to comfort you but my journey calls.  I have delayed too long.  The Lady of the Lakes is near.  Yet I give this pledge in exchange for my freedom: If it comes to my means to release you of this spell, it will be done.  Farewell.

LEONA:  Be gone for I am too old for hollow wishes.  Yet know this: I have seen your true love.  She is fair and so are you.  Farewell.

[Lights fade.  Exit LEONA.  Spot up on MAGI.]

MAGI:  Within a heartbeat he reached the water's edge and at once, from the island of the largest lake, which formed the top of the sacred trinity, Terra appeared to him, circling as in the vision in radiant blue light.  She extended her hands to welcome him and the light sprang forth to lie at his feet.  Before her majesty he bowed and knelt.

[TERRA appears above wrapped in blue light.]

TERRA:  At last you come before me!  Rise and make account.

ARMON:  I am Armon, son of Talmus, king of the light dwellers.  I am summoned by a vision of Ringed Women of whom you are one.  I have come to free my people of ancient laws that bind our will and blind our visage. I have come to strike down the great wall that divides our kingdoms.

TERRA: I am the Lady of the Lakes and protector of the deep forest. I know your father the king and persuaded him by all that is good to ban the light dwellers from this realm.

ARMON: By all that is sacred why? Forgive my insolence but I have journeyed long and hard. A good and kindly father I have made to suffer at your call. Why would you prevent our people from venturing beyond our realm? Why do you cry out to us yet block our passage?

TERRA: Know first that sight is drawn to that which is forbidden. That which is now darkness shall be light. We have summoned you at this juncture because now it is right when once it was right to stop you. The light dwellers were of another cloth. They chose the way of destruction. All that lay before them that they could not command was laid barren and rendered desolate. Like you when you arrived at our gate they could think of nothing but their own sorrow. The light dwellers were not worthy to walk among us. They journey must prepare your people to respect the light of darkness and all its beings.

ARMON: Forgive me, ringed goddess of wisdom and light, I am jealous of the knowledge that remains withheld. I know I am but small beneath your radiance. Your wisdom and your greater purpose are as the sea to the fisherman. I will uphold your law, defend your honor and abide your will as if it were my own.

TERRA: When it is your own your journey will be complete. Until then we can only help you on the path. But tell me, fair prince, what has passed since our last encounter? I have counted four moons.

ARMON: Is it four? I am lost in time. I am undone. Since last you counseled me I have encountered a false guide yet escaped the maze of confusion with your heavenly assistance. I have been guided by a wise man who I believe is known to you and I have yielded to the temptation of an enchantress. This last I fear will keep me from my journey's end.

TERRA: What have you learned by these encounters?

ARMON: That there is good and wonder in all things.

TERRA: Would you be as a brother to all things?

ARMON: I would, great lady.

TERRA: Even to one who deceived you and by that deception stayed you on your path?

ARMON: Even to she as there is goodness within her.

TERRA: Even to one who plotted so artfully to cast your soul into an endless void from which none could escape?

ARMON: Even to he for it is his path to teach by these means.

TERRA: Would you be brother to the lost souls and creatures of the forest?

ARMON: Yes for they are my equals beneath your lofted vision. But would they be brothers to me?

TERRA: Without their blessings you could not have reached these sacred lakes. Even the wind sings praises to the light dweller who walks softly with eyes that turn both inward and outward, forward and behind.

ARMON: I am honored by their blessings.

TERRA: Let it be so. You have won passage through the Deep Forest to the Land of the Lakes. You have sworn brotherhood and your word is true. You shall have my blessing for the last phase of your journey. This much and one thing more for you have shown yourself a worthy soul. You may have one wish and one that is yours alone.

ARMON: It is my oath I now deliver. Free the enchantress from her spell.

TERRA: It is done. Though she has served us well we now release her that she may resume her journey on a different path. It is the way of the circle by which all things are one.

ARMON: I am humbled by your grace.

TERRA: And I am humbled by your gratitude. You hold

the sacred crystal of my sister, Sira.

ARMON: I hold it with both hands close to my heart. It is her blessing and her love.

TERRA: It is good to hold it dear but not too tight. The time may come when it is better given than received. Fear not my sister's jealousy for her love is secure and she is bound to higher loyalty.

ARMON: I understand even in ignorance.

TERRA: You will stay here one day, bathe in our waters, eat at our table, sleep beneath our cover and in the morning receive a gift – one that has long awaited you – to prepare for the road ahead.

ARMON: I thank you.

[ARMON bows, lights fade. Spot up on MAGI.]

MAGI: Thus Prince Armon was welcomed to the family of the Deep Forest and the three Kingdoms of the Inner Light. He bathed in the waters of the sacred lakes and it shielded him from mortal harm. He consumed fruit of the sacred vine and it gave him the strength of ten mortal men. He slept beneath the enchanted roof and was given sleep that restored his soul with dreams of wonder and awe. When he awoke all that had been was no more. Before him lay a sword, more glorious than any he had seen. The path to the highest peak where Ariel – Goddess of the Heavens, Sister of the Moon, the Sun and the Stars – now beckons.

The path was steep and hard. His pace stiffened against winds of mortal time. The thirteenth moon in this enchanted land was close at hand yet he neither hurried nor hesitated. He fixed his mind to strengthen his resolve and slow his pace upward, like the mountain goat, slow and sure of foot, when at last, in the great distance, at the very edge of his view, the veiled peak of Ariel appeared shrouded in mystic clouds of light and shadow. His heart filled with hope and wonder. He started and stopped three times before he found again the pace that was his own.

When he returned to himself in patience and resolve he heard a cry of helplessness and despair. His friend the wind whispered: He is lost that hesitates. He did not hesitate but answered the call as befits a warrior and worthy prince. He did not worry that it carried him far from his path. Fleet of foot and sword drawn he came to this scene: A fair lady whose beauty rivaled even that of the Ringed Women was bound and tethered to a horned beast with iron talons and jagged teeth, hunched and bent to admire his captive in her distress. Between Armon and the beast the earth opened in a great divide. He did not hesitate but leapt the chasm and came upon the startled beast.

[Spot fades. Lights up on the scene.]

ARMON: Let this fair lady go or face the sword of your reckoning!

BEAST: [shocked] What? Would you let her throw herself to death in the chasm?

ARMON: Do not deceive for I will not be deceived. You are her torturer!

BEAST: I am her savior! This line is all that holds her from a cruel fate! But do not take the word of a beast. This maiden has a voice and may speak freely.

ARMON: Fair lady, whose voice even in despair sings sweet melody to my ears, whose vision holds the beauty of moonlight on sacred waters, whose sorrow pierces the heart and blinds me to reason, have no fear for I have none. Speak freely for I am eager to save you from this cruel beast.

ELENA: Brave and kind lord, I know not whereof you come that my cries should fall upon your ears. They were meant for heaven that the great Goddess should take pity and release me from this hold so that I may seek the very fate my master describes as cruel. To me it is kindness – a final sleep in the earth's divide that ends all sorrow.

# RANDOM PLAYS

ARMON: This is a strange tale that keeps me from my journey's end. The great lady Ariel watches us even now with keen interest. It is a test – the last and greatest. I cannot leave you. My eyes have welcomed my heart. You are the love that is not chosen. It chooses me. Our paths cross and our destinies are joined. If you choose the chasm to Sira's realm below, I will follow. Yet I implore you to join me on the path above.

BEAST: Hold a spell, lover that would be. Forget your cause but forget not me. I am not the sentimental kind but I am her master and she is mine.

ARMON: By what right do you hold this maiden?

BEAST: By all that is fair. I traded for her.

ARMON: What fairness makes property of a princess?

BEAST: Princess? Her value grows. Soon she will be queen.

ELENA: Sweet prince, my heart beats as yours. Were this another mountain and ours another time, I would throw myself to your embrace and pray that I am welcome there. For my eyes are pleased as yours and beseech my heart to join you. The greater my sorrow for I am bound to this beast by honor and by trust.

ARMON: Tell me how this came to pass.

ELENA: My father is a good man, though neither brave nor strong of will. He sought closeness to the stars and so brought my mother and I to this mountain. At this very spot we camped for the night. As we slumbered the earth shook and split apart. From the open wound out crawled the beast that stands before us. He struck a bargain with my poor father: Safe passage if I am left to be his bride.

ARMON: Unworthy father to strike such a deal.

ELENA: It was not his choice but mine. Yet he is not my husband and I am not his bride for I revised the contract thus: I would stay with him and serve no other while I lived or until the fates released me from his hold.

ARMON: By my word and the fates that guide us, you

are released. This was not fairly bargained and cannot bind you to a fate that is not yours.

ELENA: By my word and promise I remain bound. His word alone can release me.

BEAST: Hear me now and know that I am not easily impressed. I am a man as you are, entombed in this beastly disguise. I seek a treasure that will once again endear me to my queen that she may lift this unkind fate that follows me and takes my part against my will. In the lusty greed of youth I took a precious stone that was not mine to take. I have returned a thousand precious stones in my remorse but none could take its place. What have you to offer? What price for this beauty who eases my pain and amuses me with tears I can no longer shed?

ARMON: What you would have of me I will give.

BEAST: You carry a finely crafted sword of rare design, one suited to a king, yet it is no use to me for I have swords enough where my hands used to be. What else do you hold?

ARMON: [hesitates] I hold a gift from the Lady Sira – a stone that bears her love and blessing.

BEAST: [incensed] If the name you give is not your own, that lie shall be your last! Who are you?

ARMON: I am Armon of the Light Dwellers.

BEAST: [bows] Forgive me, my prince. Though I am a beast that was a beastly man, I am sworn to serve and honor you. The maiden is yours.

[The BEAST releases her. ELENA moves to Armon.]

ELENA: I am Lady Elena.

ARMON: Even your name is music. [they embrace, he addresses the Beast] By this act you are more man than beast. Receive this gift, a sacred crystal. It is my honor and our Lady's love. We have felt her blessing even now. Return it that you may return to her grace.

BEAST: I feel the joy a man feels. I will descend to her,

bestow upon her this stone, and give word of your safe passing.

ARMON: My love goes with you.

BEAST: And mine with you both.

[Exit BEAST.]

ARMON: Sweet Elena, so it is written. You will be my queen or I would not be king.

ELENA: You are my king, my prince, my savior and everything. You have restored the joy and wonder that I thought I'd lost forever. My love will repay you or I will not live.

ARMON: Come, our journey calls.

[Exit ARMON and ELENA. Spot up on MAGI.]

MAGI: The eyes of heaven cried with joy as they always do when lovers find their mates. When two becomes one the will of the God and Goddess is done. It hardly matters that in his haste the beast forgot to give them passage across the divide. Armon would not be denied. He fixed the line by which the beast had bound his love to the handle of his sword and threw it across the gorge where it planted in a stone. His love upon his shoulders he crossed the breech and resumed his climb to Ariel's peak. Word went before him, from the bottom of the deep cave to the stars of heaven, and revelry ruled the forest: Armon of the Light Dwellers, son of Talmus, and Elena of the Sacred Mountain, now approached the throne of Ariel where the Ringed Women of the Sacred Forest awaited.

[Spot fades. Lights up on ARMON and ELENA bowing below and the Lady ARIEL above.]

ARIEL: Rise, fair prince and his chosen love. Long

have I yearned to look upon you. Long have I awaited you and the moment that awaits us all. The joy that springs from the very core and center of my being is more than you can know.

ARMON: Yet it is what I feel within, great lady.

ARIEL: You have chosen well.

ARMON: Elena is the love that chooses me.

ELENA: The greater my blessing to be loved by the one I love.

ARIEL: We love all our children be they winged or leaved, man or beast. Yet some we save for rare and special love. We hold them to our hearts. Such love we bestow on you for you have both shown yourselves worthy of the noble destiny by which the circle is complete.

ARMON: That it is great and noble we are sure for it is by your hand and calling. Yet we would know more.

ARIEL: Patience, good prince. Hear my tale. It is a tale most strange and dear to my heart. There is but one of the light dwellers to reach this peak before you and he is known to you. He is Talmus, your father and your king.

ARMON: Thus did the Lady Terra speak to me.

ARIEL: She might have told you more for more there is to tell. Just as Sira and Terra are my sisters, so Talmus is our brother.

ARMON: This is the circle of the wise one's counsel. It is the riddle that thirsts for more.

ARIEL: I have waited all your life to tell you what I now tell. It must be laid before you with great care. Talmus came to the forest to learn its secrets and gather is powers just as you did. His journey was long and treacherous, his lessons many and he rose to the challenge at every pass just as you did. Along the path he met and married a lady of the inner light yet she that he chose was chosen. She was the queen and ruler of this heavenly realm. Talmus joined her on the throne and together they ruled for thirteen moons. To them a son was born, a child of darkness and of light. All was harmony and balance until Talmus was summoned to the Kingdom of the Light Dwellers. Your father's father was dying, his mother dead. The throne sat vacant and wanted its rightful king. A great circle of the wise and trusted of the three kingdoms was called to the counsel of the Ringed Women before the throne of inner light. They decided that Talmus should take his only son and leave behind his queen. The Sacred Forest would be forbidden to the light dwellers until the son of Talmus and Ariel, his queen, should return to the place of his birth. Once here and proven worthy he and his chosen queen would take his place upon his mother's throne. I return to my husband's side to share the throne of the light dwellers. Worthy son, come to your mother's arms for I have embraced you only in dreams these many, many years.

[ARMON goes to her; they embrace.]

ARMON: As long as you have waited, that long have I been but half a man.
ARIEL: Our grief for what is lost we share. The absence is now filled. It is the path we did not choose yet our faith guided us through the darkness of despair and led us to the wisdom that is love. We understand though understanding not.
ARMON: Let it be so, dear mother, for my heart fills with warmth, my spirit soars and all around me sings in harmony. I cannot doubt the wisdom of the journey and bless the sacred forces that returned me to your arms.
ARIEL: You have the inner light of darkness. It shines in your eyes. There too is the flame of the lighted ones. That which burns may comfort or destroy yet without the sacred flame the ring is broken, the circle incomplete. We will no longer live apart for we are one with all. You are born to this purpose and this call: that by your hand the wall must fall.
ARMON: It is my solemn oath.

ARIEL: Fair Elena, chosen of the forest for this coupling, come forth and take your loved one's hand to become his queen.

ELENA: Great lady, it is my honor and my joy. [she does so; they embrace]

ARIEL: Ringed Sisters of the Sacred Forest, come forth and give your blessings! Unite these two in the spirit of the circle and the cause of one. Bestow them with the wisdom that is the inner light of darkness at the center of all life. Terra of the Lakes, Sira of the Deep Earth, come forth! Join us in revelry to celebrate this moment!

[Enter TERRA and SIRA to each side of Ariel.]

SIRA: Long we have waited.
TERRA: Now we have come.
SIRA: Together we unite you.
TERRA: And bind you.
ARIEL: To the cause that is the throne of inner light.
SIRA: Armon, son of Talmus and of Ariel.
TERRA: Son of darkness and of light.
ARIEL: Know that you are chosen.
SIRA: Elena of the Sacred Mountain.
TERRA: He is chosen that chooses you.
ARIEL: Seek no other call than this.
SIRA: The journey's end shall be your bliss.
TERRA: Forces of the light behold.
ARIEL: Here stands the king that was foretold.
SIRA: He that faced the demons of his own darkness.
TERRA: He that wandered through the maze.
ARIEL: He that knows his own smallness.
SIRA: He that befriends his own fear.
TERRA: He that knows the temptress of desire.
ARIEL: He that knows the beauty of the beast.
SIRA: He that battled anger and despair.
TERRA: He that learned to triumph by surrender.

# RANDOM PLAYS

ARIEL: He that found his love and would not leave her.
SIRA: He that discovers: to love one...
TERRA: Is to love all.
ARIEL: To love all...
SIRA: Is to love oneself.
TERRA: He is Armon, son of Talmus and Ariel.
ARIEL: Realm of the Sacred Mountain and the Tall Peak, here is your king.
SIRA: She is Elena, chosen of Armon and daughter of sacrifice.
ARIEL: Realm of the Moon, the Stars and the Heavens, here is your queen.
RINGED WOMEN (Ariel, Sira and Terra as one):
The earth, the air, the fire, the water: Return, return, return, return.

The earth, the air, the fire, the water: Return, return, return, return.

[The incantation continues in round as the Ringed Women speak.]

RINGED WOMEN: May the circle grow complete. May the circle be unbroken. May the circle be filled with enchantment. Earth, fire, wind and rain: Return, return, return. Wind, fire, water and earth: Return, return, return. Air, soil, heaven and flame: Return, return, return.

[Spot up on MAGI. Exit ARMON, ELENA and the RINGED WOMEN.]

MAGI: That night was spent in the sharing of the tender and painful memories of three lifetimes. For though Ariel oversaw her son and daughter's upbringing, she could not see through their young and mortal eyes. Time was short and precious for a royal marriage wants consummation. Preparations are made. A year by mortal time passes. It is the eve of the thirteenth moon. Talmus, his kingdom and his royal self shaken by his son's absence, anxiously awaits.

[Lights up on the throne of TALMUS, an empty throne beside him. Enter ARMON, ELENA and ARIEL, disguised by a cloak.]

TALMUS: You have returned, my son, at the appointed hour. Speak for I have lost my patience: Are you a stranger or a prince?
ARMON: I am neither. I am a king who returns to you your queen, my mother. She is Ariel, Lady of the Lakes and the highest peak.

[ARIEL takes down her cloak.]

TALMUS: Ariel? What sound is this that sings such melody and brings such woe? Like the opening of a floodgate, that which was so long denied rushes to my mind and fills my heart with sorrow and with joy.
ARIEL: Am I not you queen and you my loving husband?
TALMUS: Come, my love, my life, my honored queen and royal wife! You are that better part of me that has been hidden though not forgot. I have longed for you as Tristan longed for Isolde! Here is your throne, no less nor greater than my own.

[ARIEL goes to Talmus and kneels. As she takes his hand and kisses it, he guides her to his embrace.]

TALMUS: I have grown old while you appear no older than the very day love claimed me and led me to your throne.
ARIEL: I was your elder then. My love is no less now than it was then. Now we will grow old together. You have raised a good and loyal son.

# RANDOM PLAYS

TALMUS: Forgive me, Armon, for in this matter I was ignorant.

ARMON: We shared our ignorance, good father, by heavenly design. Its blessings now unfold. This is my queen, the fair and beautiful Elena, whom I rescued from the beast on the Sacred Mountain.

TALMUS: Her love shines within you as yours does within her. She is a queen most worthy as is her king. Love chooses wisely for it is the greatest wisdom.

ELENA: If love is wisdom, my husband is my sage. The greater are you, the root of this sweet flower that blossoms even now.

TALMUS: You are most gracious.

ELENA: You are most kind.

TALMUS: It was not always so. My queen is my heart and how I longed for her. She tempered the fire of my hot and youthful blood. But let us not linger on our small joys. Speak, my beloved queen, of all that is foretold.

ARIEL: I will, my love, for I have waited long for the dawning of this day. It is the time when the serpent leaves its former self. The moth emerges from its slumber to bless us all with new, inspired sight and christens this day's journey into night. The Age of Enlightenment is upon us. That which was forbidden out of fear and ignorance is embraced. Fire joins with water. Air is joined with earth. The circle is complete. The dragons of our past become our allies in this new birth. The inward light moves outward as the outward moves within. The Gods and Goddesses beyond our earthly realm rejoice. The two become one. The one becomes all. Strike down the wall that divides us. In its place a bridge will unite us. This is prophecy.

TALMUS: Let it be proclaimed. The forest that was forbidden is now sacred by divine decree. Its subjects that were our enemy are now our brothers and sisters. No more shall we fear the darkness for it is our mirrored self. No more shall we ravage our soil for want of gold or spoil the air for want of wealth. No more in servitude shall we hold our fellow beings. We are one with all. This is the proclamation of King Talmus and Queen Ariel, your royal rulers. It is the word and testament of all that we cherish. Let no one who comes before us behold it not.

[We hear the Incantation of the Ringed Women, continuing under, as the lights fade and a spot appears on the MAGI.]

MAGI: This is the story of Armon and the Ringed Women of the Sacred and Forbidden Forest. May they live long and prosper as those who lived within their realm most assuredly did. The tale is told. No more is there to tell. Let those who hear my words remember and remember well. It is told to you that you may tell your children. As long as women are women and men are mortal men, the journey that was Armon's will call to us again.

[Spot out.]

End Act Two.

# APHRODITE HOUSE

*(A Play in Two Acts)*

## SETTING

A beautifully crafted two-story house where the sun rises from gently rolling hills and the majestic oak dominates the landscape. The stage consists of the primary living space. The living room covers two thirds of the stage with a dining room down right with a round wood dining table. The kitchen is up right with a counter dividing it from the dining area. There are windows on the upstage kitchen wall. Entrances are made through a doorway on the upstage side of the dining area. A doorway leads to a music room with a piano down left and to the bedrooms upstairs. A phone and stereo are upstage in the living room.

## CHARACTERS

TOM: A working man and artist.
SARA: A singer and pianist.
CATHY: A working woman.
JASON: A writer.
RICHARD: A musician.

# ACT ONE

## SCENE ONE

(A piano plays gently under as a spotlight comes up on JASON seated stage right.)

JASON: In the early hours of a misty morning, I observe the curious presence of a full moon, still shining in all its mirrored glory. While lesser creatures of the night make haste in fearful retreat, the moon lingers as if to catch a fleeting glimpse of Hughson House in daylight. It paints itself in borrowed, golden beauty, encircled in the fantastical oranges of Hieronymus Bosch. As majestic clouds climb slowly down gently rolling hills, taking hold of the valley floor, I watch it turn a brilliant, glowing red – a likeness I have seen but once. I gaze upon glimmering drops of dew, soon to vanish, like hope itself, under the very light of observation.

As I close my eyes a vision takes hold: An inanimate, unmoving object – by its name a house – yet such a house that like the brilliant red moon is seen but once and never seen again. A house grown, like the magnificent oak, in fertile valley soil, it sits in patient silence, waiting, watching as years go by in moments. A sense of beauty and wonder that strikes deep on sight. An uncertain feeling that pierces the very heart and soul of any dreamer who dares to stop his gaze upon her. An attraction, an intrigue, an indefinable mood that reigns within her walls – as if in the presence of a legendary queen.

A house, only a house, but such a house – and such a lady – that like the brilliant red moon in the eyes of a dreamer, holds forth a sacred promise and beckons.

# JACK RANDOM

[Spot fades on JASON. Lights up on TOM and SARA seated at the candlelit dining table, sipping wine.]

TOM: I love you, Sara. I've loved you since the first time I saw you.
SARA: I know, Tom. I know.
TOM: We've been together more than a year.
SARA: And we've had a good time, haven't we?
TOM: The time of my life.
SARA: Isn't that enough?
TOM: Look, don't make this any harder...
SARA: Fine.
TOM: I've never wanted to spend the rest of my life with anyone. I never wanted to settle down, have a family or be a father...until I met you. I know you don't feel the same. I've always known it. Still, if you gave it a chance, we could make it work.
SARA: Is that what love is? Is that what it's about? Settling down, having kids? My parents settled down and had kids. My father left when I was four. I've seen him exactly three times since then. I may not know what I want but I know what I don't want.
TOM: I'm not your father.
SARA: [stands, walks away] You're a man.
TOM: All men are not the same.
SARA: [turns back] I didn't mean they were.
TOM: It doesn't have to be that way.
SARA: It won't be because I won't let it happen.
TOM: I promise you I'd never leave you.
SARA: Don't make promises you can't deliver.
TOM: I swear.
SARA: I believe you. I just don't want the life you're offering. I like being free. I like that I can go wherever I want and do whatever I feel like doing without feeling guilty about it. I like being with you, Tom, but if I ever felt like being with someone else, it's my right. I won't apologize for

being who I am and I won't feel guilty. I've done that. It doesn't work for me. [goes to him, hugs] I know it's hard but I want you to understand: I love my freedom more than I could ever love any man. Why do people have to belong to each other? Why can't we just enjoy each other and live moment to moment?

TOM: I do understand. I've said it myself. But there comes a time when it isn't enough. It happened to me and one day it will happen to you. You're young and beautiful. You're every man's dream and every man's desire. But someday you'll look in the mirror and realize you've gotten older. Your beauty will fade and then you'll begin to wish you had someone – someone who remembers and still sees it as clearly as ever, someone who knows how special you are and always will be. I want to be that someone, Sara. That's all there is to it. I want it to be me.

SARA: Thank you. [kisses him on the forehead, the cheek and the lips] I'll never forget this night.

[SARA breaks away, crossing to the music room, stopping at the door way. TOM follows cautiously.]

TOM: I love you. I love you more than I've ever loved anyone – even my own mother.

SARA: Your mother doesn't kiss you like I do.

TOM: Thank God.

SARA: I feel like playing music. [TOM starts] No, you stay there. I'll play something for you.

[Music plays under. Lights fade. Spot up on JASON.]

JASON: At Hughson House time itself is an illusion. Just as years go by in moments, moments seem to last forever. Once heard at Hughson House, the song lingers. Once seen, the vision never fades. Once felt, the feeling is eternal. Once welcomed into her heart, yours will never be the same. At Hughson House: The heart and soul of woman one and all.

My fate cries out. It is the sweet sound of a gentle lady's voice. She sings to me of sorrow and my soul flies to comfort her. She cries and her tears are my own. She calls to me and I must go.

[Lights fade.]

End Act One, Scene One.

## ACT ONE

## SCENE TWO

(Weeks later. TOM sits reading the morning news. SARA enters, a curious smile on her face.)

TOM: What are you so happy about?
SARA: Nothing really. It's a beautiful day.
TOM: I hadn't noticed.
SARA: Stacy and I are going to the lake this afternoon.
TOM: Were you going to ask me if I'd like to go along?
SARA: Would you like to come along?
TOM: No. I just like to be asked.
SARA: Since when?
TOM: Since you stopped asking.
SARA: When was that?
TOM: Two weeks ago. I could name the day, the time, where we were standing and what we were talking about.
SARA: I think you're being paranoid.
TOM: So you're not aware that you're treating me any differently since...
SARA: What would you like me to say, Tom?
TOM: Tell me the truth, Sara. Don't play me the fool. I don't like it. I'm not accusing you of anything but things have changed between us – fundamentally. I'd like you to acknowledge it. Not that it's a big deal. I knew from the start my time would come – at least I should have known. You're like a mirage. As soon as someone gets close you fade away. I'd just like to hear it from you before I hear it from someone else.
SARA: You're so dramatic. I've just been feeling a little restless lately. That's all.

TOM: Restless? Be honest for once. I have this image of Bogie in Casa Blanca, standing alone in the rain with a silly look on his face because the woman he loves is gone and didn't even have the decency to say goodbye. I don't mind if you're feeling restless. I don't mind if you need more space. But if it's more than that...

SARA: I haven't cheated on you if that's what you mean.

TOM: No, Sara, that's not what I mean.

SARA: [waits] I don't want to hurt you.

TOM: No. You don't want to hurt anyone. You never have. But you do it anyway. You do it and then you walk away.

SARA: I never made any promises.

TOM: You think I'm not aware of that? No promises, no commitments. It's like a religion with you.

SARA: [gently] This sounds like goodbye.

TOM: It does, doesn't it? It's up to you. I can't be the one to say it.

SARA: Why couldn't you just leave it alone?

TOM: I care too much to let it go on this way. I'm losing it.

SARA: Have you made any plans?

TOM: I asked John about moving in with him. He needs a roommate to share expenses. I think it might be for the best. What do you think?

SARA: [aloof] I don't know. It might be.

TOM: Yeah. Well. He gave me until Friday to figure it out. I guess I don't need that long. [gathers coat and hat] I'll be back for my things tomorrow. [at the door] So long, Sara.

SARA: Call me?

TOM: Sure.

[TOM exits. SARA watches him drive off through the kitchen window. She then crosses to the bookshelves up left to retrieve a letter. She sits reading. Spot up on JASON.]

# RANDOM PLAYS

JASON: Dear Sara: Though I am far away and living in a world so strange and foreign to the valley, I can't stop my thoughts from drifting back to Hughson House. In my dreams I am with you. In silent moments I speak to you. Every night I pray that you hear the voice of my heart, the words I cannot speak. In the uncertain soul of a lonely dreamer you are more dear than all the fruits of this world. A vision of beauty and purest innocence. Such is my state of mind that I begin to hear your voice, calling me, beckoning. I fear I can no longer hold it back for in my heart of hearts I hear myself imploring you: Embrace me and let me live. Yours always, Jason.

[Lights fade.]

End Act One, Scene Two.

## ACT ONE

## SCENE THREE

(TOM enters with suitcase from inside doorway. Sara's roommate CATHY sits at the kitchen table reading. It is morning.)

TOM: Well, that's that.
CATHY: What's the hurry? Sit and relax a while.
TOM: I don't know, Cathy. Time to move on.
CATHY: Would you like some coffee?
TOM: [sighs, sits] Sure. Thanks.
CATHY: [delivers coffee] I don't know what you're so down about. You brought this on yourself. Actually, you should be proud. I never thought I'd see the day when someone said goodbye to Sara.
TOM: That's a laugh.
CATHY: No one's laughing.
TOM: I didn't say goodbye.
CATHY: You packed up and moved out. That was your decision. As I understand it, Sara didn't ask you to go and I certainly didn't. The way I see it, that's a pretty effective way to say goodbye.
TOM: Maybe but I don't feel like celebrating.
CATHY: Of course not. But you don't have to go into mourning either. You had a choice and you made it. I think you did the right thing. Accept responsibility and move on.
TOM: I made a decision to leave. That much is true. Whether I'm responsible is another story. Sara didn't ask me to leave. She wouldn't be that cold. I didn't do anything wrong. But she didn't ask me to stay either and she knew I would have.

# RANDOM PLAYS

CATHY: Maybe you expected too much.

TOM: You know her better than I do.

CATHY: I've lived with her longer.

TOM: Right and it doesn't hurt to be a woman. She confides in you. She never confided in me. I don't know if any man can really know Sara. We're not allowed to see beyond the surface. We only see her external beauty and we imagine the beauty within. But we never see it. It's off limits, virgin territory, untouched by the hands of man. The one thing I learned about her is that she says more in silence than she does in words. She expects you to know what's going on through telepathy.

CATHY: Of course. She's a woman.

TOM: I knew the exact moment when everything changed. She didn't have to say anything and she didn't. I knew even though I didn't want to know. Still, I would have liked her to say it.

CATHY: What good would that have done? You only would have tried to talk her out of it. The way it is, you have your pride.

TOM: You think that's important? The male ego. The problem is: It's too easy. It shouldn't be that easy for anyone.

CATHY: It's always been that way – at least for Sara. It's her mystique. That's what attracted you. It attracts all men. It makes you want to solve her. The problem is she can't be solved. She's illusive. She's a dream. You loved her for it and yet you expected her to change. I'm sorry, Tom. You're a good man. I could have told you but you wouldn't have listened.

TOM: You're right. I only saw what I wanted to see. I fell in love before I could think about it. Then I stopped thinking until it was over. The strangest thing about it is: I don't regret it even now.

CATHY: Maybe you haven't accepted it.

TOM: You know what? Maybe I haven't.

# JACK RANDOM

[SOUND: Car approaching. CATHY rises, crosses upstage to look out the kitchen window.]

CATHY: Well, I'll be... It's Jason.
TOM: Jason?
CATHY: You remember. He's a friend of John's.
TOM: Right. I thought he was in New York.
CATHY: So did I.
TOM: What's he doing here?
CATHY: Ask him yourself. [a knock at the door, she answers it] Jason! I don't believe it! [embrace] Come on in. You remember Tom?
JASON: Sure. [shakes hands] How are you?
TOM: Great and you?
JASON: Recovering. You still playing that old Martin?
TOM: Not really. As a matter of fact I haven't been doing much of anything.
CATHY: Have a seat. Stay a while. Coffee?
JASON: [sitting at the kitchen table] I will and I'd love some. Thank you.
CATHY: When did you get in?
JASON: Last night.
CATHY: Where are you staying?
JASON: I'm with my folks for now.
CATHY: What's your plan?
JASON: I may be moving in with Charlie.
TOM: Small world. I'm moving in with John upstairs.
JASON: You're kidding.
TOM: I wish I were.

[Awkward silence.]

CATHY: So how was New York?
JASON: Great. The metropolis is a good place to look at life and figure out where you belong.
TOM: So why did you come back?

# RANDOM PLAYS

JASON: A lot of reasons. I loved New York but New York couldn't make her mind up about me. I saw myself working hard to get nowhere. I found myself in the winter of discontent. Not a new feeling. More like an old ghost. But for the first time in my life I felt something pulling me back to this valley – something more than family. I couldn't shake it so I swallowed my pride and bought a ticket home.

CATHY: If you're going to be unhappy you might as well be unhappy in the company of friends.

JASON: Strange, isn't it? You have to go away to discover your roots. This place doesn't let go. I thought I could make it out there. I thought I belonged to the world. Turns out I'm just another valley boy.

CATHY: You may be a valley boy but your not just another one. So tell us about it. What did you see? Where did you go? What did you do and who did you know?

JASON: "I came upon a magic city, it's promises untold; but found it to a lonely dreamer insensitive and cold."

TOM: Sounds like a woman.

CATHY: He's a little jaded at the moment.

TOM: I've always been jaded. Right now I'm a little more so.

JASON: [waits] Is there something I don't know?

TOM: I've got a feeling there's a lot we don't know. [rises] Cathy can fill you in. I've got to move. Good to see you, Jason. Welcome back.

JASON: It's good to be back.

TOM: Tell Sara I'll call.

[Exit TOM stage right. Awkward silence.]

JASON: Where's Sara?

CATHY: Upstairs. She didn't want to come down while Tom was here. It's complicated. [crosses for more coffee] She got your letter, you know.

JASON: I didn't know.

# JACK RANDOM

CATHY: Does it bother you?

JASON: I asked John not to give it to her.

CATHY: As long as Tom and Sara were together. I know. I guess he couldn't resist. Under the circumstances he didn't think you'd mind.

JASON: The circumstances?

CATHY: Everyone but Tom knew they wouldn't last much longer. Your letter just made it easier.

JASON: There are no secrets.

CATHY: I walked in one evening and Sara was in the den. She didn't hear me come in. She was reading your letter aloud and I couldn't help but listen. It was lovely. You stole her heart.

JASON: You're forgiven.

[SARA appears at the doorway stage left.]

SARA: Hello, Jason.

JASON: I've waited so long to see you.

SARA: And I've wanted to see you.

JASON: [approaching, taking her hands] I was afraid.

SARA: Don't be.

JASON: I was afraid I'd imagined too much of your beauty. I was afraid that seeing you, touching you, looking at you... I was afraid no one, not even you, could equal the vision of my dreams.

SARA: Are you disappointed?

JASON: No. A thousand times no. Now I realize how foolish I've been. My dreams couldn't touch your beauty.

SARA: You take my breath away.

CATHY: Welcome back, Jason!

[KATHY exits SR. JASON and SARA stare into each other's eyes, then kiss and embrace. Lights fade. Spot up on JASON down right. Music under.]

# RANDOM PLAYS

JASON: I hear no voice but that which flows as music from her lips. I see no beauty in the world but that which begins with Sara. Through her eyes, I see myself undone. I am enchanted. Until now I've walked as a blind man through endless fields of wildflowers. Until now I've lived without cause or reason. Until now I've never loved. Sara. Sweet, gentle Sara. So precious and pure. I live to be graced by your affection. In return I give you this eternal promise: That you will never have need or reason to doubt my love. It is as pure as your beauty, as deep as hope, as true as any man may know. If ever I should love but you, then day is night, wrong is right and all the universe is out of joint. I love you. I've always loved you. I will always love you. This or life, itself, I swear.

[Spot out.]

End Act One, Scene Three.

# ACT ONE

## SCENE FOUR

(CATHY sits in the living room, reading, listening to music. TOM enters enraged. She remains seated.)

TOM: Where are they?

CATHY: Who?

TOM: Sara and her new boyfriend! You know, the kid, the king of romance, the prince of pastureland! Don't play games with me, Cathy. His car is outside!

CATHY: Are you drunk?

TOM: Not even close. [edges toward the doorway that leads upstairs] Are they up there? Are they fucking up there? If I go up there right now...

CATHY: You'd find an empty bedroom.

TOM: [waits] Right. [starts out]

CATHY: I knew you couldn't do it. You're not man enough.

TOM: [stops] What are you talking about?

CATHY: I knew you couldn't just leave her. You have to make a scene! Yeah, Tom, you're the big man now! Maybe you can scare him off with this tough guy act but you won't get her back. You'll only end up begging for her forgiveness.

TOM: I'm not begging anything from anyone. [yells] Not this time, baby! If anyone should worry about forgiveness it's her!

CATHY: What did you expect? Did you think she'd take a vow of celibacy? She doesn't love you anymore. You have to accept it. It's over.

TOM: [laughs] Accept it? Hell, I accepted it before it

began. It's got nothing to do with it.

CATHY: Doesn't it?

TOM: No! You fucking women think you know everything! You don't know shit!

CATHY: We do.

TOM: What?

CATHY: We do know everything. The sooner you learn that the better off you'll be.

TOM: Bullshit!

CATHY: That's it. Play the raging bull in the china shop of his own fragile ego. What are you raging against? Can you tell me that?

TOM: You want to know? You really want to know? Women! All women from Aphrodite down! All of you!

CATHY: I see. So you have no responsibility? You'd rather blame half of humanity – the better half.

TOM: Damn right!

CATHY: Okay, Tom. I'm listening. How have women conspired to make you unhappy?

TOM: Hell if I know. I can't explain what I don't know. That doesn't mean it isn't true!

CATHY: Maybe you're right. It's complicated. But I'm sure when you calm down and think this through you'll understand it's just something that happens in life. It happens all the time.

TOM: I'm tired of understanding. I've spent most of my life being understanding and I've had it! I'm sick of you and your fucking advice! I'm sick of Sara and her phony innocence! [mocking] *He's just a friend, Tom. It's all in your imagination, Tom.* It's all bullshit! It's all lies! I've had it with this house and everything in it!

CATHY: This is my home, Tom – mine and Sara's. If you don't like it, get out.

TOM: Not before I've seen Sara.

CATHY: I'm telling you to get out of my house!

TOM: I'm sorry, Cathy.

CATHY: You're not but you're going to be.

TOM: [softening] I'm sorry.

CATHY: Maybe you are and maybe you're not but at least you're calming down. Maybe now you can listen to reason.

TOM: I'll try.

CATHY: That's all I ask. When it comes right down to it, Tom, you're jealous.

TOM: You think it's that simple?

CATHY: Isn't it?

TOM: Absolutely not.

CATHY: If Sara wasn't seeing someone, would you be here? Is it so bad that she is? Is it so wrong? Jason is a good guy. He's gentle and poetic and in his eyes Sara is the best thing that's ever happened to him. He's in love. I was wrong when I said you'd scare him off. He won't scare. He'd die for her.

TOM: The day will come when he prays to God he had.

CATHY: Don't be so dramatic.

TOM: You know what's going on. Sara casts her spell and he's caught in it. He has no idea what he's getting into. He can't tell the difference between the dream and reality. We both know that reality will come smashing down on him like it did me – only worse.

CATHY: Is that why you're here? To save Jason? To rescue him from his own passion?

TOM: I couldn't save him if I tried. But I do feel for him. I know what's happening here. I can read the future. So can you. Do you really think he deserves it?

CATHY: Why don't we ask him?

TOM: Right.

CATHY: Okay, let's ask someone who's been through it. The last time I talked to you, you didn't regret a moment. What makes you think it's any different for Jason?

TOM: Because he's different. For Christ's sake, he really thinks she's innocent. He's just a dumb, naïve kid who believes in the power of love to change history and rewrite the laws of nature. Sara will eat him alive. She'll use him up and throw him away. And where will that leave him? You think I'm beat up? It'll destroy him.

CATHY: That's very moving, Tom. But your compassion for Jason doesn't explain why you barnstormed in here wanting to catch them in bed, does it?

TOM: [waits] Okay. Maybe I am just a little bit jealous. Maybe I'm having trouble getting over the rage. I keep going back and forth between anger and depression. I don't know which is worse. [shakes his head] I'll never love anyone like I did her.

CATHY: Don't be foolish. Of course you will. You just need time. We've all had heartaches. Most of us recover. If we didn't, we'd have all stopped loving a long time ago.

TOM: Maybe we have. A lot of us anyway. We just didn't notice.

CATHY: There's still something I don't quite understand. You know its over. There's no going back. So what is it you want of Sara now?

TOM: The truth. The real, honest-to-God truth. I think I've earned that much.

CATHY: Do you honestly think she knows the truth? More than anyone I know, she lives day to day. She doesn't know any more than you do.

TOM: If that's how it is, I'd like to hear from her.

CATHY: What do you think the truth is?

TOM: I think she's a spoiled child. She doesn't care or doesn't know how much it hurts to love her. I don't think she's ever loved anyone. She never loved me or anyone else. [waits] For what it's worth, I hope I'm wrong.

CATHY: Right or wrong, if she told you would you believe her?

TOM: She never lied to me. [waits] Are they up there?

CATHY: Have I ever lied to you?

TOM: I don't know. Are they?

CATHY: They went out with Stacy.
TOM: [crooked grin] Stacy?
CATHY: You find that amusing?
TOM: He's being initiated.
CATHY: What does that mean?
TOM: House rules. He's learning how to share Sara's affection. He's tasted her treasure and now he begins to pay the price. He's learning that he can't get too close or he'll get burned. He's only one of the many satellites that revolve around her beauty.

[The sound of a car approaching, followed by laughter.]

CATHY: [crossing to kitchen window] Well, Tom, if you want a scene this is your chance. You can go out with a bang or a touch of class. Your choice.

[Enter SARA alone.]

SARA: Hello, Tom.
TOM: Hello, Sara.
CATHY: Where's Stacy and Jason?
SARA: I asked them to wait outside.
TOM: Are you afraid they'll witness something they shouldn't? Afraid I'll throw a fit and challenge Jason to a duel?
SARA: I'm not afraid of anything. I'd just like to talk to you alone.
CATHY: I was just about to go for a walk.

[Exit CATHY stage right.]

TOM: I've gone through this a hundred times. It's an old story. I'm real brave as long as I don't have to look into your eyes. I guess you knew that.
SARA: I know you still care about me. And I still care

about you.

TOM: I guess there's no chance…

SARA: No, Tom, don't think that way. We had something good and true but now it's time to get on with our lives.

TOM: I won't get in your way. Believe it or not I'm looking forward to my own life. I've been obsessed with you way too long. Do you realize how much I've done for myself since with I've been with you? I used to be an artist. I don't know what I am now.

SARA: I'm sorry. I never asked you to give up your art. I never asked you to give up anything.

TOM: I know you didn't. You don't ask for anything but you inspire it and you expect it in a man. I gave you what I wanted from you: devotion. Maybe that's the key to your mystique. It's human nature to want what we can't have. You're untouchable. We can't reach you. We can't get inside and that makes us want you even more.

SARA: I don't know what to say. I'm not responsible for what a man wants. I suppose I'd be disappointed if you didn't try to capture my heart but I'm not to blame if you don't.

TOM: Everyone thinks you're so innocent. I'm not so sure. You might have been. You probably were. You wear it so well it had to be yours at one time. But you're not innocent any more. You've seen it play out too many times. You know how it ends.

SARA: I never mislead you or anyone else.

TOM: I'm not saying you did. I am saying that if you cared about me you'd have let me go a long time ago. There's no way I could have loved you so much if you didn't let me – if you didn't make me feel loved.

SARA: I did love you. Love isn't something you can turn on or off. It continues…from one love to the next.

TOM: What is this thing you call love? You can pass it from one person to another as if it didn't even matter that these are real people? No. I don't believe you ever really loved me. You're in love with love. You love being loved. You love having a devoted lover, someone who worships you and can't get enough of your affection, someone who can't give enough of his own. You need someone who lives just for the possibility of your love…and dies a little when he knows he's lost it. No, Sara, you never loved me. You just kept me around to keep loving you.

SARA: You don't believe that.

TOM: You can't tell me what I believe – not any more.

SARA: You're angry. You're bitter and jealous.

TOM: It's not that simple.

SARA: Isn't it? Then tell me: What do you want? If you want me to feel bad, I do. If you want me to say I'm sorry, I will. I have. But if you want me to feel guilty for how I feel, I refuse.

TOM: I don't want you to feel anything. I want the truth.

SARA: The truth? The truth is you left me. You weren't happy and you left. I've moved on and you haven't. You're stuck in the past and you have to get beyond it. It happens every day to a million people. You have to accept it. That's how it is.

TOM: I do. It's not easy but I do. I just want to hear you deny it.

SARA: Deny what?

TOM: The truth. Did you ever love me?

SARA: Fine. If that's what you want to hear: By your terms I never loved you. I thought I did but maybe I didn't – not the way you wanted me to. Is that enough? Is that what you need to move on?

TOM: Don't trouble yourself over that. I'll be just fine. There is one more thing I'd like to know. [waits] Do you love Jason?

SARA: [coy] We hardly know each other.

TOM: You know him. Whether he knows you is another

question. Do you love him?

SARA: [considers] Yes. I do.

TOM: You're not just fooling yourself like you did with me?

SARA: No. I love him.

TOM: [considers] Maybe you do or maybe you think do. I guess it doesn't really matter. [waits] This is going to sound strange coming from me: If you do love him, stay with him. Give him the promise you never gave me. Be true to him. If you can't do that then leave him alone.

SARA: Jason is not a child. He doesn't need you to look after him.

TOM: He's not like me. He's not like anyone you've ever known.

SARA: You think I don't know that?

TOM: He's innocent. He really is. He lives in a dream world and right now he thinks you're the answer to all his prayers. If you break his heart, he'll crawl into a cave and never come out.

SARA: Stop it. Just stop.

TOM: I've gotten to know him. I like him. I probably like him better than you do. For all his talk about frustration he has more hope than anyone I know. If you destroy that you'll destroy him. You'll kill his spirit.

SARA: You don't care about Jason! You just want to get back at me. You want to hurt me. Deep inside, you still believe I might come back to you but I won't.

TOM: I'm not naïve. I've lost. I know it. I accept it. I just want to save someone I happen to like from the same fate.

SARA: I don't believe you.

TOM: Just think about it. That's all. Jason helped me get through this just by being himself. Everyone else wanted to play the analyst. We just talked. As it turns out, I don't hate him. I don't even envy him. I feel sorry for him. I can't tell him what I think about you. I can't warn him. He wouldn't listen any more than I would have. So I'm talking to you.

SARA: You have no business interfering. I love him.

TOM: Prove it. Marry him. Promise him forever.

SARA: I can't do that.

TOM: Then leave him before it's too late. If you leave him now he'll get over it.

SARA: What is this obsession with forever? Why can't we just enjoy life today?

TOM: You know better. You've been through it too many times.

SARA: You think I've never had a broken heart, don't you? You think I've never suffered. I have. There was a time I might have listened to you. I would have locked myself in a room and cried. Not now. I've decided I have a right to happiness just as much as you. I have a right to be loved like anyone else. I have a right to be free too. If Jason wants to be with me and I want to be with him, I won't turn it down just because it doesn't last forever. Nothing lasts forever. The only thing we can be sure of is that everything changes.

TOM: It's a good philosophy and I understand it. Now try to understand me. I've tried to tell you before but you've never listened. Maybe you'll listen now. You're young and beautiful, like a flower in bloom, but the time will come when your beauty fades...

SARA: I can't, Tom.

TOM: You can.

SARA: No. I can't.

TOM: If that's true, God help him.

[Exit TOM. Lights fade. Spot up on JASON. Blues plays under.]

JASON: In the name of love, friendship is betrayed. Dressed in passion, honor is obscured. Of what value is virtue if virtue so easily and often turns against itself? Of what virtue is love so burdened with the shroud of guilt? Is it the test of love that we must choose it above all other virtue? Or is there no choice? Need we only say "I love" and all will follow? Then my choice is already made: I love...and live for the moment she gives those same precious words to me. Then life itself becomes a dream and paints itself in the fantastic colors of a master artist. Never again will I be content with less than true beauty. Never will I settle for less than the love of a lovely lady. Sara, sweet Sara, gentle princess, the light of a Parrish moon, the warmth of a summer breeze, the comfort of an ocean view, forever twilight in my heart.

[Spot fades.]

End Act One, Scene Four.

# ACT ONE

## SCENE FIVE

(A piano plays, starting and stopping. SARA enters from stage left, crosses to the kitchen, pours a drink, walks back to the living room, glances at a magazine, walks to the stereo, turns the radio on, dials several stations, turns it off, settles on the couch and thumbs through the magazine. A car approaches. SARA crosses to look out the kitchen window and returns to sit on the couch. Enter CATHY with a bag of groceries.)

CATHY: [unpacking] Hi!
SARA: [aloof] Hi.
CATHY: My, you certainly are effusive!
SARA: Am I?
CATHY: I'm being sarcastic.
SARA: Oh. Right.
CATHY: Okay. What's the problem?
SARA: Nothing. I'm just not feeling well. [CATHY crosses, places her hand on Sara's forehead] It's nothing.
CATHY: I see. [returns to kitchen] You don't want to talk about it.
SARA: It's not that.
CATHY: What is it then?
SARA: I just feel like getting in my car and driving as far as I can go.
CATHY: Restless?
SARA: [sighs] Yeah.
CATHY: Any idea why?
SARA: No. I mean, I have an idea.
CATHY: Can I help you figure it out?

# RANDOM PLAYS

SARA: Please.

CATHY: [crosses, sits] What are friends for? Let's see, what's going on in your life that might upset you? One man walked out and another walked in.

SARA: Nothing new there.

CATHY: Even so it can be unsettling – especially if the one who's walking out is a friend of the one who's walking in. That and he didn't exactly leave on good terms. What did he say to you?

SARA: A lot of things. I didn't give him a chance. I've never really loved anyone but myself.

CATHY: Is that all?

SARA: He said the day would come when I lose my beauty and then I'd wish things were different. Then I'd wish I stayed with someone.

CATHY: Someone like him.

SARA: He asked me to leave Jason alone.

CATHY: That's a little bold. Did it surprise you?

SARA: No but it bothered me.

CATHY: It's an old story. Boy loses girl to his good buddy. Boy warns his buddy to stay away for his own good. But what he's really thinking is: Maybe she'll come back.

SARA: He wanted to marry me.

CATHY: Wow! That *is* bold. Did you think about it?

SARA: No. I don't love Tom. Not anymore. I'm not sure I ever did.

CATHY: What I don't understand is why you're letting it get to you. It's not like this is the first time someone has tried to make you feel guilty. You crossed that bridge a long time ago.

SARA: I thought so too.

CATHY: Now you're not so sure. What's different this time?

SARA: Maybe it's Jason. He's different. He's sensitive and innocent. He really trusts me. He believes that love will protect him.

CATHY: More like a woman than a man.

SARA: I never thought of it that way.

CATHY: If you really care for him, Sara, give him a chance. He knows what he's getting into. He jumped in with his eyes wide open. If he's willing to take the risk, let him.

SARA: That's what I told Tom.

CATHY: You were right. You just needed someone to remind you what you think.

SARA: Thanks.

CATHY: Any time.

SARA: You know what really worries me?

CATHY: I thought that's what we were talking about.

SARA: You know me better than anyone. You know what freedom means to me and how hard it was for me to learn that about myself.

CATHY: I know. I was there.

SARA: What if I change my mind?

CATHY: You're kidding. [crosses, sits] This is serious.

SARA: Jason is different. It's as if he has some secret knowledge. He sees things others don't see. He understands things in a way that no one else does.

CATHY: Do you really believe that?

SARA: I do. He has a gift. But he needs someone to help him or he'll keep it locked away.

CATHY: Someone like you?

SARA: Why not?

CATHY: You really like him.

SARA: It's more than that.

CATHY: Of course it is. [rising, crossing to kitchen] I wouldn't worry about. It'll all work out.

SARA: You're not taking me seriously, are you?

CATHY: I don't want to hurt your feelings, Sara. I just don't think this is the end of the world. I don't have your flair for the dramatic. Jason's infatuated and you're intrigued. Enjoy it while it lasts. I don't think it will change your life and I'm sure we'll all survive.

# RANDOM PLAYS

SARA: Maybe you're right.

CATHY: Or maybe not. I've been known to be wrong once in a blue moon. In that case, you'll just have to take your chances.

SARA: I don't know if it's worth it.

CATHY: Of course it is. It's always worth it.

SARA: I'm not so sure.

CATHY: Have a little faith. Whatever happens, take it on. Don't be afraid. You don't wear it well. [waits] Call him. It'll make you feel better.

SARA: I will.

[SARA crosses to pick up the phone. Lights fade to black.]

End Act One, Scene Five. End Act One.

## ACT TWO

## SCENE ONE

(Music plays as the light of morning filters through the kitchen window. Spot up on JASON stage right.)

JASON: There is such beauty in the world. There is such wonder in the rising sun or the falling moon in morning light. There is such awe in being, breathing, seeing, feeling. There is such hope in a lover's eyes. Time itself stands aside as days go by in moments and moments last forever in a lover's heart. At Hughson House, love reigns and all lives are enchanted.

[The sound of a car approaching. A knock at the door. Lights up as TOM enters, looking around.]

TOM: Anyone here?

[He scans the living room, discovers a journal on an end table, sits and begins to read. He hears someone descending the stairs off left, replaces the journal as JASON appears at the doorway in jeans and tee shirt.]

JASON: Hello, Tom.
TOM: Jason! [rises] I didn't think anyone was here.
JASON: [glances at his journal] So you let yourself in.
TOM: Old habits.
JASON: Find anything interesting?
TOM: [glances at journal] I'm sorry. That's why I'm here: to apologize for how I behaved last time I was here. Looks like I'm on a roll. Look, maybe I should leave.

# RANDOM PLAYS

JASON: That's up to you.
TOM: You don't mind?
JASON: It's not my place.
TOM: You do mind.
JASON: No.
TOM: [sitting] Where's Sara?
JASON: I just woke up. You haven't seen her?
TOM: No.
JASON: Maybe she's out back.
TOM: How are things?
JASON: Couldn't be better.
TOM: Really?
JASON: What do you mean?
TOM: Your writing. The creative juices aren't quite flowing. You go to the well but the rope's too short....
JASON: You're familiar with it.
TOM: I used to be a prolific artist. That was before I became a regular person.
JASON: Lucky you. I have a theory.
TOM: Tell me yours and I'll tell you mine.
JASON: It's an old story.
TOM: The older the better.
JASON: I'm not sure that's the case but here it is: Discontent is the blood of creativity. There's too much happiness in my life right now.
TOM: Hard to take?
JASON: I'll survive.
TOM: I'm sure you will. Here's mine: Sara is not like other women. She's an obsession worse than any drug. One taste and you'll always come back. You can't get enough. She dominates your life, your thoughts, your desire, everything. She doesn't leave enough of you for anything else.
JASON: [considers] I know you're not completely wrong but the obsession isn't Sara, it's love. She inspires love. She breathes it into your life. If it's an addiction so be it.

Without it we wouldn't be human.

TOM: [cynical] Maybe you're right. How is she?

JASON: As beautiful as ever. She's full of energy. She's almost bursting with life. It's hard to keep up.

TOM: No signs of restlessness?

JASON: Not that I can see.

TOM: You'd see. How's Cathy?

JASON: Fine.

TOM: Stacy?

JASON: Fine.

TOM: Sara's parents?

JASON: [waits] I wouldn't know.

TOM: Ever ask her about them?

JASON: No.

TOM: Aren't you curious?

JASON: Should I be?

TOM: It's natural. You've been with her for a while now. You talk about the people in your life – friends, brothers, sisters, old lovers, whoever. Sara talks about her mother sometimes but not once did she mention her father. Doesn't that strike you as odd?

JASON: I don't talk about my parents much.

TOM: Neither do I but I don't avoid talking about them.

JASON: [waits] What's up with all the questions?

TOM: Forget it. It's nothing.

JASON: Right. So tell me then: What's the great mystery about Sara's father?

TOM: I just wanted to see how far you got. Apparently you didn't get very far. Would you like me to fill you in?

JASON: It can wait.

TOM: Now you're thinking it's something terrible and it isn't. It's as common as leaves on a tree. It's something you're bound to find out anyway so I might as well tell you: Her father left when she was three or four. She doesn't remember. The only thing she remembers is: He wasn't there. As far as she's concerned, she never had a father.

# RANDOM PLAYS

JASON: You're right. It's very common.
TOM: Very. I can't quite figure it out though.
JASON: What's that?
TOM: Whether she resents men because of her father – the kind of man he was – or she imagines the father she never had and expects us to live up to an impossible ideal. Maybe her imaginary father was always strong and understanding, patient and loving: the image of an ideal man.
JASON: You've given this a lot of thought.
TOM: I have.

[Laughter announces the entrance of CATHY and SARA in good spirits. They are not surprised by Tom's presence.]

CATHY: [hugging him] Tom!
SARA: [sitting by Jason] How have you been?
TOM: Good. Great.
SARA: [to Jason, kisses him] Good morning.
JASON: Morning.
SARA: Did you have a nice talk?
JASON: We talked.
TOM: I just stopped by to apologize.
SARA: Forget it.
CATHY: Don't worry about it, Tom. We understand.
SARA: Jason, could you go down to the store to pick some things up for the barbecue?
JASON: [stands] Sure. Give me a few minutes to clean up and get dressed.

[Exit JASON stage left. A moment passes.]

SARA: So what did you talk about?
TOM: Nothing!
SARA: Come on, Tom.
CATHY: [crossing in from the kitchen] Look! Someone's been in the cookie jar.

SARA: Not me.
CATHY: Want one, Tom?
TOM: Sure.
CATHY: It'll cost you.
TOM: Okay, I confess. We talked about Sara.
SARA: What did you tell him?
TOM: Nothing he didn't know. The affect you have on men, how you become an obsession, whatever. I managed to catch a glimpse of his journal.

[CATHY hands him a cookie.]

CATHY: Sweet, isn't it?
TOM: He's completely obsessed. Infatuation squared.
SARA: [momentarily] Have you two gotten together?
CATHY: We didn't have to. It's obvious to everyone but you and Jason. No one is that much in love.

[Enter JASON. He acknowledges the silence.]

JASON: Well... I'm on my way. See you in a bit.

[Exit JASON stage right. A moment passes in silence.]

SARA: What else did you say?
TOM: I asked if he met your parents.
SARA: My parents?
TOM: Yeah, you know: your mother and father.
CATHY: My, my.
SARA: Why would you do that?
TOM: Curiosity.
CATHY: Bullshit, Tom. You're stirring up trouble.
TOM: [rising] As I said, I just dropped by to apologize. I've got to go. I'm meeting someone.
CATHY: Mary?
TOM: How did you know?

SARA: Small world.
CATHY: Isn't it?
TOM: In this valley anyway. [exiting] Well, so long, ladies.
SARA: I still think about you.
TOM: I think about you.
SARA: You got over it soon enough.
TOM: It only seems that way.
CATHY: Don't be a stranger.
TOM: I won't.

[Exit TOM. Silence.]

CATHY: That was interesting.
SARA: Yes, it was.
CATHY: Care to join me in a swim?
SARA: Maybe later.

[Exit CATHY. SARA crosses to Jason's journal and sits reading. Lights fade to black.]

End Act Two, Scene One.

## ACT TWO

## SCENE TWO

(Months have passed. Spot up on JASON writing in his journal.)

JASON'S VOICE: Looking forward, time moves like an old man in the dead of summer. Looking back, it rushes with the force of four strong winds. Nothing remains pure forever. As time relentlessly moves on, nothing but the purest beauty remains unscarred. None but the purest heart beats true. Nothing but the purest love gathers strength and nothing but the purest dream lives on.

[Spot fades as general lighting comes up. Enter SARA.]

JASON: [closing his journal] Hi.
SARA: Hey. What are you writing?
JASON: Nothing. Notes.
SARA: How much of nothing is about me?
JASON: [smiles] All of it.
SARA: Anything I should know about?
JASON: You know how I feel about you.
SARA: [crosses, picks up journal] May I?
JASON: Sure.
SARA: [sits, reads aloud] "Sweet, gentle Sara... I give you this eternal promise: that you will never have need or reason to doubt my love... as pure as beauty, as deep as hope, as true as any man may know." [smiles] You really are infatuated.
JASON: Is that what you believe?
SARA: Jason, please, don't be hurt. I love your writing.

# RANDOM PLAYS

I do think you're a little unrealistic about me. I'm not perfect and I'm not as innocent as you imagine. I want you to love me for who I am, not for who you imagine me to be.

JASON: I don't know if you can understand this but I don't want to be realistic about you. I want to feel what Tristan felt. I love you for who you are and if that love is infatuation so be it. Maybe that's what love really is.

SARA: It's not what love is. It's not real. You've created this vision, this fantasy, and you've made me a part of it. What do you see when you look at me?

JASON: I see such beauty I never knew existed.

SARA: I'm a woman, Jason. Just a woman. Love me for who I am.

JASON: I do. I'm not blind. I know who you are. I know you've been with other men. I know you don't like to be tied down. I know you've broken hearts. Tom is a friend of mine. He told me more than I wanted to hear about your darker side.

SARA: Did you listen?

JASON: He was bitter. He still is.

SARA: Maybe he told you the truth.

JASON: He told me what he thought was true but it isn't the truth. It's only a small part of it. He can't see it the way I do. He's cynical. Everything he sees is clouded.

SARA: You're a dreamer and everything you see is like a dream.

JASON: There's nothing wrong with that.

SARA: It's only part of the truth.

JASON: Why look at a rose and see only the thorns?

SARA: You should know they're there.

JASON: I'll risk it. Just believe I love you.

SARA: Oh, Jason.

JASON: I wouldn't say it if it wasn't true.

SARA: "As true as any man may know."

JASON: As true as the moon and the stars, as true as the beat of my heart: I love you.

SARA: I know you believe it.
JASON: Still you doubt.
SARA: I'm not a fool.
JASON: And I am?
SARA: You believe in a lot of things. Some of them are real and some of them aren't. I want to believe in you but you haven't proven your love.
JASON: Love doesn't have to be proven.
SARA: Doesn't it?
JASON: [waits] I'd die for you.
SARA: [waits] I almost believe you.

[They embrace.]

JASON: It would be too easy.
SARA: How would you feel if…I saw another man?
JASON: Is that the test? Could I survive jealousy? Could I accept seeing you in the arms of another man?
SARA: I would never do that.
JASON: Meaning?
SARA: I'd be discrete. I wouldn't bring another man to this house – not while you were here. You'd never see him.
JASON: This is what Tom meant.
SARA: Yes. Only then you were the other man.
JASON: I'd rather die.
SARA: Don't say that.
JASON: I'll do what I have to, Sara. I'll understand and accept whatever it is you need, if that's what it takes to stay with you.
SARA: You'll understand?
JASON: Yes.
SARA: You promise?
JASON: Yes.
SARA: [takes his hand] Come on.
JASON: Where are we going?
SARA: Upstairs. Maybe this time we'll make it to the

bedroom.

[Exit SARA and JASON stage left. Lights fade. We hear soft piano under. Spot up on JASON.]

JASON: If a man loves too much, he's not to be believed. If his love is too pure, too deep, too devoted, the world must deny it, mock and belittle it. If a man is young they will call it infatuation. To call it love would be to admit that what they call love is a lesser emotion – a sense of need, loneliness or desire. It is not love. It is less than love. They've become jaded because they have lost the ability to love. Never having known what it means they have forgotten how to feel in full. They blind themselves to protect themselves and deny the truth: They are afraid. The price of true love is too great. So when they see it in someone else, some star-crossed lovers on a movie screen, they scoff and say it isn't real. Somehow it makes them feel better.

Do not believe them, dear lady. Do not. Believe nothing but the rhythm of your own heart as I believe mine. I love you. I have always loved you. And I will always love you. This or life itself, I swear.

[Spot out.]

End Act Two, Scene Two.

## ACT TWO

## SCENE THREE

(Weeks later. A piano plays off stage left. Lights up to reveal JASON reading and CATHY speaking on the phone.)

CATHY: Okay. I look forward to seeing you. [listens] I will. [listens] No, it's not a problem. [listens, quietly] Did she tell you about Jason? [listens] Good. It's all set. See you soon.

[CATHY hangs up and crosses downstage to the living room. The piano is silent. SARA appears at the doorway.]

JASON: Who was that?
CATHY: An old friend. He's on his way over.
SARA: Richard?
CATHY: Yeah, he was making sure it was okay.
JASON: Why wouldn't it be?
CATHY: That's what I said.
SARA: I think it's nice of him.
JASON: Who's Richard?
CATHY: An old friend. Didn't I say?
SARA: An old boyfriend. There's nothing between us now.
CATHY: I'm looking forward to seeing him. How long has it been?
SARA: A long time. Two years?
CATHY: That is a long time. I wonder what he's up to these days.
SARA: He's been in LA doing studio work.
CATHY: Have you been keeping secrets?

# RANDOM PLAYS

SARA: I don't think so.
CATHY: Is he still playing country?
SARA: I'm not sure.
CATHY: Sure you are.

[SARA looks to JASON as if to inquire how he feels about this.]

JASON: It's fine, Sara. I understand old friends – even old boyfriends. It's fine.
SARA: Really?
JASON: Really.
CATHY: Well, what's the latest?
SARA: He's moving to Mendocino to put a new band together.
CATHY: Country? Folk?
SARA: More like top forty and rock. He wants to make some money.
CATHY: Don't we all. I guess people do change.
SARA: He has a new song he wants me to hear. He wrote it for me. He wants me to sing it.
CATHY: The plot thickens. How flattering.
SARA: It is. He says it's perfect for me.
CATHY: Jason, could you run to the store for some wine?
JASON: No problem.

[JASON exits stage right. SARA exits left to resume playing piano and CATHY crosses to the kitchen as a car approaches. Enter RICHARD.]

CATHY: Richard! I don't believe it. [they embrace; he walks in and looks around] Make yourself at home.
RICHARD: Some places never change.

[SARA appears at the doorway.]

RICHARD: Hello, Sara.
SARA: Hello, Richard.
RICHARD: You still play as beautiful as ever.
SARA: Thank you.
RICHARD: I met Jason outside. Seems like a nice guy.
CATHY: He is. As nice as they come. So how the hell are you?
RICHARD: Great! Working, playing, nothing could be finer!
CATHY: Still with Julie?
RICHARD: 'Fraid not. Ended a while back. She just got tired of looking at me I guess.
CATHY: Anyone new?
RICHARD: Two or three depending on which way the wind blows. You know me. I like to keep my options open.
CATHY: Some things never change.
RICHARD: That's sure. Damned good thing too. Look at Sara here. I don't think you've aged a day.
SARA: I wish that were true.
RICHARD: It is true. God put pretty things on this earth to be appreciated.
CATHY: What did he put the rest of us here for?
RICHARD: To do the appreciatin'.
CATHY: How fulfilling.
RICHARD: I don't mean to give the wrong impression. I appreciate the both of you. You know that.
CATHY: Don't worry about it. I have thick skin – like a rhinoceros. But I do like to be acknowledged. Sara's not the only lady in this house.
RICHARD: I'll do my best but you all know I've always had a weak spot for the little lady.
CATHY: [smiles] Shore do. I'm just giving you a hard time. Don't pay it any mind.
SARA: Would you like something to drink?
RICHARD: Sure would. It gets mighty dry out there on the open highway. I ain't as young as I used to be.

# RANDOM PLAYS

CATHY: Who is? Got any more words of wisdom to share with us?
RICHARD: I got a whole basket of 'em but I'd rather hear the lady sing.
SARA: Do you have the lyrics?
RICHARD: [pulls out a folded piece of paper and hands it to her] Of course. That's why I'm here. Well, that's one reason anyway. Give it a look while I get my axe.

[RICHARD exits SR to get his guitar.]

CATHY: How do you think Jason will take all this?
SARA: [reading] What do you mean?
CATHY: You want to play dumb? Fine. Don't say I didn't warn you.

[SARA crosses to SL to the music room, turns back at the doorway.]

SARA: Would you mind opening a bottle of wine?
CATHY: I asked Jason to get some.

[Enter RICHARD with guitar case.]

RICHARD: Where is she?
CATHY: Who's that?
RICHARD: The little princess, darling.

[SARA begins playing piano off left. RICHARD starts toward her.]

CATHY: Any sign of Jason out there?
RICHARD: [stops, turns back] No, m'am. Didn't see him. You expecting trouble?
CATHY: What do you think?
RICHARD: Depends. She love him?

CATHY: I think so.
RICHARD: Then there ain't nothing to worry about.
CATHY: I don't know. She's in one of her moods.
RICHARD: Is that what it is?
CATHY: How do you mean?
RICHARD: I sense something in the air. I felt it when I first drove up. I thought it was the house but...
CATHY: Maybe it was.
RICHARD: There's always been something about this house. Can't put my finger on it.
CATHY: Jason says it's magical.
RICHARD: He might be right. Well, I don't want to keep the lady waiting.

[Exit RICHARD stage left. JASON enters stage right. During the following exchange, music, laughter and indecipherable conversation is heard.]

CATHY: Finally! It took you a while.
JASON: I went for a little drive.
CATHY: They're in the den. [she opens the wine, gathers glasses] Would you like to take them some?
JASON: Sure.
CATHY: [pours and hands him two glasses] Are you all right?
JASON: I'm not sure.
CATHY: He's just an old friend.
JASON: He seems like a nice guy. It's not him.
CATHY: [sits at the dining room table] Would you like to talk about it?
JASON: [sitting] I don't know if I can. [beat] There's something I can't get out of my mind. [beat] It's a conversation I had with Sara some time back.
CATHY: Believe me, I know.
JASON: I made her a promise.
CATHY: Now you don't know if you can keep it.

# RANDOM PLAYS

JASON: I promised I wouldn't mind if she decided to see someone else. I'd understand and accept it.

CATHY: Do you think that's what's going on here?

JASON: I'm not sure but I see her looking in my eyes, trying to gauge my reaction. [beat] I can't hide what I feel.

CATHY: What do you feel?

JASON: Anger, jealousy…my heart aching. [breaking down] Lord God, I've never known such pain.

CATHY: [places her hand on his shoulder] I'm so sorry, Jason.

[CATHY comforts him, repeating "It's alright" as a mother would her child. Lights fade, music fades.]

End Act Two, Scene Three.

# ACT TWO

## SCENE FOUR

(Late morning. Weeks later. Spot up on JASON stage right. Solemn music under.)

JASON: The four walls of my life, my love, my world and my universe come crashing down on all sides. The warmth of summer past retreats as the chill of autumn invades my soul. The once enchanting fog now holds too long, clouding my vision, dulling every sense, filling me with doubt and fear. I cannot sleep and without sleep I cannot dream. My eyes are drawn to shadows as if to discover some dark spirit that haunts me without mercy, the ghost of my unsettled mind, the curse of love betrayed.
  Who am I when I dread to hear the beating of my own heart? Where is the light? Where is the wonder, where is the charm and where is the comfort I once knew? Where is the magic of the majestic oak? Only her beauty remains and that is what I most fear.
  Tired. So tired. The air that once fed my dreams, injecting me with hope and joy, now poisons me, draining me of life with every breath. I'm dying but I do not fear death. It calls to me with a promise of solace: peace of mind, body and soul.

[Spot fades. Music fades. Lights up to reveal SARA up left on the phone as JASON enters from stage left. She acknowledges his presence with a wave of her hand as he grabs a cup of coffee from the kitchen and sits at the table.]

SARA: [on phone] It's a beautiful song. [listens] Really.

# RANDOM PLAYS

[listens] That would be nice. [listens] Please, don't flatter me. [listens] Thank you. [listens] No, I don't mind. [listens] Really. [listens] I'll think about it. [listens] I'd like to but… [listens] Right. [listens] Okay. [listens] I will. [listens] Bye.

[SARA hangs up and waits. JASON remains silent.]

SARA: Good morning.
JASON: Good morning.

[SARA starts to exit left.]

JASON: I think we need to talk.
SARA: [turns back] About what?
JASON: Who was that?
SARA: It's not polite to answer a question with a question.
JASON: Who was it?
SARA: As if you don't know? It was Richard.
JASON: What did he want?
SARA: You're jealous.
JASON: What did he want?
SARA: You're going to push this, aren't you? He wants me to play a concert in Santa Clara.
JASON: Nice. Is that all?
SARA: He'd like me to record his song.
JASON: A couple of weeks on the beach?
SARA: Don't do this.
JASON: You'd like that, wouldn't you?
SARA: Why not? What's wrong with that?
JASON: It's very romantic.
SARA: He's a friend.
JASON: I see how he looks at you and you didn't exactly discourage him.
SARA: Are you sure you want to do this?
JASON: Don't turn it around. It's not me. It's you.

SARA: You don't know what you're talking about.

JASON: I'm talking about you and Richard.

SARA: He's a musician. He likes my music and I like his. There's nothing wrong with that.

JASON: Don't expect me to play the fool. He's interested in a lot more than your music.

SARA: [turning to go] Stop it, Jason. Just stop it.

JASON: Are you planning to sleep with him?

SARA: Damn you!

JASON: Or have you already?

[SARA picks up a vase and hurls it at him.]

SARA: [in tears] Get out!

JASON: You knew this was coming!

SARA: I didn't! I thought you were different. I thought you were better. I thought you'd understand.

JASON: Understand what?

SARA: That no one can possess me! I'm free! I'll always be free! But I was wrong. You're worse than other men because you made me think you were different. Get out of this house!

JASON: Do you mean it?

SARA: Get out!

[SARA moves to grab a lamp. JASON moves swiftly to hold her arm as she lifts it to hurl it at him.]

JASON: I'm sorry. Please! I'm sorry.

SARA: [enraged] Don't ... touch me!

[JASON's complexion is changed from anger to sorrow. He slowly releases her arm. He moves his hand delicately toward her face and SARA instinctively slaps him. He stands motionless.]

# RANDOM PLAYS

JASON: [finally] Please. I'm sorry.
SARA: I don't want you here!
JASON: I can't leave you like this.
SARA: You promised! You promised!
JASON: [devastated] I know. I know.
SARA: You shouldn't have.
JASON: I meant it.
SARA: You shouldn't have promised.
JASON: Sara, please listen. All my life I've never wanted anything but to love and be loved by someone like you. You're the only woman I've ever known whose beauty spoke to my soul.
SARA: Why did you promise?
JASON: I thought I could keep it. I thought my love would give me the strength. I thought I could endure it but I couldn't. No one could.
SARA: I thought you were different. I thought you loved me that much.
JASON: I did and do. But my love was eating me alive. It didn't make me stronger. It fed my jealousy. It poisoned my soul. It made me want to die.
SARA: [waits, calmly] I want you to leave now.
JASON: [waits] You don't believe me. [he slowly approaches and wipes away her tears] Tears? For me? I have a thousand for every one of these. All this time, I've never seen you cry. I almost didn't think you could. Forgive me.
SARA: Why? How could you?
JASON: I'm dying, Sara. It's killing me.
SARA: [turning away] I don't know what to think.
JASON: I can't help how I feel. Look at me. [she does not] I don't blame you. I can't look at myself. Remember the first time I saw you? Remember the first time you smiled at me? I was so full of life. I couldn't wait to get up every morning. I couldn't wait to see this house, this magical house, and the most beautiful lady I've ever seen.

Everything here gave me hope and joy. God, I loved you, Sara. I must have loved you before I ever saw you. I was born to love you.

SARA: [moving to him, embracing] Oh, Jason, did I do this to you?

JASON: No, it's not your fault. Don't ever believe that.

SARA: [still holding him] Is it over?

JASON: [holding back the tears] I guess it is.

SARA: [waits] I'm sorry.

JASON: [waits] So am I. [waits] In all the world there will live no joy this night. Aphrodite weeps. The gods and goddesses, the muses and the graces, all mourn and lovers everywhere will wonder why.

[They remain in embrace as the lights fade. A piano plays the blues. Spot up on JASON stage right.]

JASON: A wise man once said: Our beginnings never know our ends. Thank God. We would miss so much of life trying to escape them. It is one of life's great ironies that the same things that give us boundless joy also move us to profound sorrow. Only those who touch our hearts can break them. Just as love, once given, can never die, so the pain of love remains forever in the soul. Or so it feels…tonight.

[Lights and music fade to black.]

End Act Two, Scene Four.

## ACT TWO

## SCENE FIVE

(Months later. Midday. Lights up as CATHY sits reading. Enter SARA from stage left.)

CATHY: All set?
SARA: I think so. Just taking a last look.
CATHY: You're going to miss it. This house.
SARA: I don't know. I've been thinking about it. There's something here. The house has its own spirit.
CATHY: Maybe it's not the house. It's the people who live here. Maybe it was you.
SARA: And you.
CATHY: I never thought you'd leave before me.
SARA: I never thought I'd leave at all.
CATHY: It's not too late.
SARA: Yes, it is.
CATHY: Well… I'm sure it's for the best.
SARA: I hope so.
CATHY: It seems like you're having second thoughts.
SARA: It's my curse. I'll always have doubts.
CATHY: Think of it as a long vacation. You can always come back.
SARA: What about you?
CATHY: I'm not planning to go anywhere.

[A car approaches. CATHY crosses to the window.]

SARA: Is it Jason?
CATHY: It sure is. What's he doing here?

SARA: I asked him to come.
CATHY: You could have seen him on your way out of town.
SARA: I wanted to see him here.

[A knock at the door.]

SARA: Would you mind?
CATHY: Of course not. I guess this is goodbye then.
SARA: Not really. No matter how things work out, I'll be back to visit.
CATHY: Promise?
SARA: Promise.
CATHY: It won't be the same without you.
SARA: [smiles] Let's hope not.
CATHY: Take care of yourself.
SARA: I'll do my best.
CATHY: [crossing SR] Call me!
SARA: I will.

[Exit CATHY. SARA answers the door. Enter JASON.]

SARA: Come on in.
JASON: Thanks. [looking around] So you're actually leaving this house.
SARA: I am. [silence] I wanted to tell you goodbye.
JASON: I'm glad. I've been thinking about you. I can't stop thinking about you. It's been…pretty hard.
SARA: I know. I've talked to Tom.
JASON: Have you forgiven me?
SARA: I have. And I want you to know: You were right.
JASON: I don't think so. It's going to take a while. I haven't forgiven myself.
SARA: You had good reason to be upset. I expected too much. I'd forgotten you're just a man.

# RANDOM PLAYS

JASON: There's no excuse for what I said to you. You didn't make me promise. You didn't expect anything that I didn't expect of myself.
SARA: I understand.
JASON: [approaches, kisses her cheek] Thank you.
SARA: I'll think of you.
JASON: I'll never stop thinking of you.
SARA: No regrets?
JASON: None.
SARA: Still love me?
JASON: I'll always love you.
SARA: Don't say another word. This is how I want to remember us.

[They look into each other's eyes a few moments. SARA kisses him gently and exits. JASON remains motionless a few moments, then takes a last long look around. Lights fade to black. Music plays. A spot comes up on JASON. Music continues under.]

JASON: New day at Hughson House. The sun still shines, the dew still glistens like heaven's tears and the valley moon still lingers in the morning light.

It seems so strange and foreign to me now. Like a fish out of water or a poet in a leisure suit... Like the dreams of youth that must inevitably yield to the forces of time. So it is with Hughson House. Nothing in nature, however precious and dear, can be possessed. We can only behold its beauty, grasp it if we can, if only for a fleeting moment, and let it go.

Yet for those who have never dared to touch the magic, to dream too vividly, to love too deeply, to care too much, I can only have pity. For though they may never know the sorrow that settles in the soul, neither will they know life itself.

As for me, the time will come when I look back in envy at a place in time called Hughson House: A vision of perfect beauty, a time of magic and a love so pure that all the world

## JACK RANDOM

for a brief moment stood still to behold its wonder. At Hughson House. Just a house yet such a house and such a lady that like the brilliant red moon, I have seen but once… and never will I be the same.

[Spot fades to black. Music fades to silence.]

End Act Two.

# SCENARIOS

*(A Play in Eight Scenes)*

## SETTING

The basement of a nondescript building on the poor side of a major city. The walls are of concrete and brick. There is a small barred window. There are exposed pipes and a single overhead, bare bulb light. There is a sofa, chairs and coffee table in one section of the room and a desk and chair in the other.

## CHARACTERS

JACKSON: A reporter in his mid forties.
SINCLAIR: An aging rogue agent.

## SCENE ONE: BEIRUT

(Lights up to reveal SINCLAIR behind his desk, leaning back in his chair. JACKSON checks his tape recorder and sits before him.)

JACKSON: So...who are you?
SINCLAIR: I suppose you could say I'm a political operator. A scientist is still a scientist when he or she retires. Is an operator still an operator when he's out of the game?
JACKSON: I suppose he is.
SINCLAIR: I worked for the party. There is only one. I sometimes worked for the Democrats and other times for the Republicans. Same paycheck, same employer. Sometimes I worked for Intelligence – there's an oxymoron if ever there was one. CIA, NSA, FBI: they're all the same. Same paycheck, same employer.
JACKSON: What exactly did you do?
SINCLAIR: I ran scenarios. Fascinating work. We had a bank of computers no one could rival. We plugged in data, events, public statements, propaganda and news accounts. We took situations, events, real and hypothetical, and we created scenarios. We ran them to their logical conclusions.
JACKSON: You contacted me – an unknown reporter for a little known paper. Why me and not the New York Times? Why not 60 Minutes or Christianne Amanpour?
SINCLAIR: Why doesn't the whistleblower report to his employer?
JACKSON: Are you implying that the mainstream media and the government are working in tandem?
SINCLAIR: I'm not implying anything. I'm telling a story. I'm providing information. Whether you believe me or not and what you choose to do with that information is up

to you. You are not the first reporter I've had down here. In fact, you are the seventh in the last three weeks. Four of them did not make it past the initial interview. The others did not get much further. I warn you: What you are about to hear may be detrimental to your career.

JACKSON: Go on.

SINCLAIR: You're sure?

JACKSON: I didn't become a reporter to run away from a story before I've heard it.

SINCLAIR: Why did you become a reporter?

JACKSON: I believe in the fourth estate. I believe that a free press is all that stands between democracy and fascism.

SINCLAIR: You believe we have a free press?

JACKSON: I do.

SINCLAIR: Go away. I have no need of you. Your naiveté is debilitating and beyond absurd. Go now. I don't have time to waste.

JACKSON: I see. This is one of your scenarios.

SINCLAIR: Exactly. You figured it out! Now go away and find another story.

JACKSON: I'd like to see how this one plays out. You said yourself you've gone through seven reporters. The word gets around. How many more do you think you'll get?

SINCLAIR: [thinks] Okay. Play on.

JACKSON: You didn't answer my question. Why me?

SINCLAIR: I ran a search for reporters who never put their name to government propaganda, who never ran with a story without the checking the facts, and who continued to ask questions even after 9-11. Surprisingly few made the list.

JACKSON: [laughs] I think you have the wrong reporter. I was at Metro. I've only been on the News desk a few weeks. I never had a shot at the hard story. I was covering little Johnny's bake sale for the Afghan refugees.

SINCLAIR: You didn't run that story. You didn't run the stories about children's terrorist nightmares or the fear of flying or the fear of leaving the house. Why not?

# RANDOM PLAYS

JACKSON: I didn't believe in those stories. They were meant to spread fear.

SINCLAIR: Exactly. You're wrong about Metro not covering the hard stories. They're all hard stories. You've managed to show some integrity and you've paid for it. You should have made the News desk a long time ago. Instead, you landed on my list.

JACKSON: Okay. So tell me your story.

SINCLAIR: Beirut, 1983. A handful of Shiite militia, loaded with explosives, fought their way into the American embassy and blew themselves up along with seventeen American agents, including Robert Ames, the Agency's chief Middle East analyst. No one called them cowards then. This was the ultimate sacrifice and it scared the hell out of us. How do you fight someone who is willing to blow himself up?

We ran a scenario. How should we respond? What options did we have? Carpet bomb Lebanon, Iran, Iraq? Reagan was president. That was a go. The victims were not civilians. That was a stop. They were intelligence agents. The last thing we wanted was a congressional inquiry. The things we were doing in the Middle East couldn't come to light. End of story. We could take no official action. Any response would have to be covert.

They bombed our marine compound and we took no action. They bombed our embassy in Kuwait: still no action. They hit Beirut again and kidnapped our station chief. We had no doubt Buckley would talk so we took action. We set off a car bomb outside the home of a Hezbollah leader. He wasn't there but we killed eighty bystanders and hit the congressional inquiry button. The whole operation was a total disaster and everyone involved got burned.

JACKSON: You said the CIA was doing things that couldn't come to light. What kind of things?

SINCLAIR: You remember the hostage crisis? The first demonization of the Arab world. The infamous Ayatollah.

# JACK RANDOM

You're a journalist. Did you ever wonder why the hostages were released on Inauguration Day? Did you think that was a coincidence? There are no coincidences in my world. This was politics. Truth be told, it was borderline treason. Ah, well, at least nobody died – unless you count the marines who went down in the failed rescue. Would you like to know what the odds of success were on that mission?

JACKSON: Not very good.

SINCLAIR: Zero. The agency had no intention of making Jimmy Carter a hero. It wasn't in our best interest.

JACKSON: I can't believe the agency has that kind of power. The military was involved. The generals were in charge.

SINCLAIR: When I say the agency I mean something far greater than the CIA. I'm talking about a broad coalition of forces: naval intelligence, army intelligence, the FBI and the NSA. There are private contractors and foreign agencies involved. But there is a reason it's called *Central* Intelligence. The agency is the hub. It is the ultimate authority in the hierarchy of power. When Reagan appointed his DCI, do you know who he chose?

JACKSON: William Casey.

SINCLAIR: His campaign manager. He was taking no chances.

JACKSON: Let me get this straight. The agency sabotaged Carter's rescue attempt and conspired with the Iranian government.

SINCLAIR: In 1982 we broadcasted anti-Khomeini propaganda from Egypt to Iran four hours a day. At the same time we courted the Ayatollah's favor by providing a list of his political opponents. They were supposed to be our allies inside Iran. More than a thousand people were rounded up and executed. Everything the agency did was designed to create instability and foment violence. Reagan was in bed with the Ayatollah. The Ayatollah was in bed with the Islamic fundamentalists. Everyone was playing the game

# RANDOM PLAYS

and innocent people died. This is all in the public record.

JACKSON: I don't think so.

SINCLAIR: It's all there if you make the effort.

JACKSON: I will. So what happened next?

SINCLAIR: That was the beginning of a chain of events that nearly took down President Reagan. It was known as the Iran-Contra affair.

JACKSON: Of course.

SINCLAIR: You say that as if you know something.

JACKSON: Who doesn't? It nearly destroyed the Reagan administration.

SINCLAIR: Treason! The word is treason!

JACKSON: Let's not get carried away. It was a classic case of executive abuse. No one went to jail.

SINCLAIR: Correction. One person went to jail.

JACKSON: Really?

SINCLAIR: His name was Bill Breedon. He lived in the same town as John Poindexter. When the town named a street for Poindexter, he stole the sign and held it for ransom. He served three days in the local jail, making him the only person to serve time over Iran Contra. Ollie North, the little rightwing Gestapo twerp, became a talk show host, an eternal hero to the conservative movement. Everyone else was reassigned, receiving a nice promotion and a bump in pay.

JACKSON: It was the Reagan years.

SINCLAIR: With malice aforethought they defied an act of congress. That, my friend, is an impeachable offense. The president subverted the official foreign policy of the nation and the expressed authority of the constitution.

JACKSON: The Supreme Court didn't see it that way.

SINCLAIR: They never got the chance.

JACKSON: So you believe Reagan should have been impeached.

SINCLAIR: If ever there was a case for impeachment, this was it. Reagan lied to the American people, he lied to the press and he lied to congress. He tipped the balance of power. He supported military despots all over the world and he finally became one. The party of opposition folded and the trial of the century never happened. Those who died under Reagan's reign of terror are forgotten. Instead, an airport is named in his honor. He will forever be known as the man who brought down the evil empire. He did no such thing.

JACKSON: I don't believe you.

SINCLAIR: Come again?

JACKSON: I don't believe you're a rogue agent, a truth teller, a whistle blower. I think you're just some radical dissident in a basement looking for attention.

SINCLAIR: [waits] This interview is over.

JACKSON: [nods] That's what I thought.

SINCLAIR: [smiles] I had you going though.

[JACKSON packs away his notes and recorder.]

JACKSON: You did. I'm impressed with the depth of your knowledge. You made some valid points.

SINCLAIR: [producing a card from his pocket] Here's my card, Mr. Jackson.

JACKSON: [reads] William James Sinclair, Consultant.

SINCLAIR: [smiles] Same time tomorrow?

JACKSON: [laughs] We'll see.

[Exit JACKSON. Lights fade. End Scene One.]

## SCENE TWO: TRUE HISTORY

(Lights up. As before, JACKSON sits before SINCLAIR at his desk, setting up his recorder. A pitcher and two glasses are on the desk.)

SINCLAIR: I knew you'd be back.
JACKSON: The hell you did.
SINCLAIR: I saw it in your eyes, Mr. Jackson. You want the story. You need the story. You're desperate for it. You had me checked out?
JACKSON: I did.
SINCLAIR: So you know I'm the real deal and you're intrigued.
JACKSON: I'm fascinated. But I'm here for the story. So, for the record, you *are* a rogue agent for the CIA.
SINCLAIR: I'm a *former* agent.
JACKSON: And you're offering me the story of a lifetime.
SINCLAIR: The biggest story since the fall of the Soviet Union.
JACKSON: What year was that?
SINCLAIR: It was only yesterday. That's the trouble with Americans, isn't it? Anything that happened before 1776 is ancient history. We remember the Holocaust. We remember the Nazi's. But we decidedly do not remember the genocide involving the natives of this great land. We remember apartheid in South Africa but not slavery in the American south. We remember Vietnam but we don't remember the reasons why. It's ancient history. Get on with it. Get over it. The difficulty is the rest of world remembers quite clearly. To the Kurds and Punjabi ancient history reaches back thousands of years. They remember the world

before the Buddha, before Mohammed, before Christ, before the Tao and the Great Pyramids. To the rest of the world Vietnam happened yesterday. Beirut was yesterday. The hostage crisis, the Iranian revolution, Nicaragua and El Salvador are happening now. The fall of the wall is still unfolding. The Gulf War is in progress.

JACKSON: I'm trying to piece together your intent. Are you trying to say we shouldn't be in Afghanistan and Iraq? Are you saying the War on Terror is something else?

SINCLAIR: I'm not a protester. I make no judgments. I run scenarios. I program variables and determine the most likely outcomes and consequences of a given event. I've run literally thousands of scenarios. What I am proposing is to share with you just a few of those scenarios. You can draw your own conclusions.

JACKSON: Just the facts.

SINCLAIR: That's right. Just the stone cold facts.

JACKSON: How do I know this isn't a setup?

SINCLAIR: You don't. You won't. You'd never see it coming. That's the first thing you learn in this business. Trust no one. First, you have to figure out the game. Then you make an educated guess and you run with it. There's nothing else you can do. I'm an analyst. I analyze. You're a reporter. You report.

JACKSON: You used the present tense just now. You're an analyst.

SINCLAIR: So what?

JACKSON: It clearly implies you're still with the agency. You're an active agent.

SINCLAIR: Did I actually say I was with the agency?

JACKSON: [looking through notes] I believe you did.

SINCLAIR: Then I misspoke. What difference does it make?

JACKSON: It makes a difference to me.

SINCLAIR: You're a reporter. I have a story. Do you want it or not?

# RANDOM PLAYS

JACKSON: I'm here.

[SINCLAIR stands and paces the room. JACKSON remains seated but swivels his chair to follow him.]

SINCLAIR: Okay, fine. It appears to me you're suffering from a lack of context. You can't possibly understand without an historical point of view. You're American. That's too bad. But you're well educated. You are well educated?
JACKSON: I have an advanced degree.
SINCLAIR: So you are well educated. That cuts both ways, of course. You've been trained to analyze, synthesize, dig below the surface to find the real story beneath the deluge of distractions.
JACKSON: You're an American, too. Aren't you?
SINCLAIR: Am I? Yes, I am. I'd almost forgotten. We have so little in common. Americans have no history. I have too much history. Americans think the revolution was fought over ideals: freedom, independence, democracy!
JACKSON: Why was the revolution fought?
SINCLAIR: Economics. Yes, there were individuals with the highest ideals but the root was clearly economics. But let that pass. Americans think the civil war was about slavery. Let that pass. Americans think the First World War was the war to end all wars – whatever that means – and the second was to stop genocide and fascism. We forget that our own country was born in genocide. A native population of forty to fifty million was reduced to 600,000 by the end of the $19^{th}$ century. Manifest Destiny! But let that pass. Americans think Vietnam was a tragic misunderstanding having something to do with the Red Menace. Millions of Southeast Asians lost their lives and Americans lament that we were not fully committed to the war. Can you imagine? How many more lives would have been lost had we been fully committed?

# JACK RANDOM

JACKSON: I've never heard those numbers.

SINCLAIR: You think I'm making them up?

JACKSON: It doesn't matter what I think.

SINCLAIR: It certainly does. Do you homework, man! How can you write a story if you don't know the facts? [pours a glass of water, drinks] But let that pass. To most Americans it's all an abstraction. Move on. Get over it! You can't change the past. But to the rest of the world, history is a living thing. It's alive and they're still living with the consequences.

JACKSON: Granted, Vietnam was wrong.

SINCLAIR: Bravo!

JACKSON: It was immoral.

SINCLAIR: It was amoral.

JACKSON: A failed application of a flawed theory.

SINCLAIR: Dominoes? You're invoking dominoes?

JACKSON: Of course I am. The Domino Theory. We thought we were fighting the spread of communism.

SINCLAIR: Since the end of the Second World War we were spending more on weapons than the rest of the world combined. Vietnam was nothing less than a demonstration of our massive military might.

JACKSON: It began with a lie and ended in failure. End of story.

SINCLAIR: How can you be so lame?

JACKSON: We were on the wrong side.

SINCLAIR: We were the wrong side!

JACKSON: Fine. What more can I say?

SINCLAIR: Thousands of innocent civilians – men, women and children – die every year from the unexploded munitions of our bombing in Laos and Cambodia. To them the war has never ended.

JACKSON: Compare that to the millions killed by Pol Pot and the Khmer Rouge.

SINCLAIR: We created the Khmer Rouge! We put Pol Pot in power!

# RANDOM PLAYS

JACKSON: We cut him loose when...

SINCLAIR: When he no longer served our purpose. Have you ever heard of Operation Phoenix?

JACKSON: I have a feeling I'm about to.

SINCLAIR: The agency rounded up 20,000 South Vietnamese civilians and executed them. No trial, no judicial process. We were supposed to be fighting for them.

JACKSON: My Lai, free-fire zones, Agent Orange, carpet bombing: We know all about it. War is hell.

SINCLAIR: If war is hell, who is the Great Satan?

JACKSON: You've gone too far.

SINCLAIR: I haven't even gotten to Nixon.

JACKSON: I think we can cut the history lesson short. I understand where you're coming from. I understand why you think it's necessary. Now it's time for the story.

[SINCLAIR calmly pours a glass of water steps center stage and drops it. It shatters.]

SINCLAIR: What is this?

JACKSON: The hell if I know.

SINCLAIR: It's gravity. The solemn and powerful effect of gravity. Get out of my office. Come back when you have some appreciation of it.

[JACKSON packs up his recorder and notes.]

JACKSON: What makes you think I'll come back at all?

SINCLAIR: I could hardly care less.

[Exit JACKSON. Lights fade. End Scene Two.]

## SCENE THREE: THE MANUAL

(Lights up. As before, JACKSON sits before SINCLAIR at his desk, setting up his recorder.)

SINCLAIR: I knew you'd come back.
JACKSON: The hell you did.
SINCLAIR: It's all about the story and you're willing to put up with my eccentricities to get it.
JACKSON: I suppose. To a point.
SINCLAIR: That attitude will never get Pulitzer.
JACKSON: Probably not.
SINCLAIR: Nicaragua 1983.
JACKSON: We're really going back to Nicaragua?
SINCLAIR: The less you interrupt, the less time it will take. We were fighting against the Sandinistas who were fighting for the people. They *were* the people but they were not in the best interest of our government. We chose to support a ruthless military dictatorship. The Contra's were losing so the agency sent an operative from Laos and Cambodia to take over the operation. He wrote the operational manual with the title: Psychological Tactics in Guerilla Warfare. This is important. Write it down. [JACKSON does so] Suddenly our people turn against one of their own – a man who's been involved in the goon squads and the terror units. The agency cuts him loose and he goes to the press. He releases the Operational Manual. Now that is a disaster.
JACKSON: I can see how it would be embarrassing but a disaster?
SINCLAIR: It should have been titled: How to Subvert a Popular Government using Terrorist Tactics.
JACKSON: Could you be more specific?

# RANDOM PLAYS

SINCLAIR: Create an atmosphere of fear with random looting, rape and murder. It's better if it all seems random. That way you can always deny it. Why would we do such a thing without any apparent method or strategy? The manual suggests assassination. It spells out torture and intimidation techniques. It suggests creating martyrs by having leaders on your own side killed. It was all too revealing and should have been much more than embarrassing.

JACKSON: What happened?

SINCLAIR: The press never published the good parts. They were far more cooperative than the agency ever imagined. This was the eighties, of course, before all the news organizations – the papers, the cable networks, the broadcasting networks – were bought by international corporations. If they wouldn't publish the truth then, what chance is there today?

JACKSON: It's a benevolent dictatorship. They own us but they don't control us.

SINCLAIR: Really? Maybe that's why you're in Metro.

JACKSON: Hard to tell.

SINCLAIR: Drink?

[SINCLAIR pulls glasses and a bottle of brandy out of his desk, crosses to the sofa. JACKSON follows.]

JACKSON: Why not?

SINCLAIR: The implications are staggering. A manual for overthrowing a democratic government and upholding despotism. Think about corporate interests. Think about the implications of hiring criminals and thugs. Think about Nixon and Watergate, Reagan and Iran-Contra, Kennedy and Lee Harvey Oswald.

JACKSON: It took a while but I knew you'd get around to it.

SINCLAIR: Don't tell me you're one of the three or four intelligent beings on the planet who actually believes

# JACK RANDOM

Kennedy was shot by a lone gunman?

JACKSON: Eight.

SINCLAIR: I beg your pardon.

JACKSON: There were seven members of the Warren Commission. That makes at least eight of us.

SINCLAIR: I said intelligent. That rules out Ford. The rest were merely masquerading.

JACKSON: Of course they were.

SINCLAIR: You're staking your argument on the Warren Commission?

JACKSON: I'm not making an argument. I tend to be skeptical of conspiracy theories.

SINCLAIR: You can't believe that the agency would use their own techniques on their own government. What's good enough for Guatemala is good enough for the US of A!

JACKSON: The CIA is bound by law not to interfere in domestic affairs.

SINCLAIR: Assassination, creating martyrs out of our own leaders, overthrowing governments not in the agency's interest. We lost Kennedy and got LBJ. You tell me: Who benefited? Who won and who lost? Did you know there were places in Texas that cheered the news of Kennedy's assassination?

JACKSON: Kennedy was no saint.

SINCLAIR: Neither was LBJ.

JACKSON: He made a lot of enemies.

SINCLAIR: That he did. One of them may or may not have been a little man named Oswald who did contract work for the agency. Fact.

JACKSON: Fine. Let's stipulate that the CIA killed Kennedy. What then?

SINCLAIR: Sirhan was a prototypical product of mind control. Imagine coming to the conclusion that killing Bobby would someone forward the cause of the Palestinians. Ludicrous. Then, of course, there's the strange case of James Earl Ray, a textbook patsy. Every assassination of the tumultuous sixties had the agency's signature. Fact.

JACKSON: I don't mean to patronize but you're diluting your case.

SINCLAIR: It's not easy to undo an entire lifetime of indoctrination. Americans have the best propaganda machine ever unleashed on the species. You think I like reviewing history to someone who by all rights should know better? It's necessary. I have to shake up your smug insistence that you know what you clearly do not.

JACKSON: I'm an American. I'm proud to be an American. I believe in democracy and justice and freedom of the press and I'm not about to sell my country out because someone claims I'm ignorant.

SINCLAIR: Is that what you think? You think I want you to betray this nation?

JACKSON: Tell me you don't want to overthrow the government.

SINCLAIR: If I can persuade you of anything it should be this: There is an infinite distance between the government and the nation. The nation is a construct, a body of ideals that represent the people. Despite the indoctrination and the constant propaganda the people still believe in democracy, the Bill of Rights, equal justice and opportunity, freedom of thought, speech and religion. When a government betrays those fundamental ideals, it is the duty of every American to oppose them. In this country we still have the opportunity to change governments every two to four years.

JACKSON: Or not.

SINCLAIR: We have the choice. And that choice depends largely on the information we are given.

JACKSON: The press. That's where I come in.

SINCLAIR: Or not.

JACKSON: I feel like a student in a college civics course.

SINCLAIR: It's the best education you're ever likely to get.

# JACK RANDOM

JACKSON: I'm still here.

SINCLAIR: [standing, pacing] Very well. It's the second term of the Reagan administration. By this time the old man was pretty much a shell. Everyone who paid attention to the debates with Carter knew something was missing. We only later learned it was Alzheimer's. He was not in command if he ever really was.

JACKSON: That's a little harsh.

SINCLAIR: It would be harsher if he were in command. In fact, it would be criminal. The Reagan Doctrine was carte blanche to invade any country if it advanced military or economic interests. What held him back were a congress and an electorate that had no appetite for war. They were forced to resort to covert operations, guerilla warfare, propaganda and terror. They concentrated their efforts in Latin America.

JACKSON: El Salvador.

SINCLAIR: El Salvador, Guatemala, Chile, Grenada, Panama, Columbia, Nicaragua, Argentina, Peru, Mexico.

JACKSON: Mexico?

SINCLAIR: The agency trained Mexican agents to deal with the Indian uprising in Chiapas. We also infamously used the drug trade to finance dark operations.

JACKSON: Distribution of crack cocaine in East LA.

SINCLAIR: Yes. It should tell you something about the agency's reluctance to engage on domestic soil.

JACKSON: What can you tell me about El Salvador?

SINCLAIR: How much do you know?

JACKSON: I was involved in some protests regarding the church ladies and the Archbishop.

SINCLAIR: Oscar Romero? You're Catholic?

JACKSON: I was raised Catholic.

SINCLAIR: You found the religious martyrs in El Salvador disturbing so you took to the streets in protest?

JACKSON: Back in the eighties I was more engaged than I am today.

SINCLAIR: Protests in the decade of disco? You must

be kidding.

JACKSON: Very amusing.

SINCLAIR: El Salvador. It was a typical example of our Latin American policy. Like so many others, its government was an oppressive military regime. Carter funded them and Reagan quadrupled the effort. We supplied their military, trained their goon squads and applied our special methods of persuasion. Something was in the air and it worked its way into the church. Incredible really. The church was always complicit as it is today but for a moment in time... Archbishop Camara once said: *When I fed the poor they called me a saint; when I asked why they were poor they called me a communist.* So...the church decided to ask why. They organized the poor and Archbishop Romero was at the heart of it. No one really knows how many died in El Salvador. Tens of thousands? No more than the dead in Columbia, Nicaragua, Guatemala and Chile. But in El Salvador they included six Jesuit emissaries, four American missionaries and the Archbishop Oscar Romero. [reflects] The manner of their deaths was horrifying. [silence] Go home, Mr. Jackson. I'm through for the night.

JACKSON: [packing his things] Did you know him?

SINCLAIR: I had the pleasure of meeting him. [deeply moved] We shook hands.

[Exit JACKSON. Lights fade.]

## SCENE FOUR: EAST TIMOR

(Lights up. As before, JACKSON sits before SINCLAIR at his desk, setting up his recorder.)

SINCLAIR: Indonesia.
JACKSON: Christ! Really?
SINCLAIR: Strange that you should invoke his name – you being a Catholic and all.
JACKSON: Do you intend to recite the entire history of American military interventions?
SINCLAIR: I can assure you it is only a modest sample. You would not begin to believe the number and scope of operations since the end of World War II. It assaults the mind, dulls the senses and leaves an impression that nothing can be done to satiate America's desire for domination.
JACKSON: Fine. Let's hear it.
SINCLAIR: Indonesia. This one covers half a century but I'll be succinct. It begins with Sukarno – not to be confused with Suharto the butcher. He comes later. Sukarno became leader of Indonesia when the Dutch were cast out. He wisely advocated neutrality in the Cold War and that to the agency was unforgivable. We tried political sabotage and that failed. We attempted assassination and that failed. We led an invasion that was crushed, leaving Sukarno stronger than ever. He reigned for eight more years but the agency never forgets an enemy and we didn't forget him. We waited until the eyes of the world were on Vietnam when a military coup successfully supplanted Sukarno with General Suharto who became one of the most brutal mass murderers in all of history. In the mid-seventies Suharto invaded East Timor, a small rural nation of about 700,000 peasants. Suharto massacred nearly ten percent of the population while the

world stood by and watched. In the late nineties, after three decades of genocide, we got reports that the General was losing his mind. We asked him to step down and he politely complied. As an unintended consequence, East Timor reasserted its independence.

JACKSON: This was during the Clinton administration?

SINCLAIR: Does that surprise you? Like Carter before him, he promised to reduce military spending. He in fact increased it. He promised to rein in the agency and he did not. The myth that Clinton dismantled the intelligence community is pure fantasy. He loved intelligence. He loved covert operations. The trouble is: He couldn't control it.

JACKSON: At least he ended Suharto's reign.

SINCLAIR: Yes, he did. His successor, one B.J. Habibie, fully funded and supported by the Clinton administration, with agency trained troops, immediately reinvaded East Timor. Word of the massacre that followed slipped out before the press was expelled. There was one particularly moving story about sixty people, mostly women and children, hiding in a church. They were summarily executed. We did nothing. We said nothing while a quarter of the population was erased from the world.

JACKSON: That's heartbreaking. But you can't blame America for everything that happens. We are not responsible for what the leader of Indonesia does.

SINCLAIR: You hear me but you don't listen. They were our people. They did what we wanted them to do.

JACKSON: What should we do? Go to war every time something goes wrong in the world? We'd never stop fighting! I thought you were against interventionism.

SINCLAIR: Wrong? Nothing went wrong. East Timor was a troublesome little nation. We got what we wanted and, frankly, who cares?

JACKSON: [waits] What about Kosovo? We intervened to stop Milosevic from carrying out genocide: ethnic cleansing, rape, torture and mass murder. He was a monster!

Does that count for anything? Or doesn't it fit your image of American brutality?

SINCLAIR: Kosovo is a fascinating case. The agency was against intervention. Any war in the Balkans is messy and unpredictable. But Clinton needed something to distract the people – the Monica Lewinski business – so we bombed the hell out of them. We stopped the Serb massacre of the Croats and Muslims and stood by while the Muslims and Croats returned the favor. Genocide on genocide. We turned Kosovo into a living hell. And that's your example of American humanitarian interventionism.

JACKSON: We just can't win with you, can we? We might as well throw down our arms and accept whatever happens. Who knows? Maybe peace will rise from the ashes!

SINCLAIR: [waits] I am no pacifist, Mr. Jackson. There is a time and a place for military action. Kosovo was such a time and place. Clinton got what he wanted. He finished his presidency. Unfortunately for the Serbs, it was not in our interest to prevent counter-genocide. As for East Timor, we only had to raise an objection. We did not. We ran a scenario. Do you know what it said? Nobody cares. Nobody that counts anyway. [waits, takes a deep breath] That's it for today. Go home.

[JACKSON packs up, crosses to door.]

JACKSON: These sessions are hard on you, aren't they?
SINCLAIR: More than you know.
JACKSON: It's personal with you – as if there's more at stake than the story.
SINCLAIR: [shakes his head] It's all about the story.

[Exit JACKSON. Fade lights.]

## SCENE FIVE: SECOND THOUGHTS

(Lights up. As before, JACKSON sets up his recorder.)

JACKSON: Who are you anyway?

SINCLAIR: I've already said. I was an operator. Now I'm not. I'm a man without a country.

JACKSON: That's not what I mean. Who are you when you leave this space? Who are you when you're not playing agency games? Who are your family, friends, hobbies and interests?

SINCLAIR: Is this really necessary?

JACKSON: Was East Timor really necessary?

SINCLAIR: Very well. Once upon a time I had family, friends and all the activities and interests that go with them. I joined a country club, went to church and participated in social functions. My wife was a conventional woman who ultimately did not appreciate my line of work.

JACKSON: No children?

SINCLAIR: My wife wanted children. I did not. We put it off until it went away. We parted amicably enough. She remarried, had two kids, and I renewed my vows to the agency. We're no longer in touch.

JACKSON: You severed all ties.

SINCLAIR: It's better this way.

JACKSON: Better for whom?

SINCLAIR: For everyone involved. Now that I've broken from the agency, there's no one. I'm very much alone.

JACKSON: You still have contacts.

SINCLAIR: I do. Strictly business. Need to know.

[SINCLAIR reaches out and turns the recorder off.]

JACKSON: Surely we're not finished. We still have the Gulf War and the history of the Middle East.

SINCLAIR: I'm having second thoughts.

JACKSON: About?

SINCLAIR: Everything.

JACKSON: It's a little late for that.

SINCLAIR: Decades.

JACKSON: What exactly are you saying?

SINCLAIR: I'm considering my options.

JACKSON: What options? Going back to the agency?

SINCLAIR: That bridge crumbled long ago.

JACKSON: It seems to me you have no options.

SINCLAIR: If I've learned anything it's that we always have options.

JACKSON: Spell it out for me.

SINCLAIR: I'd like to see the world one more time before it's too late.

JACKSON: Too late?

SINCLAIR: In a year or two no American will be welcomed anywhere in Asia, the Middle East or Eastern Europe. In three or four years it may be dangerous to travel anywhere outside our own borders.

JACKSON: If you really believe that you're in a unique position to do something about it.

SINCLAIR: What would you have me do? Tell the truth? Who would believe it? Who the hell cares about the truth? It's unpatriotic. We change governments but the war goes on. Republican or Democrat, the war must go on! I've come to the conclusion it does not matter which party is in power. It's all the same.

JACKSON: Go outside the traditional parties.

SINCLAIR: Oh, there's a solution! Name a successful challenge to the two-party system and win a trip to the heart of Africa!

JACKSON: Nader could have made a difference.

SINCLAIR: Where is he today? Now that we're at war

with the Arab world, does anyone even remember that an Arab American ran for president on the same ticket as a Native American woman? There was sweet poetry in that. I appreciate the effort even if it was hopelessly idealistic.

JACKSON: We made a difference in Vietnam. We helped stopped the war.

SINCLAIR: Maybe. Even though Nixon gets the credit. How's that for irony!

JACKSON: We got rid of Nixon. Change is possible. In fact, it's inevitable if you take the long view.

SINCLAIR: Speaking of irony, I have the precise opposite view. Change only happens on the short term. The long view remains the same.

JACKSON: It's incremental. You should know that. If one person fails to do his or her part it sets the whole process back. You're lucky! You know your part. Just do it!

SINCLAIR: Listen to you, the little revolutionary! You've taken your lessons to heart.

JACKSON: I've been doing my homework. I know you're right about most things.

SINCLAIR: What things?

JACKSON: True history. Imperialism 101.

SINCLAIR: Chomsky and Zinn.

JACKSON: The People's History. Propaganda and the Public Mind.

SINCLAIR: Two of the greatest minds of our time. They've pretty much been silenced since the war on Terror. Have you noticed? Has anyone? Where are the dissenting voices?

JACKSON: We're still here. If you know where to look.

SINCLAIR: Really?

JACKSON: The voices of protest. There are thousands of us. More every day. We're waiting for a chance to rise up and express our outrage.

SINCLAIR: What's holding you back?

JACKSON: We need something to fuel the fire. Like

# JACK RANDOM

Daniel Ellsberg's Pentagon Papers. Something everyone can understand. We need a glimpse of the truth.

SINCLAIR: You need the inside story.
JACKSON: Exactly.
SINCLAIR: It is all about the story.
JACKSON: It is.
SINCLAIR: I underestimated you.
JACKSON: Thank you.

[SINCLAIR turns the recorder back on.]

SINCLAIR: Let's talk about the Middle East.
JACKSON: Good.
SINCLAIR: Iraq, Iran and Afghanistan. Pop quiz: Who was the Great Evil before Osama bin Laden?
JACKSON: Saddam Hussein.
SINCLAIR: Who was the Great Evil before Saddam?
JACKSON: The Ayatollah Khomeini.
SINCLAIR: [up and pacing] Very good. Iran, Iraq, Afghanistan and back again. When Iran was the enemy we supported Iraq. We gave birth to their biological warfare unit. When Iraq was the enemy we sent arms to Iran. Long before the Soviet invasion, our policy was to promote instability – mainly by propping up third party resistance. Throughout the region that meant supporting Islamic militants. So we financed and encouraged terrorist cells. We supplied arms and built networks. We provided the best training money could buy. We created fucking Al Qaeda!

Do you remember Muammar Gaddafi? He was Reagan's fixation. He bombed Gaddafi's compound, killing his infant daughter and dozens of civilians. Talk about acts of terrorism! Do you remember when Clinton bombed Iraq over an alleged assassination attempt on the elder Bush?

JACKSON: I do.
SINCLAIR: Do you know what we called it?
JACKSON: Counter-terrorism?

# RANDOM PLAYS

SINCLAIR: Not at all. It was a joke.
JACKSON: How do you mean?
SINCLAIR: We hated Clinton. He loved us but we hated him. We told him about this secret assassination plot just to see what he'd do. I ran a scenario and won the pool. Clinton loved it. Bombing civilians to defend the honor of George fucking Bush! Precious!
JACKSON: Incredible.
SINCLAIR: The key to the Middle East, of course, is Israel and Palestine. Who do you suppose is blocking the peace process and the establishment of a Palestinian state?
JACKSON: You'll probably say Sharon. Someone else would say Arafat.
SINCLAIR: The only difference between Sharon and Arafat is that Sharon is the head of a sovereign nation.
JACKSON: A sovereign nation can't commit acts of terrorism.
SINCLAIR: Exactly. But the real reason there is no Palestinian state is that the United States does not want one. We like the way it is. Israel remains our satellite. How long would that last if Israel and Palestine were at peace?
JACKSON: You ran a scenario.
SINCLAIR: I did. The people of Israel would turn against us but first they would turn on their own government. You remember the assassination of Rabin?
JACKSON: The peace candidate.
SINCLAIR: Indeed. He might as well have signed his own death certificate.
JACKSON: An inside job?
SINCLAIR: Even you should know that much.
JACKSON: The agency?
SINCLAIR: A joint operation. Israeli intelligence is quite good.
JACKSON: Do you believe we could mandate a Palestinian state unilaterally?
SINCLAIR: It would require one sincere statement: End

the occupation and create a Palestine with real borders and sovereignty or all US aide ends today. Do you know what Israel would do?

JACKSON: Shit.

SINCLAIR: After that. Let's just say, the American president would be at grave risk.

JACKSON: And the agency?

SINCLAIR: A dilemma. Israeli intelligence is like our little brother. Would we allow them to...? We'd have to run a few scenarios.

[Lights fade. End Scene Five.]

## SCENE SIX: THE GULF WAR

(Lights up. JACKSON sits before SINCLAIR. The tape recorder is running.)

JACKSON: Can we talk about the Gulf War?
SINCLAIR: Yes. It's time. Why do you think Bush chose to fight in Iraq?
JACKSON: According to Bush, it was a response to unprovoked aggression. Saddam invaded Kuwait.
SINCLAIR: You don't believe that.
JACKSON: I don't but you tell me: Why did we fight the Gulf War?
SINCLAIR: Iran, Iraq, Afghanistan: What do they have in common?
JACKSON: Oil.
SINCLAIR: Congratulations! The Pulitzer is yours! Three reasons actually: Oil, Vietnam and politics. The American economy and the president's popularity were in steep descent. It is important to note that the Gulf War was the first since the great World War in which the media was under complete and absolute control. It would not be the last. Remember the bombing of Al Jazeera in Kabul?
JACKSON: They were allegedly harboring terrorists.
SINCLAIR: Al Jazeera is the Middle East equivalent of CNN. Think back to Shock and Awe! The first day of the war. There was a fascinating story about the plight of the Kuwaiti refugees.
JACKSON: I remember.
SINCLAIR: Absolute rubbish. Kuwait is a nation of ultra wealthy Shakes and Sheiks. It maintains no military. It relies solely on America for security. At the first sign of trouble, the Kuwaitis phoned Washington and left for Monte

Carlo. The refugee story was agency propaganda. Now I ask you: How could CNN have fallen for such an outrageous lie?

JACKSON: It couldn't.

SINCLAIR: And yet there was no retraction. There was no apology. We were treated to the grand spectacle of the smart bomb and the awesome might of the American military machine. Iraq was utterly destroyed. An estimated forty percent of our smart bombs missed their targets. The unintended casualties of war. Tens of thousands of Iraqis lost their lives against a few hundred American soldiers. But everyone knows: Arabs do not value life like Americans do.

JACKSON: Hearts and Minds.

SINCLAIR: Do you know what cross drilling is?

JACKSON: I'm afraid I don't.

SINCLAIR: It's a relatively new technique in the oil business for drilling in one place to tap oil in another. Would you like to know what Saddam's problem with Kuwait was?

JACKSON: Let me guess: Cross drilling.

SINCLAIR: Bingo! Saddam cleared the invasion with the State Department – or at least he thought he did. Bush wanted the war. He needed it. When it was over he basked in the glory and announced to the world: *The specter of Vietnam has been buried forever in the desert sands of the Arabian Peninsula.*

JACKSON: We left Saddam in power. It seems to me that was a monumental mistake.

SINCLAIR: Was it? We had crushed the Iraqi army. We had destroyed their infrastructure. The Kurds were in open rebellion and Saddam was holding on by a thread. We not only let him off the hook, we enabled him to slaughter the Kurds. Why? The worst-case scenario was not Saddam but democracy. Democracy would mean instability – very probably civil war – and that was not in our interest. Further, there was an antiwar movement building in the states. Bush did not wish to become LBJ locked away in the White

House, afraid to show his face. Beyond that the international coalition was falling apart. The last thing the Arab world wanted was an American occupation. At war's end, the world demanded that we lift sanctions against Iraq. We refused. A half a million Iraqi children died as a result.

JACKSON: What can you tell me about the Gulf War Syndrome?

SINCLAIR: Who knows? Our soldiers came home with all the signs of a neurological disorder: impaired muscular control, nausea, loss of appetite, chronic fatigue. Our government refused to acknowledge the condition. Too costly. Was it chemical or biological warfare, the effects of an experimental vaccine? It's hard to investigate a sickness that does not officially exist.

JACKSON: It hit them pretty hard.

SINCLAIR: Yes. But the Gulf War was a resounding military victory and it served notice: We are the world's sole superpower. We possess the most destructive force the planet has ever witnessed and by God we're willing to use it!

[Lights fade. End Scene Six.]

## SCENE SEVEN: AFGHANISTAN

(Lights up. As before. The tape is rolling.)

SINCLAIR: The Soviet Union invaded Afghanistan in December 1979. Over the next eight years we pumped eight billion dollars into the resistance. We supported the freedom fighters, the Mujahadeen. We recruited the holy warriors of Islam from all over the world. We set up training camps. We taught our techniques of terror. We armed them and fed their rage. It was our hope and intent that after the war they would become a force against the red army on every continent. Who knew then that the Soviet Union would fall and scatter into a thousand pieces?

JACKSON: Did the fall of the Soviet empire disappoint you?

SINCLAIR: [smiles] You'd like that, wouldn't you? How easy it would be if I turned out to be a traitor, a communist sympathizer, a Russian spy? Unfortunately for you, I am none of these things. I happen to believe in democracy, the one form of government the agency has always feared. I will say this: Had the Soviets not fallen, it is unlikely 9-11 would have occurred.

JACKSON: Please elaborate.

SINCLAIR: The butterfly effect. Change a single element and everything else changes. Without the fall the holy warriors are still fighting the Soviet beast. Bush the elder doesn't go to war in the Gulf. Osama bin Laden isn't betrayed and the attack on the towers never happens.

JACKSON: How did we betray bin Laden?

SINCLAIR: We promised to leave Saudi soil as soon as the war ended. We did not. We left our military planted on holy ground. To men like bin Laden it was an unforgivable offense. You wonder why they hate us?

JACKSON: Not any more. You've taught me that much. There are many reasons why and it's measured in human lives.

SINCLAIR: Yes, the numbers game. Do you recall the death count after 9-11? The toll kept rising. Four thousand, five, six and counting. Then the Times questioned the numbers. The towers were in their city and they couldn't locate that many victims. They were right of course. They stopped the government from selling a false number.

JACKSON: What difference would it make? Whether it's three or five thousand, what does it matter?

SINCLAIR: It matters because at some point very soon we will pass that number in retribution. We probably already have. It matters because at some point the people will ask: How many is enough? Ten thousand, a hundred thousand, a million lives? Sooner or later we have to say: This is enough. We have our revenge.

JACKSON: [reflective] Numbers matter.

[SINCLAIR begins pacing. He is distracted.]

SINCLAIR: I've been trying to run the numbers. It's hard because we don't count the enemy dead. We used to but not any more. It's not in our interest. But sooner or later some organization arrives at a number. Best guess. Two hundred thousand in East Timor. One hundred fifty thousand in Guatemala. Fifty thousand in Columbia, Nicaragua and El Salvador. One hundred thousand in Iraq. Do we count death by sanction? Another five hundred thousand. Do we count Vietnam? Yes? No? Best guess: We are responsible for two million deaths since Vietnam. In the same span of time we have sacrificed approximately five thousand soldiers. Two million against five thousand. [stops pacing] I am not a sensitive man. I don't cry at movies. But the numbers, the sheer numbers, make me feel…shame.

# JACK RANDOM

JACKSON: We've already had our revenge.

SINCLAIR: Should we decide which victims were innocent and which were not? Should we estimate the relative worth of human life? Should we count the tears?

JACKSON: We've already taken more than our share.

SINCLAIR: We sponsored the Mujahadeen! We created Al Qaeda! We chose the Taliban to rule Afghanistan! They were our best bet for an oil pipeline.

JACKSON: Look, don't go too far. Listen to me: This is good advice. Don't make it sound like you're defending Osama bin Laden.

SINCLAIR: Bin Laden? Damn him! Damn the Taliban! I do not condone terror! I do not believe in subjugating women or suppressing religion! I believe in democracy, a free press and freedom of speech!

JACKSON: Good. Good. Settle down.

SINCLAIR: But damn us, too. We are not innocent of crimes against humanity. Our hands are not cleansed of innocent blood. After we created this evil we cannot turn around and claim the moral high ground. It has nothing to do with justice or democracy. It has everything to do with power.

JACKSON: Okay. Relax. I understand.

SINCLAIR: We didn't lay it out. Maybe we didn't intend so many to die. But we put the wheels in motion.

JACKSON: Then we sat back and watched it happen.

SINCLAIR: [sighs] Yes.

[Lights fade. End Scene Seven.]

## SCENE EIGHT: UNSPEAKABLE

(Lights up. As before. Tape rolling.)

SINCLAIR: There's a question you should have asked by now.
JACKSON: What's that?
SINCLAIR: What is terrorism? What is an act of terrorism?
JACKSON: An act of unprovoked violence designed to create widespread panic?
SINCLAIR: Too broad. Too inclusive. It would include far too many of our own military interventions.
JACKSON: An act of unprovoked...
SINCLAIR: The question of provocation is interesting. It's entirely subjective. Ask bin Laden if he believes the 9-11 attack was unprovoked. Ask Reagan if his bombing Libya was unprovoked. Ask Clinton about Kosovo.
JACKSON: Let's try again. An act of violence against a civilian population designed to create widespread...
SINCLAIR: [shaking his head] Infinitely too inclusive. It would certainly include Indonesia's invasion of East Timor, our invasion of tiny Grenada, the bombing of Laos, on and on. Much too broad.
JACKSON: One more time. An act of violence against a civilian population, designed to create fear, and not related to war between nations.
SINCLAIR: Closer but not quite. The question of war is troublesome. The constitution gives the power of war to congress. Does it matter that congress has delegated that power to the commander? Does it matter that the Vietnam War was never declared? Does it matter that the so-called war on terror has not been declared? No. An act of terrorism

is a violent attack on civilians, designed to create fear, by an individual or collective not affiliated with a sovereign nation.

JACKSON: Of course.

SINCLAIR: So when Israel uses an American missile to assassinate a Palestinian leader, it is self-defense. When the Palestinians answer in kind it is an act of terrorism.

JACKSON: So what you're saying is that the war on terror will target only individuals and groups not affiliated with a sovereign nation.

SINCLAIR: It depends on the nation. If the agency determines that your nation is a sponsor of terror then you're a target. Of course, that standard will not be applied to allies like Saudi Arabia. It may be applied to American citizens. What it really means is: America and her allies, in general, and intelligence agencies, in particular, are exempt.

JACKSON: So that's the beauty of it. It's a moving definition. If Al Qaeda does it, it's terrorism. If we do it, it's not.

SINCLAIR: Correct. [reflects] As you know, I started running terrorist scenarios way back in Beirut. As the years went by we added more and more variables. What if? What if they attacked in London or Paris? What if they bombed our embassy? What if they killed a senator or president? What if? Well, in January 1996 I completed an analysis on a very interesting scenario. It was the usual attack with a twist. A simultaneous attack on multiple sites within the United States. This attack would target civilians: the Washington Monument, Disney World and the World Trade Center. I didn't dream these things up. I took them from the public record. Trial transcripts from the embassy bombing and the first attack on the Towers. I gathered them from interviews of terrorists by prominent journalists. It wasn't my job to dream things up. It was my job to gather information and run realistic scenarios through our probability quotients.

JACKSON: You ran this scenario and submitted it to your superiors in the agency?

SINCLAIR: Of course. That was my job.

JACKSON: How did they react?

SINCLAIR: They liked it. I could tell they liked it. It appealed to their sensibilities.

JACKSON: Can you be more specific?

SINCLAIR: My supervisor was a stoic man, very conservative and controlled. He came to me very excited. He was suddenly interested in my work. He talked about a pay raise and promotion. He said my work was getting notice up above. Then he asked me to add one element to my latest scenario. They wanted a face to symbolize the enemy. I did as I was told. I came up with an obvious face, an Arab face. He had been in Afghanistan, he had worked with the agency and his name kept coming up in connection with various attacks.

JACKSON: Let me guess: Osama bin Laden.

SINCLAIR: Yes. The feeling in the agency was that he was more a figurehead than an operator, more propagandist than fighter. We knew him. After the war in Afghanistan we forgot all about bin Laden and his freedom fighters but they never forgot about us.

JACKSON: I assume your superiors liked it.

SINCLAIR: Liked what?

JACKSON: The Osama element.

SINCLAIR: They loved it. Americans demand a face for the enemy. Bin Laden was perfect. It had a significant positive effect on the numbers.

JACKSON: Support for the coming war on terror?

SINCLAIR: It was all in the analysis. Cost versus benefit. The costs were in lives lost and dollars spent. Damage to the economy, the insurance industry, the tourist industry and the airlines. All significant costs. The benefits were in the outcomes.

JACKSON: Expand.

SINCLAIR: Increased military spending, expansion of the intelligence apparatus, increased powers of surveillance, virtual control of the internet, access to financial records, political domination, on and on. We projected at least seven more years of a Republican White House, control of congress, on and on. By far the most important outcome, however, was a replacement for the Cold War. It would go on for decades.

JACKSON: You gave this to them?

SINCLAIR: Yes.

JACKSON: You can document it?

SINCLAIR: Yes.

JACKSON: Astonishing. [reflects] But it still falls short.

SINCLAIR: I broke with the agency in 1996. Imagine my surprise when I awakened early on the morning of September 11, 2001. There it was: my scenario. It was being played out before my eyes. So I started backtracking, putting the pieces together. I recalled a security briefing with the brass after the embassy bombings. There was this general running on and on about these goddamned Arabs. These animals. These terrorists. The scourge of civilization! The Great Evil of the $21^{st}$ century! Finally, we'd had enough. One of my colleagues confronted him and what he said silenced him point blank. Do you know what he said?

JACKSON: I can't imagine.

SINCLAIR: He said: "They're your best friends, General. We created them, financed them and kept them going. The day will come when you thank God for them. They're your ticket for forty years of war: bloated military budgets, unlimited covert operations and public adulation. They're your best friends and, deep down, you know it. So save your preaching for the congregation."

JACKSON: I don't suppose you have a recording?

SINCLAIR: I do not.

JACKSON: Too bad.

SINCLAIR: On December $13^{th}$, three months after the fact, we produced the tape that proved we were right all along: Osama bin Laden did it. But they announced it on

# RANDOM PLAYS

September 11th. The question is: How did they know? What did they know? If they had proof all along why did they hide it? To protect our sources? The agency has a thousand ways to protect sources. The real reason is that they had to shield the fact that the evidence pre-dated the attack and if it pre-dated the attack why didn't we stop it?

JACKSON: Are you saying we knew?

SINCLAIR: We knew what they were planning years in advance. It's in the trial transcripts. It's in the interviews. It's a matter of public record.

JACKSON: The information was there. That doesn't mean they knew.

SINCLAIR: Incompetence? Don't be absurd. I worked with the agency for three decades. I have a lot of choice words to describe them but incompetence is not one. They recruit the best of the best, the brightest of the bright, and they provide the best technology money can buy. Incompetence? No, that won't do. Look at the facts.

JACKSON: What facts?

SINCLAIR: We knew who the suicide bombers were. Their pictures were on CNN before the dust settled. They were known terrorists. They were on the watch list. They were being monitored. We knew who they were and what they intended but we let them go to flight school. We failed to alert the Border Patrol. We failed to inform the airlines. Christ, the least the might have done was to secure the cockpits! How hard could it have been?

JACKSON: All this is after the fact.

SINCLAIR: On December 13th House Democrats dropped a proposal for an external review of intelligence failures. The first rule of accountability is to assess past measures but for the most spectacular failure in American history there was no review. Why?

[SINCLAIR pulls a large, bulging envelope from his desk and lays it down.]

# JACK RANDOM

JACKSON: What is this?

SINCLAIR: Transcripts, taped conversations, memos, emails, written communications: names, places, dates and times. It's all there.

JACKSON: My God.

SINCLAIR: I cashed in all my chips on this one. It's unconscionable, unthinkable, unspeakable but here it is. Take it if you've got the guts.

JACKSON: [freezes] If I take that package, what can assure me there won't be two agents waiting for me outside the door?

SINCLAIR: You still doubt my integrity. Very well.

[SINCLAIR pulls a stack of news stories from his desk and lays them out. Certain passages are highlighted.]

SINCLAIR: Take a look. [points to a passage] There.

JACKSON: [reads] "A former agent who prefers to remain anonymous..."

SINCLAIR: [pointing] And there.

JACKSON: "Analyst William Sinclair points to the oil reserves..."

SINCLAIR: And there.

JACKSON: "An inside source stated that the American government is well aware of the Gulf War Syndrome and its devastating effects..."

SINCLAIR: And here.

JACKSON: [looks up] What is this?

SINCLAIR: An obituary. [reads] "William Sinclair, Jr., age 27, of Arlington, Virginia, died at St. Jude's Medical Center. He was a veteran of Desert Storm. He is survived by his mother, Ruth Sinclair Walton, of St. Augustine, Florida, and his father, William Sinclair, Sr., of Delaware." [waits, sets the article down] He shot himself after he passed the sickness to his fiancé. He was just a dumb kid.

JACKSON: I thought you didn't have children.

SINCLAIR: I lied.
JACKSON: That's why you left the agency.
SINCLAIR: Yes.

[JACKSON picks up the envelope and crosses to the door.]

JACKSON: I have a confession.
SINCLAIR: You never read Zinn.
JACKSON: No.
SINCLAIR: You contacted the authorities.
JACKSON: Yes. A friend of a friend knows someone in the FBI.
SINCLAIR: [waits, smiles] Congratulations! You passed the test. [presses a button on the underside of his desk] We're off the record.
JACKSON: I knew it. You're still with the agency.
SINCLAIR: You know what they say. Once you're in you can never get out.
JACKSON: You had me going. You were so sincere.
SINCLAIR: That's what made me the man for the job.
JACKSON: Everything you said was true.
SINCLAIR: [nods] I'm afraid so.
JACKSON: Your son?
SINCLAIR: Tragically.
JACKSON: [the envelope] Is this real?
SINCLAIR: No.
JACKSON: Is there anything we can do?
SINCLAIR: We've crossed that bridge, I'm afraid. From this point forward, we do what the agency wants us to do.
JACKSON: What could we do anyway?
SINCLAIR: No one would believe it.
JACKSON: No? I did.
SINCLAIR: Dust in the wind.

# JACK RANDOM

[JACKSON turns to the door.]

SINCLAIR: There's one thing you should know: Your employer is complicit.
JACKSON: I'm not surprised.

[JACKSON exits. SINCLAIR makes a note. Lights fade to black. End Scene Eight.]

# REASON'S RECKONING

*(The Age of Tom Paine)*

## SETTING

A sparse stage with several projection screens left, center and right. Slide presentations and voiceovers supplant the words of the characters on stage. Props and set pieces include a writing desk, a wooden chest, a small table and chairs, and two podiums. The first act calls for a tavern, Paine's study and a campfire. The second act summons a study in London, quarters in Paris, the Luxembourg Prison and the guillotine.

## CHARACTERS

THOMAS PAINE:  Revolutionary author of Common Sense, The American Crisis, The Rights of Man and The Age of Reason.

EDMUND BURKE:  Traditionalist author of Reflections on The French Revolution.

## ACT ONE

(A slide presentation begins with Romney's portrait of Thomas Paine. The following quotations are displayed with voiceovers accompanied by portraits and depictions of historical events.)

"His name is Paine, a gentleman about two years from England – a man whom General Lee says has genius in his eyes." – John Adams, Second President of the United States.

"His writings certainly have had a powerful effect upon the public mind." – George Washington.

"I have always regarded Paine as one of the greatest of all Americans. Never have we had a sounder intelligence in this republic. He was the equal of Washington in making American liberty possible. I consider Paine our greatest political thinker." – Thomas Edison.

"Without the pen of Paine, the sword of Washington had been wielded in vain." – John Adams.

"Others can rule, many can fight, but only Paine can write for us the English tongue." -- Benjamin Franklin.

"No writer has exceeded Paine in ease and familiarity of style, in perspicuity of expression, happiness of elucidation, and in simple and unassuming language." – Thomas Jefferson.

"I never tire of reading Paine." – Abraham Lincoln.

# JACK RANDOM

"The services he rendered to his country in its struggle for freedom have implanted in the heats of his countrymen a sense of gratitude never to be effaced as long as they shall deserve the title of a just and generous people." – James Monroe.

"Filthy little atheist." – Theodore Roosevelt.

"I believe in one God and no more and I hope for happiness beyond this life." – Thomas Paine.

[Lights up. PAINE is seated at a table in a pub with a bottle and glass of brandy.]

PAINE: My adult life began and ended in the company of my fellow beings in a setting not unlike this modest pub. Some – we shall not invoke names, the likes of John Adams and Alexander Hamilton getting enough attention without my assistance – would have me discredited for carousing in such houses. My answer to this charge is simple as the truth should be: A man of common sense and common decency should seek the company of common folk. [rises, glass of brandy in hand] Here, here! Good people of Sussex – London, Philadelphia, Paris and New York – good common people of all nations and all persuasions, of every natural distinction known to humankind, fellow citizens of the world and fellow inhabitants of the known universe, a toast!

Here's to a man frequently remembered, more frequently forgotten!
Here's to his story that's often told, most often mistold!
Here's to a man of many faiths, of many battles lost and won, of many lands and many dubious loyalties, but only one cause: humanity itself!
Here's to a man of infinite wisdom and curious

# RANDOM PLAYS

superstition!
>Here's to a man of wondrous glory and shameful infamy!
>Here's to his rotting remains in an unknown grave!
>Good friends: A toast to the common man!
>God rest his weary soul!

[He drinks, crosses to a large wooden chest, opens and rummages through it.]

In the fall of the year 1774 I booked passage on the London Packet to New York. It was not my first time at sea. In my youth I found myself discontent with my father's trade of corset making. I ran off to sea, serving on the King of Prussia during the Seven Years War. From that time to the present, I have been a man of many trades: Educator, preacher, tobacconist and tax collector. None of these vocations suited my character or sensibilities. [locates a ribbon with a lock of hair] On 27 September in the year 1759 I married out of love a woman of purest innocence. Her name was Mary Lambert. She was timid and frail but to these eyes she was more beautiful than all the glories of nature. Our years of happiness counted one. It was my fate that I should never love again.

When I set sail for New York I traveled light with the exception of a large wooden chest that contained the treasures of my life – most of them on parchment. Manuscripts, poems, personal correspondence, scattered memories, amusements, thoughts and ideas. Somehow I always believed that my writings would be worthy of preservation. Vanity? Perhaps. But not entirely unfounded. The world was teeming with revolutionary ideas: Newtonian science and republican politics. Voltaire's ideas were springing to life. I sensed great change in the universe and I longed with all my heart to play a part in christening the new age, an age of reason, and an age of the common man.

# JACK RANDOM

[Having gathered a number of items, he crosses to his desk and begins organizing them.]

I therefore account it my good fortune that by the year 1774 I found myself in a state of spiritual and financial collapse. My second marriage, a marriage of convenience, having failed, my belongings sold at auction to escape debtor's prison, and recently discharged from government service for political pamphleting, I had severed every possibility of success in my native land. In the process I had managed to establish a reputation as a man of letters. It gained me an introduction to the renowned American diplomat, whose views were in harmony with my own. It was Benjamin Franklin who authored my recommendation to the new land.

[A portrait of Franklin appears overhead.]

VOICEOVER (Franklin): "The bearer, Mr. Thomas Paine, is very well recommended to me as an ingenious and worthy young man."
PAINE: I know not whether he intended sarcasm or perhaps self-flattery for in the latter part of the $18^{th}$ century a man of twenty-seven was hardly young.
VOICEOVER: "He goes to Pennsylvania with a view of settling there."
PAINE: Indeed, once there I could scarcely afford to go elsewhere.
VOICEOVER: "I request you to give him your best advice and countenance as he is quite a stranger there. If you can put him in a way of obtaining employment you will do well and much oblige your affectionate father. B. Franklin."
PAINE: [rises, crosses to bookshelf] From this humble beginning I embarked on my life's journey: A dream of three revolutions, a hand in each, a pen to stir the heart and mind; to set down on parchment for all to see the principles

## RANDOM PLAYS

of republican government; to elucidate the natural rights of man and to speak without fear of reprisal or want of compromise, the voice of reason and the tenor of common sense. [selects a bound bundle of parchments, returns to desk] The events of 1774 propelled the passage of time. By years end I established myself as a literary figure. I had published a strong condemnation to the importation of slaves, a denunciation of the general debasement of women both in England and the colonies, and an attack on the British brand of despotism.

[He sits and prepares to write, pouring a glass of brandy.]

I had made the acquaintance of a circle of free thinkers involved in Philadelphia and Continental politics, including David Rittenhouse and Timothy Matlack, Dr. Benjamin Rush and Christopher Marshall, Richard Henry Lee of Virginia and Sam Adams of Massachusetts – not to be confused with the lager or his well-read and highly powdered cousin. As you might imagine, I made my share of adversaries as well.

By March of 1775 the first reports from Lexington and Concord arrived in Philadelphia. With that singular act of barbarity all plans and proposals to settle the question by compromise were "like the almanacs of last year which though proper then are superceded and useless now."

[With quill and inkwell, he begins to write.]

Americans were in need of a call to arms. For though the enemy had reared its ugly head in a brutal show of force, the common citizen still lacked a cause that would move him to battle. They believed it was a business concern: A matter of who levies the taxes, not how much, a matter of which aristocrats rule, not if. It was a time of great danger to America. If her future depended on any one political circumstance it was in changing the sentiment of the people from dependence to independence and from the monarchy to the republican form of government. Had she unhappily split on the question she most probably had been ruined and as for me, had we failed, I know not where any home in the world would have been.

By the end of the year 1775 I completed the final draft of a modest pamphlet. It was to accomplish much toward changing the course of history and, I believe, raising the general estate of humankind. At Dr. Rush's suggestion I entitled it Common Sense. It would become my signature.

Though it would become the most widely read publication in the history of the continent, I resolved not to profit from my service. It was a decision I would not regret though it would cause me considerable hardship.

[He pens the last line, affixes his signature and rises gathering his papers and crossing to a podium, where he addresses the audience.]

Gentlemen of Philadelphia, patrons of the Indian Queen, I have been asked to address you on behalf of the cause of independence. It is a subject on which I find myself at no loss of words and yet my words can tell you no more and no less than what you know, than what you have always known in your hearts, to be true.

*I speak of the cause of freedom, which in part is the cause of America, which in great measure is the cause of all mankind. Many circumstances have and will arise which are not local but universal in nature and through which all lovers of mankind are affected. The laying a country desolate with fire and sword, declaring war against the natural rights of all mankind and extirpating the defenders thereof from the face of the earth is the concern of every man to whom nature hath given the power of feeling.*

*I shall but briefly address the nature and origin of government before pointing a few concise remarks at the*

# RANDOM PLAYS

*much-boasted constitution of England. I shall first draw an important distinction between society, which is produced by our wants, and government, which is produced by our wickedness.*

*Society in every state is a blessing but government, even in its best state is but a necessary evil, in its worst state an intolerable one. For when we suffer the same miseries by a government, which we might expect in a country without government, our calamity is heightened by reflecting that we furnish the means by which we suffer.*

*Let us suppose a small number of persons settled in some sequestered part of the earth unconnected with the rest. In this state of natural liberty necessity like a gravitating power would soon form our newly arrived emigrants into society. The reciprocal blessings of this social bond would supercede and render the obligations of law and government unnecessary while they remained perfectly just to one another. But as nothing but Heaven is impregnable to vice, it will unavoidably happen that they will begin to relax in their duty and attachment to each other, and this remissness will point out the necessity of establishing some form of government to supply the defect of moral virtue.*

*In the first parliament every man and woman by natural right will have a seat. But as society expands public concerns will likewise increase and the distance at which the members may be separated will render it impossible to meet on every occasion. This will point out the wisdom of their consenting to leave the legislative part to be managed by a select number chosen from the whole.*

*Here then is the origin and rise of government: namely, a mode rendered necessary by the inability of moral virtue to govern the world. Here too is the design and end of government: the protection of freedom and security. And however our eyes may be dazzled with show, our ears deceived by sound, however prejudice may warp our wills or interest darken our understanding, the simple voice of nature and reason will say: 'tis right!*

I draw my ideas of the form of government from a principle in nature that no art can overturn: that the simpler a thing is, the less liable it is to be disordered and the more easily repaired. With this maxim in view, I offer a few remarks on the British Constitution. That it was noble for the dark and slavish times in which it was erected is granted. When the world was overrun with tyranny, the least remove therefrom was a glorious rescue. But that it is imperfect, subject to convulsions and incapable of producing what it promises is easily demonstrated.

I realize it is difficult to overcome longstanding prejudice but if we examine the components of the English Constitution, we will find them to be the base remains of two ancient tyrannies compounded with some new republican materials.

First: The remains of monarchical tyranny in the person of the king.

Second: The remains of aristocratic tyranny in the persons of the peers.

Third: The new republican materials in the persons of the commons on whose virtue depends the freedom of England.

The first two, being hereditary, are independent of the people and therefore contribute nothing towards the freedom of the state.

To say, however, that the English constitution is a union of three balanced powers is farcical. For as the greater weight will always carry up the lesser, it only remains to know which power has the most weight for that will govern. That the crown is the overbearing part in the English constitution is obvious. That it derives its whole consequence merely from being the giver of places and pensions is self-evident. Wherefore, though we have been wise enough to shut and lock the door against absolute tyranny, we have been foolish enough to put the crown in possession of the key.

# RANDOM PLAYS

*With your leave, I shall now address the critical questions of monarch and hereditary succession.*

*Mankind being equal in the original order of creation, the equality could only be destroyed by some subsequent circumstance. The distinctions of rich and poor may in great measure be accounted for without recourse to such harsh sounding names as oppression and avarice. But there is another distinction for which no natural or religious reason can be assigned and that is the division of men into Kings and Subjects. Good and bad are the distinctions of heaven but how a race of men came into the world so exalted above the rest is worth inquiry and whether they are the means of happiness or misery to mankind.*

*Government by kings was first introduced by heathens. It was the most prosperous invention the devil ever set on foot for the promotion of idolatry. The heathens paid divine honors to their deceased kings and the Christian world has improved on the plan by doing the same for living ones. How impious is the title of sacred majesty applied to a worm that in the midst of his splendor is crumbling into dust!*

*Near three thousand years passed away till the Jews requested a king and, when reason could not dissuade them, the prophet Samuel cried out: I will call unto the Lord and he shall send thunder and rain that ye may see your wickedness in asking you a king! So Samuel called unto the Lord and the Lord sent thunder and rain and all the people greatly feared Samuel and the Lord. And the people said unto Samuel: Pray for thy servants unto the Lord that we die not for we have added to our sins in asking for a king.*

*That the Almighty hath here entered his protest against monarchical government is true or the scripture is false. And when a man seriously reflects on the idolatrous homage that is paid to kings, he need not wonder that the Almighty disapproves a form of government that so impiously invades the prerogative of heaven. And yet, as if the original sin was insufficient, to the evil of monarchy we have added hereditary succession. As the first is a degradation of ourselves, the second is an insult to posterity.*

*One of the strongest proofs of the folly of hereditary succession is that nature, herself, disapproves it. Otherwise she would not so frequently turn it to ridicule by giving us an ass for a lion! But it is not so much the absurdity as the evil of hereditary succession that concerns me. If it insured a race of good and wise men it would have the seal of divine authority. But as it opens the door to the foolish, the wicked and the improper, it has all the markings of oppression.*

*In short, good friends, monarchy and succession have laid the world in blood and ashes. It is a form of government that the word of God bears testimony against and blood will attend it. Moreover, if we inquire into the business of a king, we find that he has little more to do than to make war and give away places, which is to impoverish the nation and set it together by the ears. In plain terms: Of more worth to society is one honest man than all the crowned ruffians that ever lived.*

*I conclude my address with a few thoughts on the state of American affairs: I offer nothing more than facts, plain arguments and common sense. I have no other preliminaries to settle but that you divest yourself of prejudice and suffer your reason and feelings to determine for themselves. I hope that you will put on – or rather, not put off – the true character of a man and generously enlarge your view beyond the present day.*

*Volumes have been written on the struggle between England and America. Men of all ranks have embarked in the controversy but all have been ineffectual. Alas, the period of debate is closed. Arms as the last resort will decide the contest. The appeal was the choice of the king and the continent shall accept the challenge. For the sun never shone on a cause of greater worth. It is not the affair of a city, a county, a province or a kingdom but of a continent. It is not the concern of a day, a year or an age; posterity are virtually involved and will be more or less affected to the end of time.*

*Now is the seedtime of continental union, faith and honor. The least fracture now will be like a name engraved on the tender rind of an oak; the wound will enlarge with the tree and posterity will read it in full-grown characters.*

*Everything that is right and reasonable pleads for separation. The blood of the slain, the weeping voice of nature cries: 'Tis time to part! For though it is the good fortune of many to live distant from the scene of present sorrow, we need only let our imaginations transport us a few moments to Boston. That seat of wretchedness will teach us wisdom and instruct us forever to renounce a power in whom we can have no trust. If you say you can pass the violations over, I ask: Hath your house been burnt? Hath your property been destroyed before your eyes? Are your wife and children destitute of a bed to lie on or bread to live on? Have you lost a parent or child by their hands and yourself the wretched survivor? If you have not, then are you not a judge of those who have. But if you have and can still shake hands with the murderers, then are you unworthy the name of husband, father, friend or lover – and whatever may be your rank in life, you have the heart of a coward and the spirit of a sycophant.*

*O you that speak of reconciliation, can you restore to us the time that is past? Can you give to prostitution its former innocence? Neither can your reconcile Britain and America. The last cord now is broken. There are injuries that nature cannot forgive. She would cease to be nature if she did. As well can the lover forgive the ravisher of his mistress as the continent forgive the murders of Britain. The Almighty hath implanted in us these inextinguishable feelings for good and wise purpose. They are the guardians of his image in our hearts. They distinguish us from the herd of common animals. The social compact would dissolve and justice be extirpated from the earth were we callous to the touches of affection.*

O ye that love mankind! Ye that dare oppose not only the tyranny but the tyrant, stand forth! Every spot of the old world is overrun with oppression! Freedom has been hunted round the globe! Asia and Africa have long expelled her! Europe regards her as a stranger and England has given her warning! O receive the fugitive and prepare in time an asylum for all mankind! A situation similar to the present has not happened since the days of Noah. For we have it in our power to begin the world over again.

[PAINE bows, gathers his papers and returns to his desk. Lights shift.]

My audience then as now was restrained in response. I could not judge the effect of my words for fear shrouded sentiments of the heart and blocked any outward show of approval. My friends applauded my courage for I had most assuredly identified myself as an enemy to the king. The loyalists scoffed at my folly and vowed that the heavy hand of revenge would crush my insolence like an unsuspecting insect. Thereafter, I attempted to practice brevity in public discourse, as I did not wish to be martyred so early in the undertaking.

To the present audience I ask forbearance as I cannot with any certainty know what interest my thoughts may have. It may be that freedom is now so rooted in the world that these events have but passing interest. But if despotism continues to impose itself, like a foul weed that chokes off the life of fairer species and strips the fruit from the tree of liberty, then you would do well to acquaint yourself with the struggles of the past. That is my whole purpose and design – simple, forthright and unfettered. For you, like an unmoving, eternal ghost of unending history, are the posterity for whom I dedicate my existence. And if my destiny should decree, for thee, happily, will I lay down my life.

# RANDOM PLAYS

[He pauses to reflect, then moves to the pub setting where he pours and drinks brandy.]

It is now early in the year 1776. My plain argument begins to work a powerful change on the collective mind of our citizens. By year's end over a hundred thousand pamphlets have been distributed throughout the colonies. Many deprived of literacy gather in pubs and coffee houses to hear public readings. I am told even George Washington, commander of the Continental Army, felt the pull to the cause of liberty and democracy elicited by my modest contribution.

By the second of July the Continental Congress could no longer hold back public sentiment. Jefferson's Declaration of Independence is adopted. King George had proclaimed the rebellion fully half a year prior.

As for me, I grow impatient with Philadelphia politics. I resign my position with the Pennsylvania Magazine and enlist in the militia. On the fifth of July we march for Amboy, New Jersey. The regiment is a pitiful sight. Inadequately trained and supplied, desertions are a daily occurrence. In September, when the command expires, our soldiers hurry to their scattered homes and families without having struck a single blow to the enemy. I continue to Fort Lee where I enlist as volunteer Aide-de-Camp to General Nathaniel Greene, a man of uncompromised honor and loyalty. There I experienced my first taste of battle.

General Greene was charged with holding Forts Washington and Lee on opposing sides of the Hudson River. It was a command he upheld until the sixteenth of November when the whole of the British Army laid siege.

[He crosses to a campfire setting. Lights shift.]

The Continental Army is in disarray. Divided and defeated from Long Island to White Plains, the dark days of the New Jersey retreat are upon us. Those who do not desert merely await the expiration of their short terms of enlistment. The British are convinced, with ample reason, that one final blow will put an end to this pitiful uprising.

From Fort Lee we march for Hackensack Bridge, continuing that day and half the next when the inclemency of the weather, want of quarters and the approach of the enemy, obliges us to proceed to Aquaconack and from thence to Newark.

[He sits on a log and prepares to write.]

Though it may appear a creation of fiction, history faithfully records that the first number of American Crisis papers was written by campfire on the head of a drum. Paper and every other necessity is in short supply. So cold that I can hardly command my fingers to write, my heart is yet filled with such a powerful mixture of emotion and thought that my words cannot be contained. Having formulated the first sentence, the words flow as if my hand is guided by some divine presence without hesitation or need of revision.

The appeal cries out for an immediate hearing and on Christmas Eve, scarcely a week after publication, it is received by those most desperately in need. General Washington orders a reading before a tired gathering of soldiers on the eastern bank of the Delaware River.

[PAINE stands and reads.]

*These are the times that try men's souls. The summer soldier and the sunshine patriot will, in this crisis, shrink from the service of his country. But he that stands it now deserves the love and thanks of man and woman. Tyranny, like hell, is not easily conquered. Yet we have this consolation, that the harder the conflict, the more glorious the triumph. What we obtain too cheaply, we esteem too*

# RANDOM PLAYS

*lightly. It is dearness only that gives everything its value. Heaven knows how to put a proper price upon its goods and it would be strange indeed if so celestial an article as freedom should not be highly rated.*

[He stops reading and returns to his desk.]

The event that followed is known to all who have but casually examined the chronicles of history. An encampment of Hessian mercenaries was taken by surprise and soundly defeated. The cause of American independence at last had its first victory.

The battle closed the campaign. General Howe retreated to New York for the winter, Washington sought refuge at Valley Forge and I returned to Philadelphia. Dr. Franklin and I drafted and pushed for the adoption of a new state constitution. It provided for universal suffrage, democratic representation, religious freedom and annual elections. It was adopted in time to christen the New Year.

I was offered and gratefully accepted the position of Secretary to the Committee for Foreign Affairs of the Continental Congress. Had I known the dirty business that would follow I would surely have declined.

[He pours a brandy and begins drinking.]

The unlikely affair involved a Mr. Silas Deane, Esquire, appointed Commissioner to France. At the onset the contest involved two commissioners: Mr. Arthur Lee accused Mr. Deane of mishandling business transactions in order to make an illicit profit. I should have left them alone to settle their own dispute. It so happened, however, that I was in possession of a secret regarding supplies from abroad and the money demands of Mr. Deane. The dispatches that should have contained the information never reached Congress, blank paper arriving in their stead. The documents came into my possession with a warning that they should be kept secret even from Congress "where it is supposed England has some intelligence." That Mr. Dean was attempting a fraud was exceedingly visible to me.

Profiteering had become all too commonplace. I could not in good conscience hold the information back. On the fourteenth of December I published a letter in the Pennsylvania Packet. A firestorm of controversy followed. When the French Minister to America, a Monsieur Conrad Alexander Gerard, intervened on Mr. Deane's behalf, my position and reputation were seriously questioned. Rather than allowing the affair to do any further damage to the cause, I submitted my resignation.

[He reads.]

*To the Congress of the United States – Honorable Sirs:*
*Finding by the Journals of this House that I am not to be heard and having declared that I could not, in duty to my character as a free man, submit to being censored unheard; therefore, consistent with that declaration and to maintain that right, I think it my duty to resign the office of Secretary to the Committee for Foreign Affairs.*
*I have the pleasure of reflecting that as I came into office an honest man, I go out of it with the same character.*
*I am, Honorable Sirs, you honor's most obedient and humble servant,*
*Thomas Paine.*

[He pours and drinks. Selects a document from his desk.]

I later wrote to Dr. Franklin in Paris: [reading] *I met with a turn that, sooner or later, happens to all men in popular life. That is, I fell, all at once, from high credit to disgrace and the worst word was thought too good for me. I have had a most exceedingly rough time of it.*

# RANDOM PLAYS

It would be two long years before the truth vindicated me and restored my character. As it turned out, Mr. Deane's treachery ran deeper than anyone suspected. He had been commissioned by the British crown to disrupt the French Alliance and promote disharmony within America.

I was in Paris, attempting to secure a critical loan for the cause, when a series of letters by a Mr. Silas Deane, urging a reunion with England, were published in New York. I returned to America in time to celebrate the victory at Yorktown. The war would drag on for two more years but on the nineteenth of April 1783, the eighth anniversary of Lexington and Concord, I published the final American Crisis.

[He gathers papers and crosses to the podium.]

*The times that try men's souls are over and the greatest revolution the world ever knew gloriously and happily accomplished. But to pass from the extremes of danger to safety, from the tumult of war to the tranquility of peace, though sweet in contemplation, requires a gradual composure of the senses to receive it.*

*In the present case, the mighty magnitude of the object, the uncertainties of fate it has undergone, the numerous dangers we have suffered, the eminence we now stand on and the vast prospect before us, must all conspire to impress us with contemplation.*

*In this pause of recollection, let us look back on the scenes we have passed and learn from experience what is yet to be done.*

*Never had a country so many openings to happiness as this. Her setting out in life, like the rising of a fair morning, was unclouded and promising. Her cause was good, her principles just and her temper serene. Everything about her wore the mark of honor. It is not every country that can boast so fair an origin.*

# JACK RANDOM

*It would be a circumstance ever to be lamented were a single blot suffered to fall on this revolution, which to the end of time must be an honor to the age that accomplished it. It has contributed more to enlighten the world and diffuse a spirit of freedom and liberality than any human event that ever preceded it. But as none ever began with a fairer origin than America, so none can be under a greater obligation to preserve it. The struggle is over. She has it in her choice to do and to live as happily as she pleases. The world is in her hands.*

*It was the cause of America that made me an author. The force by which it struck my mind and the dangerous condition the country was then in, made it impossible for me to be silent. And if, in the course of more than seven years, I have rendered any service, I have likewise added something to the reputation of literature, by freely employing it in the great cause of mankind.*

*Independence always appeared to me practical and probable provided the sentiment of the country could be formed and held to its object. There is no instance in the world where a people so extended and wedded to former habits were so effectually persuaded by a turn of politics as in the case of independence. They supported their opinion through a succession of good and ill fortune until they crowned it with success.*

*But as the scenes of war are now closed and every man is preparing for home and happier times, I take my leave of the subject. I have followed it from beginning to end, through all its turns and windings, and whatever country I may hereafter be in, I shall always feel an honest pride at the part I have taken and acted. I shall always feel gratitude to nature and providence for putting it in my power to be of some use to mankind.*

*Common Sense.*

[He discards his manuscript and wanders about the stage,

as if gathering remembrances.]

The greatest event in all of history had ended. What should have followed was a life of relative ease – a pleasant yet useful passage of time in pursuit of creative and intellectual interests. What actually followed was six years of hardship and discontent.

I became engaged in scientific matters. It was the age of reason, the age of revolution and the age of invention. I designed the first single arch bridge with the intention of erecting it across the Schuylkill River. At the suggestion of my old friend, Dr. Franklin, I went to Europe to seek the approval of the Royal Society in London and the Academy of Sciences in Paris.

On the twenty-sixth of April 1787, I set sail for France. My intention was to return before the first frost of winter. I could not have known then but it would be fifteen years and several lifetimes before I would place my foot on American soil again.

[Lights fade to black. End Act One.]

## ACT TWO

(The stage is altered with the addition of a stage left representation of the French National Assembly. In place of the wilderness there is a depiction of the Bastille prison with a depiction of the guillotine upstage. PAINE sits at his desk.)

PAINE: My departure from America was accompanied by mixed emotions. I felt intense pride at my part in giving birth to the republican form of government. It is my conviction that the rights of man, once admitted to the sovereignty of mankind, could not be turned back until every corner of the earth is swept of its cobwebs, poison and dust, and made fit for the reception of generous happiness. For this honor, I would always be grateful to my adopted country.

And yet, as is frequently observed in nature, the extremes of pride and gratitude are often accompanied by extremes of the opposing sentiments. As I had dedicated my life to her cause from beginning to end, I could not have foreseen that my services would so soon be forgotten and my welfare neglected.

Late in the year 1783 I wrote a Memorial to Congress in hope that I could awaken that body from this unworthy slumber of neglect and ingratitude.

[reading] *I cannot help viewing my situation as singularly inconvenient. Trade I do not understand. Land I have none or what is equal to none. I have exiled myself from one country without making a home of another and I cannot help asking myself: What am I better off than a refugee and that of the most extraordinary kind – a refugee from the country I have obliged and served to that which can owe me no good will?* [discards document]

It came to pass that my hopes for an awakening were not

well founded. Years later, when I took my leave, my ambitions had changed considerably. More a man of science than a man of letters, it was my fondest dream to return to America and live out my days in happier and more peaceful times. Alas, it was not to be.

[He rises and crosses stage left, sitting on steps before the audience.]

It was spring when I arrived in France. On the road to Paris the country was teeming with abundant life – as glorious and beautiful as any display in nature's bountiful kingdom. The year was 1787. In Britain the cunning young William Pitt succeeded Lord North as Minister of King George's court. In France Louis the Sixteenth still reigned. You may recall that Louie aided the American cause and applauded our victory without pausing to consider its broader meaning and implications. For the seed that was planted in America would soon take root in the fertile soil of France.

[He rises and crosses to the pub setting, which now serves tea, wine and cheese.]

I was an international celebrity. I savored it as a gentleman savors his first taste of romance or a fine French wine. For the first time in my life, I was admitted to the privileged chambers of private discussion and public discourse. I was welcomed to my old hometown where I met with leading members of parliament: Lords Lansdowne and Shelburne, Charles James Fox and London's greatest defender of liberty, Edmund Burke. In Paris, I consulted with free thinkers and advocates of the principles of democracy: Monsieur's Condorcet, Brissot and, of course, the Marquis de Lafayette – a great hero to the American nation.

## JACK RANDOM

[He returns to his study.]

In Paris, I began the second great friendship of my life. The first, of course, was Dr. Franklin. The second was his successor as Minister to France. If Dr. Franklin was my political father, then Thomas Jefferson was my political brother. His pen gave official and powerful recognition to the unalienable rights of man. Jefferson insisted that I serve as America's unofficial representative in England – a position I upheld until my equally unofficial replacement arrived in April 1789. An embarrassing aristocrat by the name of Gouverneur Morris, he would become my most devious and dangerous enemy.

[He holds up a model of his bridge.]

My single-arched bridge was a remarkable success. Erected over the River Wear in the year 1793, it was praised for its beauty and utility. As befits my various misfortunes on this earth, I received neither profit nor credit for the venture.

By the summer of 1789, however, the rapid turn of affairs in France [discards bridge] commanded the attention of all and all the monarchs of Europe trembled in trepidation. On the seventeenth of June, a National Assembly was formed to draft a new French Constitution. On the twelfth of July the king raised an army of 30,000, composed largely of mercenary soldiers, to march on Paris and destroy the assembly. Within a moment's time a cry of "To arms!" went up across the whole of Paris.

[Rallying cries are heard in the background, torches marching through crowded streets...]

Arms had they none, nor scarcely any who knew how to use them. But desperate resolution, when every hope is at stake, supplies for a while the want of arms. Piles of stone were drawn up to attack the cavalry. A party of the king's guard rushed from their quarters to join the people. With night coming on, the king's army retreated.

The night was spent in providing themselves with every sort of weapon they could make or procure: swords, blacksmith hammers, carpenter's axes, pikes, pitchforks and clubs. The numbers with which they gathered the next morning and the still more incredible resolution they exhibited astonished their enemy. Accustomed to slavery themselves, they had no idea that liberty was capable of such inspiration.

In this state of suspense the Parisians remained through the next night. The king's army made no further advances and every moment was employed in collecting arms and concerting plans. But defense was not the only object of the citizens. They had a cause on which depended their freedom or their slavery. The object that now presented itself was that bastion of royal despotism, which would be prize or prison to its assailants: The Bastille.

They marched to the Hospital of the Invalids, adjoining the city, and seized a large magazine of arms. Thus supplied, they marched on to the Bastille.

That the Bastille was attacked with an enthusiasm of heroism, such as only the highest animation of liberty could inspire, and carried in the space of a few hours, is an event that the world is fully possessed of. Thus did the Bastille fall on the fourteenth day of July in the year 1789, a day that will be remembered by all lovers of liberty to the end of time.

[He sits and pours a brandy.]

Before the month was out, Lafayette was appointed Commander of the National Guard. In August the National Assembly adopted A Declaration of the Rights of Man and the Citizen, a document that I and my associates – Condorcet,

Jefferson, Brissot and Lafayette – had a hand in writing. In September, Lafayette presented me with the key to the Bastille for delivery to the newly elected American president, George Washington. I pronounced it: *The first ripe fruits of American principles transplanted into Europe.* I wrote to Washington: *A share in two revolutions is living to some purpose.*

But I secretly yearned for a third revolution on my native soil to be followed by another and another until despotism was abolished from the universe. For the first time in history, the prospect of worldwide revolution seemed within reach. It was my duty and destiny to rally the people to their own cause, to awaken in them their natural love of liberty and a spirit of intolerance for that ancient form of government that denied them their rightful place in a free society.

[He gathers papers and takes his place at the lectern stage right.]

When I returned to London I found the friends of aristocracy alarmed and the monarchy in panic. I was not surprised – though I might have been – by news of Edmund Burke's impassioned plea before the Commons, condemning the events in France. I had been forewarned.

[BURKE appears at a lectern stage left in a pool of light.]

BURKE: Dear Sir: You are pleased to call for my thoughts on the late proceedings in France. I will not give you reason to imagine that I think my sentiments of such value as to wish myself to be solicited about them. They are of too little consequence to be very anxiously either communicated or withheld.

PAINE: [in a pool of light at his lectern] Withhold them, then, and retain for yourself a seat in the House of Liberty.

# RANDOM PLAYS

Or if you will not, send them forth and afford those who would still reside there the honor of reasoned refutation.

BURKE: I would not so readily be unseated, Mr. Paine. It is the fashion of popular leaders to express grand, swelling sentiments of liberty; to speak of revolution and freedom as if the two were one. The effects of their incapacity are to be covered with the all-atoning name of liberty. In some people I see great liberty indeed. But what is liberty without wisdom and without virtue? It is the greatest of all possible evils for it is folly, vice and madness without tuition or restraint. Those who know what virtuous liberty is, cannot bear to see it disgraced by incapable heads on account of their having high-sounding words in their mouths.

You see, Mr. Paine, I do most heartily wish that France may be animated by a spirit of rational liberty.

PAINE: By rational we may presume you mean that liberty should be rationed like a commodity – and that by a royal monarch who assumes his authority by reason of his exalted birth.

BURKE: I fear you mean to entice me, Mr. Paine. Yet I will take up the challenge.

One of the first and most leading principles on which the commonwealth and laws are consecrated is that they should act as if they were the entire masters; that they should not think it among their rights to cut off the entail or commit waste on the inheritance by destroying the whole original fabric of their society. By such unprincipled facility of changing the state as often as there are floating fancies, the whole chain and continuity of the commonwealth would be broken. No generation could link with another. Men would become little better than the flies of summer.

To avoid, therefore, the evils of inconstancy we have consecrated the state; that no man should look into its defects but with due caution; that he should never dream of beginning its reformation by its subversion; that he should approach the faults of the state as to the wounds of his father, with pious awe and trembling solicitude. By this wise prejudice we are taught to look with horror on those children of France who hack that aged parent to pieces and put him into the kettle of magicians in hopes that they may regenerate the paternal constitution and renovate their father's life.

PAINE: I have now to follow Mr. Burke through a wilderness of rhapsodies, a sort of descant upon governments, in which he asserts whatever he pleases on the presumption of its being believed, without offering either evidence or reasons for so doing.

BURKE: Allow me, Mr. Paine. [PAINE nods] Society is indeed a contract. It is a partnership in science, in art, in virtue and in all perfection. As the ends of such a partnership cannot be attained in many generations, it becomes a partnership between those who are living and those who are yet to be born. The contract of each particular state is but a clause in the eternal contract of society, linking the lower with the higher natures, holding each in their appointed place. This law is not subject to the will of those who, by an obligation above them, are bound to submit their will to that law. It is the first and supreme necessity, a necessity that is not chosen but chooses, a necessity paramount to deliberation. It admits no discussion and demands no evidence. But if that which is only submission to necessity is made the object of choice, the law is broken, nature is disobeyed and the rebellious are exiled from this world of reason and order into a world of madness, discord and unavailing sorrow. These, my dear sir, are, were and long will be the sentiments of not the least learned and reflecting part of this Kingdom.

PAINE: If I may inquire, sir, what is the source of this eternal contract?

BURKE: The source is most sacred and that which cannot be denied.

PAINE: Come, Mr. Burke, would you rest your case on the scriptures for I would most happily oblige.

# RANDOM PLAYS

BURKE: As I am not a priest and this is not a pulpit, I would rest my case on the sound foundation of law. If you would have precedence, Mr. Paine, I will educate you.

[PAINE nods, takes notes.]

The law by which the royal family of the House of Hanover is specifically destined to the succession is the twelfth and thirteenth of King William. The terms bind us, our heirs and our posterity to them, their heirs and their posterity to the end of time. I quote: "The Lords spiritual and temporal and Commons do, in the name of all the people aforesaid..."

PAINE: Meaning the people of England then living.

BURKE: Of course. [clears throat] "...most humbly and faithfully submit themselves, their heirs and posterities forever; and do faithfully promise that they will stand to maintain and defend their said Majesties to the utmost of their powers," etcetera. So far is it from being true, as Mr. Paine has suggested, that we acquired by the Revolution of 1688 a right to elect our Kings; that if we possessed it before, the English nation did at that time most solemnly renounce it for themselves and for their posterity forever.

PAINE: [clears throat] As I am not a man of the bar and this is not a courtroom, I will found my argument, as always, on plain truth and common sense. Mr. Burke conceives his point sufficiently established by producing these aged precedents that exclude the right of the nation forever. Yet not content with making such declarations, he further states "that if the people of England possessed such a right before the Revolution, the English nation did at that time renounce it not only for themselves but for all posterity."

As Mr. Burke applies the poison drawn from his horrid principles not only to the English but to the French as well, I shall, sans ceremony, place another system of principles in opposition.

## JACK RANDOM

The English Parliament of 1688 did a certain thing, which for themselves and their constituents they had a right to do. But in addition to this right, which they possessed by delegation, they set up another right by assumption: that of binding and controlling posterity to the end of time.

I reply: There never did, never will and never can exist a parliament possessed of the power to bind and control posterity to the end of time. Therefore, all such clauses, acts or declarations are null and void. Man has no property in man and a generation has no property in the generations that follow. Every age and every generation must be as free to act for itself as the ages and generations that preceded it. The vanity and presumption of governing beyond the grave is the most ridiculous and insolent of all tyrannies.

Those who have quitted the world and those who are not yet arrived in it are as remote from each other as the utmost stretch of moral imagination can conceive. What possible obligation can exist between them? What rule or principle can be laid down that two nonentities – the one out of existence and the other not yet in it – that the one should control the other to the end of time?

In short, I am contending for the rights of the living and Mr. Burke is contending for the authority of the dead over the rights and freedom of the living. A greater absurdity cannot present itself to the understanding of man than what Burke offers to his audience. He tells you and the world to come that a certain body of men a hundred years ago made a law and there does not exist and never will the power to alter it. Under how many absurdities has the divine right to govern been imposed on the incredulity of man! And yet, in this manner, would Mr. Burke urge you to abdicate your true and natural rights.

BURKE: Your argument, Mr. Paine, is made to simple and unthinking minds. Those that practice it know that government is a complicated matter. When we hear the simplicity of contrivance aimed at by this new school of republican thought, we are at no loss to decide that the artificers are either grossly ignorant or negligent of duty. Government, Mr. Paine, is not made in virtue of natural rights, which may and do exist in total independence of it. Rather, government is a contrivance of human wisdom to provide for human wants. Men have a right that these wants should be provided by that wisdom.

PAINE: If we allow for the moment that government is "a contrivance of human wisdom," it must follow that hereditary succession can make no part in it because it is impossible to make wisdom hereditary. And that cannot be a wise contrivance which, in its operation, may commit the government of a nation to the wisdom of an idiot. The ground Mr. Burke now takes is fatal to every part of his cause.

BURKE: Indeed, Mr. Paine. The wisdom to which I refer is the wisdom of antiquity. It is rather in the form of the thing than in the person of the king. That wisdom would hardly deny the rights of men and far am I from so doing. In denying false claims I do not mean to injure those that are real. If civil society is made for the advantage of man, all the advantages for which it is made become his right. These are often in balance between differences of good and in compromises between good and evil or, indeed, sometimes between evil and evil. Political reason is a computing principle: adding, subtracting, multiplying and dividing, morally and not metaphysically true moral denominations.

PAINE: [sighs, smiles] As the wondering audience, whom Mr. Burke supposes himself talking to, may not understand all this learned jargon, I will undertake to be its interpreter. The meaning, good people, of all this is that government is governed by no principle whatsoever, that it can make evil good or good evil as it pleases. In short, that government is arbitrary power. As it is without origin and its power without authority, it is usurpation – plain and simple.

BURKE: I see by your answer, Mr. Paine, that you

would rather mock the author than attend to his argument. For myself, I would no longer engage this mockery of reasoned discourse on the nature of government. I would rather turn my visage to the disgraceful affairs of France. All your high sounding talk of liberty and right is but a cruel disguise to your true purpose: the total destruction of civil and ordered society.

Plots, massacres and assassinations seem to some people a trivial price for obtaining a revolution. A cheap, bloodless reformation, a guiltless liberty, appear flat and vapid to your tastes. There must be a great change of scene, a magnificent stage effect, a grand spectacle to rouse the imagination, grown torpid with the lazy enjoyment of sixty years security and prosperity. The preacher finds them all in the French Revolution!

PAINE: Mr. Burke should recollect that he is recording history, not writing plays. He never speaks of plots against the revolution and it is from these that all the mischiefs have risen. It suits his purpose to exhibit consequences without their causes. It is one of the arts of the drama to do so. If the crimes of men were exhibited with their sufferings, the effect would be lost and the audience would be inclined to approve where it is intended they should commiserate.

BURKE: If I am inclined to the dramatic, Mr. Paine, it is because my heart cries out at cruelty and senseless horror. As things now stand, one is forced to apologize for harboring the common feelings of a man. But it is only natural that I should feel thusly because we are made to be affected at such spectacles with melancholy sentiments, because in those natural feelings we learn great lessons. Our passions instruct our reason. When kings are hurled from their thrones by the Supreme Director of this great drama, and become the objects of insult to the base and of pity to the good, we are alarmed.

Tears might be drawn if such a spectacle were exhibited on the stage. Indeed, the theatre is a better school of moral sentiment than churches when the feelings of humanity are thus outraged. In the theatre the first intuitive glance would show that this method of political computation would justify every extent of crime. The audience would soon see that criminal means once tolerated are soon preferred. When perfidy and murder are approved for public benefit, public benefit soon becomes the pretext and perfidy and murder the ends. Such must be the consequences of losing, in the splendor of these triumphs of the rights of man, all natural sense of wrong and right.

This, my dear sir, was not the triumph of France. I must believe that, as a nation, it overwhelmed her with shame and horror. For you have rebelled against a mild and lawful monarch with more fury, outrage and insult than any people against the most illegal usurper or most sanguinary tyrant.

PAINE: This is one amongst a thousand other instances in which Mr. Burke shows that he is ignorant of the springs and principles of the French Revolution. It was not against Louie but against the despotic principles of government that the nation revolted. The monarch and the monarchy are distinct and separate things. It was against the established despotism of the latter that the revolt commenced and the revolution has carried. As to the tragic paintings by which Mr. Burke has outraged his own imagination, they are very well calculated for theatrical representation: where facts are manufactured and accommodated to produce a weeping effect. But Mr. Burke should be informed that his audience will expect truth and not the spouting rant of high-toned declamation. It is painful to behold a man employing his talent to corrupt himself. Nature has been kinder to Mr. Burke than he is to her. He pities the plumage but forgets the dying bird.

BURKE: [pointedly ignoring Paine's argument] It is now sixteen years since I saw the Queen at Versailles, and surely never lighted on this orb, which she hardly seemed to touch, a more delightful vision. I saw her just above the horizon, decorating and cheering the elevated sphere she just began to move in, glittering like the morning star, full of life and splendor and joy. O what a revolution and what a heart must I have to contemplate without emotion that elevation and that fall.

Little did I dream that she should ever be obliged to carry the sharp antidote against disgrace concealed in that bosom; little did I dream that I should live to see such disasters fallen upon her in a nation of gallant men. I thought ten thousand swords must have leaped from their scabbards to avenge even a look that threatened her with insult.

But the age of chivalry is dead! That of sophisters, economists and calculators has succeeded and the glory of Europe is extinguished forever! Never more shall we behold that generous loyalty to rank and sex, that proud submission, that dignified obedience, that subordination of the heart, which kept alive the spirit of an exalted freedom. The unbought grace of life, the cheap defense of nations, the nurse of manly sentiment and heroic enterprise is gone! It is gone, that sensibility of principle, that chastity of honor, which felt a stain like a wound, which inspired courage whilst it mitigated ferocity, which ennobled whatever it touched, and under which vice itself lost half its evil by losing all its grossness.

PAINE: [aside] I know a point in America called Point-no-Point because, as you proceed along the shore, gay and flowery as Mr. Burke's language, it continually recedes and presents itself at a distance. But when you have got as far as you can go, there is no point at all.

BURKE: [as before] But now all is to be changed. All the pleasing illusions, which made power gentle and obedience liberal, which harmonized the different shades of life and incorporated into politics the sentiments which beautify and soften private society, are to be dissolved by this new conquering empire of light and reason. All the decent drapery of life is to be rudely torn off, leaving exposed the defects of our naked and shivering nature.

On the scheme of this barbarous philosophy, which is the offspring of cold hearts and muddy understanding, a king is but a man, a queen is but a woman, a woman is but an animal not of the highest order – for all homage paid to sex is regarded as romance and folly – and laws are to be supported only by their own terrors, for terror only can support that which wisdom and tradition denies.

PAINE: Is this the language of a rational man? Is it the language of a heart feeling, as it ought to feel, for the rights and happiness of the human race? When we see a man dramatically lamenting that the Age of Chivalry is over, that the "unbought grace of life" – if anyone knows what it is – "the cheap defense of nations, the nurse of manly sentiment and heroic enterprise" is gone! And all this because the Quixotic age of chivalric nonsense is gone, what opinion can we form of his judgment and what regard can we pay to his facts? In the rhapsody of his own imagination he has discovered a world of windmills and his sorrow is there are no Quixote's to attack them. But if the age of aristocracy and monarchy and despotism, like that of chivalry, should fall, then Mr. Burke, trumpeter of the order, may continue his parody to the end and finish with: Othello's occupation is gone! The question, which must sooner or later be answered, is whether we should profit by the wisdom acquired of knowledge and experience, or whether we should invest the happiness of mankind on the virtue of poetic liberty. Little wonder that Mr. Burke's musings "admit no discussion and demand no evidence" for in the world of reasonable minds they can have no part.

BURKE: [yawns] But I grow tired of debate. I have spoken my thoughts in good faith and I have given your arguments fair reading. I will not attempt, in the smallest degree, to refute them. This will be done – if such seditious writings shall be thought to deserve any but the refutation of criminal justice – by others who may think as I do.

# JACK RANDOM

[Spot fades to black. PAINE gathers his papers and returns to his study.]

PAINE: There is something rather odd and somewhat ludicrous in the spectacle of the great conservative philosopher breaking off from the most momentous debate of his time to summon the intervention of criminal justice.

As it happened, the Pitt Ministry needed no prompting from Mr. Burke. Failing reasoned refutation they summoned a hack writer, using the pseudonym of Francis Oldys, to publish a false and libelous biography. My answer was the second part of the Rights of Man. It enjoyed an even greater run than the first, which, if I may say so, was unprecedented in the history of letters.

In that work I envisioned a global society of republics and a European Congress to settle international disputes. I envisioned an age of enlightenment in which elected governments went beyond simple representation to provide care for the indigent, the old and the young – not as a matter of grace but of natural right. I proposed to pay for such care through taxes on the wealthy – not in the nature of charity but rather of responsibility.

In May a royal proclamation was issued against not only the writing but also the printing, publishing and dispersion of "wicked" and "seditious" writings. I was presented a summons and my trial was to be held in June. The minister hoped that I would flee the country. When I did not the trial was postponed. I thereby improved the occasion by issuing an appeal to the people of England to elect a convention for the purpose of drafting a new constitution. In September I received an unsolicited honor. I was elected to the National Assembly of France.

[Reading] "Come, friend of the people, to swell the number of patriots in an assembly which will decide the destiny of a great people, perhaps of the human race. The happy period you have predicted has arrived. Come! Do not

# RANDOM PLAYS

deceive their hopes."

I could not refuse.

[He crosses stage left to a representation of the French National Assembly.]

On September 13 I left England for the last time. Never more would I see the white cliffs of Dover or experience the spirited interchange that so often occasions the workingman pubs of London. In December I was tried and convicted of sedition in absentia and banished from my homeland forever.

[The sound of a mob grows and images of protest, a hanging in effigy, torches and disruption appear on screen.]

I am told the Court hired instigators to incite a mob. They burned my books, hanged my image in effigy and fixed my inscription to the soles of their shoes so that they could stamp out the Rights of Man with each step. I thank God I was not there to witness such a spectacle.

I was given a hero's welcome in France. The nation was in the midst of great turmoil. Sensing an opportunity, Prussian and Austrian armies marched on Paris. The citizens of Paris once again rallied to her defense. In their passion and zeal they initiated a purge of the priesthood and royalist elements. Fearing enemies within and without, the Revolution took a bloody turn in the events that would be known as the September Massacres.

I cannot judge whether such extreme measures were necessary but it cannot be denied that despotism, founded in antiquity, is not easily uprooted. If the price of liberty be a thousand lives or more, it is a price we must pay if not happily then dutifully, for our children deserve no less.

Still, I prayed that the innocent should be spared and that the massacres of September would not beget the Great Terror that followed. Though I never lost hope that the principles of the Revolution would prevail not only in France but throughout Europe, it would be some time before I could believe I would witness that glorious scene in my lifetime.

[He moves to a long table, surrounded by chairs, with a document upon it.]

I was appointed to a committee of eight, including Citizens Condorcet and Brissot, charged with drafting the constitution. Brissot had become the leader of a moderate faction seated to the right of the Assembly floor. Their opposition sat on the high ground to the left. They were called "Le Montagnard" or the Mountain. Citizens Danton and Robespierre sat with them, vying for the loyalty of the sans culottes. Condorcet and I took the middle ground or "plain" of the Assembly floor.

Condorcet took the lead in drafting the constitution, selecting as his model the Pennsylvania constitution written by Dr. Franklin and myself. By April the document was complete but the politics of Paris had shifted dramatically. The Mountain had control of the assembly and would not allow a constitution for which they could not take credit. They drafted a new version, which was adopted shortly thereafter. Of the original committee of eight, six would not survive the summer of 1794.

[We see an image of the guillotine in operation and hear the roar of the mob witnessing an execution.]

The French had adopted a new and "humane" method of public execution. One by one, I saw my comrades and friends summarily executed. Others were hauled off to prison on a daily basis. The intolerance of the religious persecutions was transferred to politics. The Revolutionary Tribunal supplied the place of the Inquisition and the guillotine that of the stake. As he might have foreseen,

# RANDOM PLAYS

Robespierre would himself kneel before the instrument of his own horrific creation but for two solemn years he held firmly to it reins.

As to my own fate, in the mind of Robespierre and his comrades, it was sealed when I opposed the execution of Louie. As you will recall, the French monarch had helped secure liberty for America and I felt a debt of gratitude.

[He takes to the lectern and reads.]

*My language has always been that of liberty and humanity; and I know by experience that nothing so exalts a nation as the union of these two principles. I know that the public mind of France has been heated and irritated by the dangers to which they have been exposed. But could we carry our thoughts into the future, what today seems an act of justice may then appear an act of vengeance. If, on my return to America, I should employ myself on a history of the French Revolution, I had rather record a thousand errors dictated by humanity than one inspired by a justice too severe.*

[He discards his notes on his desk.]

My appeal fell on deaf ears. The deposed king was executed and I was soon escorted to the Luxembourg Prison on the charge of being a foreign alien. I would spend ten months and nine days in that former palace of aristocrats. I did not know daily whether I would live to greet another day.

[He is now in a prison setting.]

From the middle of March to the end of July, the state of affairs was a constant horror. No man could count upon life for twenty-four hours. To such a pitch of rage and suspicion were Robespierre and his committee arrived that it seemed they feared to leave anyone living. Hardly a day passed in which ten, twenty, thirty, fifty or more were taken out, carted before a pretend tribunal and beheaded before nightfall.

All the horror of the times could not match the terror of the gruesome scene that passed before me that fateful June. It happened that one hundred and sixty eight persons were taken from Luxembourg in a single night and a hundred and sixty guillotined the next day – of which I know I was to be one and the manner I escaped that fate is curious indeed.

The room in which I was held was on the ground floor and the door opened outward and flat against the wall, so that when it was open the inside of it appeared outward and the contrary when it was shut. When prisoners by the score were to be taken out it was always done in the night and those who performed the office had a private mark by which they knew what rooms to go to and what number to take. I had three fellow prisoners with me and the door of our room was marked with the number four in chalk. But it happened that the mark was put on when the door was open and flat against the wall. It thereby came on the inside when we shut it at night. Thus did the destroying angel pass us by.

In the nights that followed I died a thousand deaths; a thousand times I mounted the scaffold, arms bound behind me; a thousand times I knelt below the guillotine's monstrous blade; a thousand times I heard its swift descent and saw, from Heaven's gate, my own severed head in a pool of blood below; a thousand times I witnessed the approving roar of the mob as my deathly visage, marked in terror, was held up for display. From that day forward, I could not fear. I could not fear!

[He crosses from the prison to his study, pours and drinks.]

I would later learn how unnecessary it all was. America had only to claim me as its citizen and I would have been released. But at that time, the American Minister to France was my nemesis, Gouverneur Morris. His betrayal is what history will record but what of my American friends? What of Washington and Jefferson? That they chose to do nothing and avoid a political controversy is what I fear and suspect. They did not wish to offend the British ministry. It broke my heart.

But lest I should sound too despondent, I should note that on the 29$^{th}$ of July 1794, the body of Citizen Robespierre – and not that of Paine – was separated from its master. In August, Mr. Morris was replaced by Mr. James Monroe who alas procured my release.

[Manuscript in hand, he returns to the lectern.]

*Fellow Citizens of the United States of America:*
*I put the following work under your protection. It contains my opinion upon religion. You will do me the justice to remember that I have always supported the right of every man to his own opinion. He who denies to another this right makes a slave of himself to his present opinion because he precludes the right of changing it.*

*It has been my intention for several years to publish my thoughts upon this subject. I am well aware of the difficulties that attend it and from that consideration have reserved it to a more advanced period of life. I intend it to be the last offering I should make to my fellow citizens of all nations and at a time when the purity of motive could not admit of question. For it happened that the people of France were running headlong into atheism, rendering a work of this kind necessary, lest in the general wreck of superstition, of false systems of government and false theology, we lose sight of morality, of humanity and of a theology that is true.*

*I had this work translated into their own language to stop them in that career and fix them to the first article of every man's creed who has any creed at all: I believe in God.*

# JACK RANDOM

As several of my colleagues have given me the example of making their voluntary professions of faith, I will make mine – and I do so with all the sincerity and frankness with which the mind of man communicates with itself.

I believe in one God and no more and I hope for happiness beyond this life.

I believe in the equality of man and I believe that religious duties consist in doing justice, loving mercy and endeavoring to make our fellow creatures happy.

But lest it should be supposed that I believe many other things, I shall declare the things I do not believe and my reasons for not believing them.

With respect to what are called denominations of religion, if everyone is left to judge of his own religion, then is there not such a thing as a religion that is wrong. But if they are judge of each other's religion, then is there not such a thing as a religion that is right. Therefore, all the world is right or all the world is wrong. As either is an affront to common sense, I do not believe in the creed professed by any church I know of.

The most formidable weapon against errors of every kind is reason. I have never used any other and I trust I never shall. My own mind is my own church. All national institutions of churches appear to me no other than human inventions set up to terrify and enslave mankind.

With respect to religion itself, without regard to names, and as directing itself from the universal family of mankind to the divine object of all adoration, it is man bringing to his maker the fruits of his own heart. And though these fruits may differ like the fruits of the earth, the grateful tribute of every one is kindly accepted.

I do not mean by this declaration to condemn those who believe otherwise. They have the same right to their beliefs as I have to mine. But it is necessary to the happiness of man that he be mentally faithful to himself. Infidelity does not consist in believing or disbelieving; it consists in professing *to believe what one does not believe.*

*It is certain that all the nations of the earth and all religions agree: All believe in a God. The things in which they disagree are the redundancies annexed to that belief. Therefore, if ever a universal religion should prevail, it will not be by believing anything new but in getting rid of redundancies and believing as man believed at the first. Adam was created a Deist. But in the meantime, let every man follow, as he has a right to do, the religion and the worship her prefers.*

[Discards manuscript and crosses to pub setting.]

Some would suggest it is unfortunate I did not expire on the scaffold beneath the blade of the guillotine. I should have exclaimed some glorious tribute to truth, liberty and reason. I should have bid the community of all mankind, which I have faithfully served, a final dramatic farewell.

But destiny decreed that I should live. I remained in Paris nine more years and then returned to New York. My final years in the land I loved were neither pleasant nor eventful. Many of my former friends had either perished or refused to associate with the world's most renowned infidel. Once again I was the target of unceasing abuse in the public papers.

Of course, I continued writing but the great works of my career had already been written. By June of the year 1809, I was a very old, very poor and very tired man. As I lay on my deathbed, I was visited by those who call themselves religious persons. I was asked to recant my religious beliefs. Each time I wondered: Was ever a man more faithful and less understood than Tom Paine?

On the eighth day of June I left this world to a most uncertain future.

[He stands and crosses down center.]

## JACK RANDOM

I had not intended to leave so much of the work undone. And yet, as I believe in the power of good and the strength of reason, I trust that succeeding generations have made great progress toward an age of enlightenment.

As long as a man has a heart to feel and a mind to think, he need not be instructed as to his duty. It presents itself. Yet I will leave you with a challenge:

*To see it in our power to make a world happy; to teach mankind the art of being so; to exhibit on the theater of the universe a character hitherto unknown; and to have a new creation entrusted to our hands: These are honors that command reflection and can neither be too highly esteemed nor too gratefully received.*

With this, my friends, your most humble and obedient servant bids you adieu.

[He bows. Lights fade to black. End Act Two.]

## ABOUT THE AUTHOR

Jack Random has lived at once an ordinary and extraordinary life. His roots firmly planted in the fertile central valley of California, he has marched the streets in protest, haunted jazz town bars, read poetry in cafes and town squares, strutted his hour upon the stage, crisscrossed the country by air, rail, highway and thumb, mourned at Wounded Knee, gazed into the eyes of the crow at Grand Canyon, and paid tribute at the grave of Geronimo. He has labored in the fields of plenty, toiled on the assembly line, pursued higher education and attempted to enlighten children in the public schools. He has been a pilgrim and a seeker of truth. He is married to the love of his life. All the while he has chronicled his thoughts and revelations in words: plays, poetry, novels, stories and essays.

## OTHER BOOKS FROM CROW DOG PRESS

***Wasichu: The Killing Spirit*** – A Novel by Jack Random. A modern telling of the life of Crazy Horse recalls the history of Native America and its most revered leader.

***Number Nine: The Adventures of Jake Jones and Ruby Daulton*** – A Novel by Jack Random. A woman on the run picks up a hitchhiker and takes us on an adventure that winds its way to New Orleans in the summer of Katrina.

***A Patriot Dirge*** – A Novel by Jack Random. Political genius Roman Mason takes on the political and economic forces that rule our lives (Jazzman Series).

***Jazzman Chronicles: Volumes I-X*** – Essays by Jack Random. Political commentaries from 2000 to 2014.

***A Mother's Story*** – **Stories, Art and Reflections** by Artis Brown Miller. A mother of eight children reflects on a life of hardship and love.

***Pawns to Players: The Stairway Scandal*** – A Novel by Jack Random. An aristocrat and a billionaire play a chess match to determine the fate of the American government.

***The Grand Canyon Zen Golf Tour*** – A Memoir by Jack Random. Two friends embark on a journey of golf, music, poetry and family in the summer of 1993.

***Hard Times: The Wrath of an Angry God*** – A Novel by Jack Random. Not with a bang but a whimper the end of days comes.

***Pawns to Players: A Match for the White House*** – A Novel by Jack Random. Part two of the Chess Series.

***Apache Jack: Native Visions & Stories*** by Jack Random. A collection of short works surrounding Indian culture.

***Random Jack: Tales from Jazztown & Beyond*** by Jack Random. A collection of short stories.

***D'Arc Underground & Other Plays*** by Jack Random. The first of two volumes of plays.

*Crow Dog Press*

www.ingramcontent.com/pod-product-compliance
Lightning Source LLC
Chambersburg PA
CBHW060148050426
42446CB00013B/2730